# The Moment

# Praise for *The Moment*

"While the world was hearing about Rev. Jeremiah Wright and his potential spiritual, and perhaps political, influence on then–presidential candidate Barack Obama, the voices of Rev. Wright's parishioners were silent. They have found their voices in *The Moment* with the help of Carl and Shelby Grant. A must-read for the curious and those who want to know more than the media presentation regarding this moment." —**Percy Bates**, University of Michigan

"*The Moment* powerfully documents an often forgotten aspect of racial politics in the United States—the voices of the community. Carl Grant and Shelby Grant offer a stunning counter-narrative of the confluence of race, theology, class, ideology, history, and media within the 2008 ascendance of Barack Obama." —**Anthony Brown**, University of Texas at Austin

"This narrative speaks to the lives and souls of a black community and its most powerful institution—the black church. Grant and Grant provide a history ignored by the media and, in doing so, reveal the story that needed to be told. Through the voices of the Trinitarians, the authors reveal a belief that the 'media firestorm' was larger than the Wright and Obama relationship. There were those who believed they were witnessing an attack by the white power structure on their most essential and sacred institution. This book may move us closer to having that conversation about a post-racial society—such a conversation is clearly long overdue." —**Beverly M. Gordon**, The Ohio State University

# The Moment

*Barack Obama, Jeremiah Wright, and the Firestorm at Trinity United Church of Christ*

Carl A. Grant and Shelby J. Grant

ROWMAN & LITTLEFIELD PUBLISHERS, INC.
Lanham • Boulder • New York • Toronto • Plymouth, UK

Published by Rowman & Littlefield Publishers, Inc.
A wholly owned subsidary of The Rowman & Littlefield Publishing Group, Inc.
4501 Forbes Boulevard, Suite 200, Lanham, Maryland 20706
www.rowman.com

10 Thornbury Road, Plymouth PL6 7PP, United Kingdom

British Library Cataloguing in Publication Information Available

**Library of Congress Cataloging-in-Publication Data**

Grant, Carl A.
The moment : Barack Obama, Jeremiah Wright, and the firestorm at Trinity United Church of Christ
/ Carl A. Grant and Shelby J. Grant.
p. cm.
Includes bibliographical references and index.
ISBN 978-1-4422-1997-7 (cloth : alk. paper) — ISBN 978-1-4422-1999-1 (electronic)
1. Obama, Barack. 2. Obama, Barack—Friends and associates. 3. Presidents—United States—Election—2008. 4. Wright, Jeremiah A., Jr. 5. African American clergy. 6. Trinity United Church of
Christ (Chicago, Illinois) 7. African American churches. 8. United States—Race relations—Political
aspects. 9. United States—Race relations—Religious aspects. 10. Chicago (Ill.)—Politics and
government—1951– I. Grant, Shelby J. II. Title.
E908.3.G735 2013
973.932092—dc23
2012023526

Printed in the United States of America

This book is dedicated to the many people whose voices often go unheard or unacknowledged . . . especially those who sit in the pews at Trinity United Church of Christ.

*American whites and blacks both possess deep-seated resistances against the Negro problem being presented, even verbally, in all of its hideous fullness, in all of the totality of its meaning. The many and various groups, commissions, councils, leagues, committees, and organizations of an interracial nature have consistently diluted the problem, blurred it, and injected foggy moral or senti-mental notions into it. This fact is as true of the churches as of the trade unions; as true of Negro organizations as of white; as true of the political Left as of the political Right; as true of white individuals as of black.*
—Richard Wright, *12 Million Black Voices* (1941)

*I know I was there that day for that particular sermon but he had a much larger point to make. The snippet they took made it sound like he was con-demning the United States of America. . . . He was condemning a cystic evil within society that perpetuates all kinds of oppression. He's always preaching liberation and he used an example from the Bible and showed a very clear example of how that same thing happens here in the United States and has happened over and over again. They just took that one piece. It was that the United States has indeed been complicit in the oppression of many people and that's a fact. Anybody who denies that is looking at history with rose-colored glasses. He has reminded us of that time after time after time not in an effort for us to be anti-American; but for us to have a clear picture of what is going on in the world so we can make critical decisions about how we function in the world, how we vote and how we do ministry. He wants to make sure we see both sides of the coin. Historically, you know yourself the story has always been one-sided. We as a nation have never done anything wrong. We didn't rape the land from the Indians. We didn't do any of that but Pastor Wright always tells the real story good, bad, and indifferent. He helps us and provides an opportunity for us to think critically and that sermon was just one example of what he did every single Sunday. What's so interesting he's not the only pastor that does it. There are many African American pastors who present the same way about the same kind of issues across the nation all the time. He's not the only one! There's a prophetic message being preached Sunday after Sun-day. It just happened to be that particular time and in that particular context at that particular moment in history. He got caught I guess.*
—Unnamed Trinitarian

# Contents

Authors' Note                                                                    xi

Acknowledgements                                                                 xiii

Introduction                                                                      xv

Prologue                                                                         xxi

**1**  Back to the Moment: March 13 to May 31, 2008                                1
**2**  Race, Migration, and Politics in the Windy City                            33
**3**  The Black Church and the African American Church in Chicago                69
**4**  Trinity United Church of Christ                                            93
**5**  The Unheard Voices of Trinity Church                                       119

Epilogue                                                                         157

Appendix: Interview Questions                                                    159

Notes                                                                            161

Index                                                                            173

# Authors' Note

The idea for *The Moment* grew out of a comment from my brother, Shelby, when we were in New Orleans in February 2011 at the Race, Gender, and Class Conference. The conference was on Obama's education policies. Long story short, during the Q&A a woman from the audience, after asking a question about Obama's education policies, asked a follow-up question about Obama and Trinity Church. To this question Shelby replied, "Let me tell you how the congregation feels." When he said that, I (Carl) immediately said to myself, "Oh My Lord! No one has ever *really* talked to Trinity congregation. We have heard from Obama, Wright, and the media, but the voices of the members of the congregation are undiscovered, marginalized, and in most cases silent."

The thought continued to haunt me, but for several days I pushed it away. I was involved in completing one book and starting another, in addition to several other professional obligations. The haunting continued for weeks. Finally, one night I said to myself, "I need to exorcise this thing: What would such a book look like?" After developing an outline, I asked several colleagues what they thought of the idea. To my surprise, I received wonderfully positive responses. I called Shelby to get his reaction and to ascertain his thinking about our being able to interview Trinitarians. He said, "Yes, let's do it. I am the Man!" He believed that the congregants would be willing to share their story. You are now about to read that story.

We conducted research for the book by interviewing members of the Trinity Church in Chicago. We also examined published news articles and interviews, available in print and online, as well as books and discussions with friends and colleagues. Only one person declined to be interviewed and most interviewees (Trinitarians) asked us to use their names. Nevertheless, we decided not to use real names, probably to the disappointment of many whom we interviewed. Hopefully, they will respect our decision, a decision made with them in mind. Occasionally quotations from the congregants have been shortened for the reader's convenience, but the content is never changed. Unattributed quotes in the book come from our interviews with the congregants.

# Acknowledgements

At the end of a challenging, but *oh so* pleasant journey, we have many to thank and to pin a rose on. At the top of the list are all the Trinitarians, and especially the members and staff of Trinity United Church of Christ who volunteered to be interviewed and offered full-throated comments. To show our immense gratitude, we would like to list each of your names individually, as many of you requested, but we feel a need to maintain everyone's confidentiality. Just know that each of your contributions made this book possible and to that we are eternally grateful. There are several Trinitarians, including staff members, who are deserving of special mention for their help: Melody Morgan, executive assistant to the pastor; Karen Cupil and Brenda Tillman, administrative assistants to the pastor; Arlington Swan, who is in charge of security; and Rudolph Brown, a member who established numerous contacts for the interviews.

Second, there are all of our colleagues and friends who were both super supportive and read and critiqued copies of the manuscript. We are forever in their debt. A good and special friend, Margaret Quinlin, is especially deserving of high praise and will be long remembered for her comment "Keep the narrative focused." Sylvia Thorson-Smith, Bernadette Baker, and Craig Werner are appreciated for their rich feedback and support. Typing transcriptions is a chore, but Jennifer Austin volunteered and did it with great efficiency. THANKS, Jennifer. Much appreciation is awarded to the MERIT staff and Jim Jonas for their willingness to help with archival research and provide computer support.

Robert Saddler did all, and more, that very good long time friends do: read and commented on the manuscript and accompanied Carl around Chicago when he came to the city to conduct research. "General," we owe you big time!

One of the privileges of being a professor at a great university is having the opportunity to work with very smart graduate students. Such was the case throughout this project. Melissa Gibson's comments were insightful and helpful, as usual. Elisabeth Zwier's scholarship and commitment were also greatly appreciated. Thanks, too, to Lauren Gould for hunting down those missing citations.

Most deserving of high, high praise for her devotion to the project is Alexandra Allweiss. Alex's untiring dedication and scholarship, her research skills, and especially her words—"Carl, do you mind if I push back?"—will always be remembered and were a distinct contribution to the project.

Finally, thanks to brothers Alvin and Ernest; son and daughter, Carl and Alicia; and nephew and niece, Paul and Sharon, for their insightful comments and support. We are also grateful to Deana Wright, for her wonderful encouragement and her journalist experience that deeply enhanced our interviews and this book.

With the generosity and support of so many during the journey, we encountered very little "turbulent air." That said, mistakes are ours alone and cannot be attributed to any who graciously helped us.

# Introduction

*Whereof what's past is prologue, what to come, In yours and my discharge.*
—Shakespeare, *The Tempest*, Act 2, Scene 1

It is our ambitious aspiration that this book can contribute to American history, filling a void that is not only unnoticed but often dismissed or dealt with on others' terms: the unheard voices of the members of Trinity Church. Here we elaborate on the purpose of the book, address challenges we encountered, discuss the reason for locating *The Moment* in a historical context, and raise questions about media ethics.

## PURPOSE AND HOPE

This book seeks to encourage critical self-reflection and critical reflection on the many social issues (e.g., race, religion, politics) that intertwine in *The Moment*. We encourage readers to ask "why?" and "what have I missed?" and "why have I missed this?" In addition, we encourage readers to reason about the condition of the legacy of the Fourth Estate (a historical way of framing the media as a "fourth branch" of the government) and to question whether Thomas Carlyle would repeat the phrase "more important far than they all"[1] today? We invite you to reason about the extent to which journalism's code of ethics is serving the United States. Finally, we hope readers reach the point that they can honestly challenge W. E. B. Du Bois's statement in 1903: "We must not forget that most Americans answer all queries regarding the Negro *a priori*, and that the least that human courtesy can do is to listen to evidence." Du Bois went on to note, "We seldom study the condition of the Negro today honestly and carefully. It is much easier to assume that we know it all. Or perhaps, having reached conclusions in our mind, we are loathe to have them disturbed by facts."[2]

## CHALLENGES

We approach this writing project as educators with three overriding challenges. The first is to record the unheard voices of the worshipers at Trinity Church where Shelby is a charter (founding) member. The second is to take back a moment that was colonized and distorted by individuals and groups within the United States as Barack Obama campaigned for the presidency in 2008. Arthur A. Schomburg correctly noted, "The American Negro must remake his past in order to make his [or her] future." The third challenge is to write about a moment in U.S. history involving three distinguished African American actors: Barack Obama during his campaign for the presidency in 2008, Reverend Jeremiah Wright Jr., and everyday black Americans who were congregants at Trinity United Church of Christ in Chicago during this time period.

## SIGNIFICANCE OF HISTORY AS A TOOL

Our narrative—especially chapters 2 and 3—uses history as a tool to assist readers in better understanding the people and events we discuss. As we use history, we think differently about politics and reject the artificial divisions between political history and social history.[3] *The Moment* is both political and social and it would not be possible to separate one from the other. To attempt this would be to present an incomplete story. By bringing these two histories together we can develop a deeper contextual understanding and illumination of the changes that have taken place in society from the days of enslavement, including their significance for how and why the society we live in came to be. History, in other words, helps us to understand people—both black and white—in the United States as a society of codes, laws, beliefs, and values. In addition, history helps to explain, to tell the story of how black and white people live as they move to Chicago from the South during the mid-1800s through today—and how and why the ways black and white people live and function in the past are relevant to the lives of people in Chicago today.[4]

The hopeful expectation is that the use of history (e.g., official statutes and mandates, written stories, poems, historical accounts) will prompt reflections on the human experiences of other cultural groups in other times and places and help us to realize that through a historical lens we can better understand which elements of our political, social, and educational institutions persist despite change. By researching black workers—female and male employees at meat-packing plants, aspiring politicians, and so forth—we learn from Peter Stern of the American Historical Association that history "provides a terrain for moral contemplation."[5] Here history becomes a rubric for assessing one's own moral sense. It enables one to compare and contrast one's life against the complexities some people as individuals and as a group have faced. In order to sharpen our historical analysis, we borrow the concept of "hidden transcript," a dissident political culture manifested in daily conversations, folklore, jokes, songs, and other cultural practices. Robin D. G. Kelley maintains that despite appearances of consent, oppressed groups challenge those in power by constructing a hidden transcript. In addition, we use the concept of *infrapolitics* to indicate the daily under-the-radar struggle of oppressed groups (such as "confrontations, evasive actions, and stifled thoughts") to push against unequal societal power relations. Kelley asserts, "Daily acts of resistance and survival have had consequences for existing power relations, and the powerful have developed immense resources in response."[6] The concepts of hidden transcript and infrapolitics aid our analysis and discussion of what takes place in Chicago's Black Belt.

In subsequent chapters we show how the hidden transcripts of resistance and infrapolitics surfaced through the ongoing struggle of black Chicagoans to redress and respond to the persistence and insidiousness of white supremacy. We draw attention to the evolution of black Chicago politics from the early 1900s to the present to see how the ongoing struggles and cultural practices of black political organizations and activism grew out of a desire to subtly challenge a Northern kind of "Jim and Jane Crow" politics. We argue that nowhere was the transcript of resistance more present than in the liberation theology of the black churches of Chicago, with Trinity Church, its members, and its leadership serving as shining examples of black hope and resistance. It is from this prophetic dissident space that we explore what has been "hidden" from the public discourse—the voices of Trinity Church.

Finally, history as a tool helps us to know who we Americans are as a people, our exceptionalisms and our warts. Using history as a tool heightens our ability to assess what we see and hear, evaluate conflicting interpretations, and assess the extent of change to problems related to race, while staying alert to the ways in which issues of inequality are nuanced into less blatant forms.[7]

That said, the authors are cognizant of Howard Zinn's statement that "anyone reading history should understand from the start that there is no such thing as impartial history." Furthermore, Zinn notes, "All written history is partial in two senses. It is partial in that it is only a tiny part of what really happened. That is a limitation that can never be overcome. And it is partial in that it inevitably takes sides, by what it includes or omits, what it emphasizes or deemphasizes. It may do this openly or deceptively, consciously or sub-consciously."[8] The history of everyday people—in this case, the congregants at Trinity Church—will serve to provide a reframing of events, a push away from a "single story" about Reverend Wright and Trinity Church.

Chimamanda Adichie's lecture about the danger of a "single story" describes how a single story affects the way people think about one another and creates or reinforces stereotypes because the *one* story becomes the *only* story. As she states, "Show a people as one thing, as only one thing over and over and that is what they become." She describes how the single story, in the case of Africa, causes people to envision a continent of poor, starving people and a place full of wild animals, making it difficult for people to imagine any other reality about Africa. "The consequence of a single story is this . . . it robs people of dignity and makes our recognition of equal human-ity difficult."[9] Here, too, is the danger of a single story of a black man. Our plan, keeping in mind Zinn's argument and using it as a guideline, is to make sure that our telling of African American history is open and offers a voice for those whose voices have been ignored in other accounts of this history.

Young Senator Barack Obama received a lesson on the significance of history when he visited Senator Robert C. Byrd in Byrd's office. In *The Audacity of Hope*, Obama says that at the outset of the meeting, after he inquired about the senator's gravely ill wife and participated in some photo-taking, he asked Senator Byrd "what advice he would give me as a new member of the Senate." Senator Byrd's comment to Senator Obama is in line with what we argue above: "Learn the rules. . . . Not just the rules, but the precedents as well. . . . Not many people bother to learn them these days."[10]

We dedicate considerable attention to describing African Americans his-torically, their migration to Chicago, and the significance of the black church, as well as how and why they arrived at their sociopolitical thought and identity. We do this to help the reader have access to the "precedents." In the United States, ethnic and racial groups have very little knowledge of each other's history. This lack of knowledge and understanding does not facilitate teachable moments on race. We keep this clearly in mind: It is not only that people and occurrences of the past have led to what is taking place today but also that what the future will bring is up to our actions.

## MEDIA ETHICS

Numerous times during the 2008 presidential campaign, and especially dur-ing the period that we identify as "the Moment," future teachers in Carl's introduction to education class raised questions about media ethics and fair-ness. More than two and a half years later, students today are still raising questions about media ethics regarding the campaign period that centered around Barack Obama and Reverend Wright. Whenever Carl is asked to discuss this project, his students' prevailing question is this: "In these days of standards and testing in schools, what standards of ethics and fairness inform the media?"

In part, this book explores the same questions that challenge Carl's students. It seeks to trouble what the world saw and heard during the presidential campaign of 2008: the images of Reverend Wright circulated on television and the Internet via video snippets, Barack Obama's reactions, and depictions of Trinity Church as racist or anti-American. We offer another perspective regarding Barack Obama, Reverend Wright, Trinity Church, and the media by presenting the unheard voices of the Trinity congregants as they spoke up about these three actors and their church. One may claim that these parishioners were "heard" in the snippets of interviews that were presented in the media, but the congregants argue that these snippets, often taken out of context, have not accurately represented their voices and opinions. We contend with them that they have not been able to give their full-throated comments until now.

## OVERVIEW OF THE BOOK

This book is organized into five chapters. The first four chapters provide essential knowledge and a pathway toward understanding and appreciating the voices of Trinity congregants in the fifth chapter. From a perspective of education theory and practice, the first four chapters provide the "readiness"—background knowledge, cultural and racial history, Chicago history, and a description and history of Trinity Church—needed to participate in a teaching and learning moment. Chapter 5 consists of the unheard and marginalized voices of the parishioners from Trinity Church. Members' voices are honest and blunt. They are offered first as independent individuals and second as members of a proud race and church.

Whose voices speak up about this moment in history? Who says yes to an interview knowing that a recording device will be placed before them? To what extent do they represent Trinity Church? We interviewed eighty Trinitarians. We paid attention to age, gender, and length of membership in the church. While we were conscious of the socioeconomic variable and its significance in social science research, other than asking the interviewees their profession/occupation and where they attended high school and college (which they readily provided), we did not inquire further. That said, a fair generalization is that Trinity congregants are working class to upper middle class, and they attend church on Sunday, especially those ages forty and older, often dressed in their "Sunday best."

We did meet the demand of our statistician to conduct at least sixty interviews for the congregation of six to eight thousand. While we paid attention to age and gender, the women outnumbered the men. In addition, we interviewed more Trinitarians who were age sixty and older; the next largest group included those ages fifty to sixty, followed by ages forty to fifty. Next was the group of ages thirty to forty, and the smallest group was congregants ages seventeen to thirty.

Some of the interviews were conducted in person, and the rest were conducted over the phone after first meeting the congregant in person and arranging a time to conduct the phone interview. Interview sessions ranged from thirty minutes to an hour (or longer), depending on how gregarious the interviewee was and whether we interviewed more than one congregant at a time. The interviews were open and dialogical; by this we mean that the interviewee(s) spoke fully and a sequence of exchanges took place as the interviewer and interviewee(s) negotiated the discussion. Although seven general questions (listed in the appendix) were asked of each interviewee, the interviewee determined the nature, time, and complexity of the response. In some cases, they said what they thought about the question(s) asked and offered comments after the interview was completed. In the majority of cases, the interviewees and interviewer negotiated the meaning of questions; that is, they didn't hesitate to seek clarification.

# Prologue

Our educational experiences taught us as students—and continue to teach our children and grandchildren—that a good deal of African American history is victim of the LSDS malady. It has been (L)ost because the contributions of African Americans to the United States were not recorded, (S)tolen because the contributions of African Americans to society were not acknowledged or were attributed to another ethnic/racial group, (D)istorted because contributions of African Americans were minimized or misunderstood, and (S)trayed because records of African American contributions did not receive safekeeping. We know that members of other ethnic groups can make similar claims.

Significant to and influencing this book are two registers that account for the way African American history is written or played out in society, especially in the schools. First, African American history is written through the life, experiences, and challenges faced by black leaders (e.g., Rev. Dr. Martin Luther King Jr.), the exceptional deeds performed by famous black people (e.g., Rosa Parks), and the brilliance and complexities of black intellectuals (e.g., W. E. B. Du Bois). Second, African American history is often told through narratives of resistance or fights for freedom (e.g., the civil rights movement). What is missing from these two registers is the history—points of view, dispositions, and stories—of ordinary African Americans. In the 1930s, the *Chicago Defender*, a newspaper primarily devoted to African American readers, reported on this omission when it stated, "The history of our people in Chicago is not so well known. . . . While there are old settlers still alive who recall the days when Abraham Lincoln's body lay in state at the Federal building, yet the social, economic, political, and religious life of our folks of early Chicago has never been chronicled and presented to the people of today."

A little more than a decade later, Richard Wright, in *12 Million Black Voices*, his authoritative narrative and pictorial account of African Americans during the Great Depression, addresses the significance of the everyday black person. Wright states:

> This text assumes that those few Negroes who have lifted themselves, through personal strength, talent, or luck, above the lives of their fellow-blacks are like single fishes that leap and flash for a split second above the surface of the sea, are but fleeting exceptions to that vast, tragic school that swims below in the depths against the current, silently and heavily, struggling against the waves of vicissitudes that spell a common fate. It is not, however, to celebrate or exalt the plight of the humble folk who swim in the depths that I select the conditions of their lives as examples of normality, but rather to seize upon that which is qualitative and abiding in the Negro experience, to place within full and constant view the collective humanity whose triumphs and defeats are shared by the majority, whose gains in security mark an advance in the level of consciousness attained by the broad masses in their costly and tortuous upstream journey.[1]

An illuminating observation about the experiences of the "school that swims below in the depths against the current" was recently brought to our attention by Stephen Tuck in *We Ain't What We Ought to Be*,[2] a provocative and compelling account of African Americans' long civil rights struggle that weaves into the content stories of ordinary black people: women, men, girls, and boys. Tuck stands against reducing African American history into a single strand and argues for an account of the role played by the everyday African American in the civil rights struggle. Equally compelling is our reflection on the following: Nathaniel Paul once said, "Through the long lapse of ages, it has been common for nations to record whatever was peculiar or interesting in the course of their history."[3] A reliance on "peculiar or interesting" events in writing history tends to silence the contributions, ideas, and experiences of everyday people. The voices of the Trinitarians (everyday people) speak back against the reliance on these "peculiar or interesting" events and focus on the experiences of those "who swim in the depths." This book, besides speaking back, also reaches forward to facilitate and encourage a constructive engagement among people around a pivotal event in American history that has yet to be explored in such a way.

*Chapter One*

# Back to the Moment

*March 13 to May 31, 2008*

*What is important is to live in the present, to stop being hoodwinked, to cast off delusions, to look clearly at this moment of time and at the same time to scrutinize the self.*

—Gao Xingjian

*God puts rainbows in the clouds so that each of us—in the dreaded moments— can see a possibility of hope.*

—Maya Angelou

## ACTORS IN THE MOMENT

There are three actors that dominate this moment: Barack Obama, Reverend Dr. Jeremiah Wright Jr., and the U.S. media (broadly conceived).

In what we are calling the "Moment," Barack Obama is a U.S. senator from the state of Illinois and one of the presidential candidates for the Democratic Party in the 2008 primaries. At issue is Barack Obama's membership and presence at Trinity United Church of Christ (UCC), his patriotism, and the perceived influence of Reverend Wright's preaching of black liberation theology, including some of his comments that are perceived to be anti-American, which were made during Obama's twenty-year membership in the church. Barack Obama's knowledge of or witness to statements in Reverend Wright's sermons about the U.S. government as an oppressor and killer of people occupy center stage in this moment.

1

Dr. Jeremiah Wright Jr. is the former pastor of Trinity UCC, a mega-church in Chicago with more than eight thousand members. It is known for its promotion of the Black Value System and a wide range of ministries that serve the church and the wider Chicago community. A renowned biblical scholar and lecturer, Reverend Wright was well respected within his congregation and the larger Chicago community. In the Moment, he is best known for snippets of his sermons that circulate on television and online, including his contention that the attacks of September 11, 2001, were proof that "America's chickens are coming home to roost" and the statement "not God Bless America. God damn America."

The media (broadly defined) includes print-based and online news reports, including major national newspapers such as the *New York Times* and the *Washington Post*, information from online videos, and Internet posts by everyday people responding to these events. Comments from the general public are revealing for what they say and also because they serve as a reminder of a fundamental American right: the freedom of speech. People's posts on media websites display an unalienable right to speak truth to power, and Edward Said reminded us that it is the "intellectual's role to speak the truth, as plainly, directly, and as honestly as possible."[1] Here we modify Said's statement to include not only the "intellectual" but also everyday women and men, girls and boys, speaking back to a presidential candidate, the media, and Reverend Wright as citizens.

Our interest in the media, besides its role as a messenger, is influenced by the significant role that it plays in maintaining and influencing a democratic self-governing society. Thomas Carlyle, in his book *On Heroes, Hero Worship and the Heroic in History*, stated, "Burke said there were Three Estates in Parliament; but, in the Reporters' Gallery yonder, there sat a Fourth Estate more important far than they all."[2] Oscar Wilde writes:

> In old days men had the rack. Now they have the press. That is an improvement certainly. But still it is very bad, and wrong, and demoralizing. Somebody—was it Burke?—called journalism the fourth estate. That was true at the time no doubt. But at the present moment it is the only estate. It has eaten up the other three. The Lords Temporal say nothing, the Lords Spiritual have nothing to say, and the House of Commons has nothing to say and says it. We are dominated by Journalism.[3]

There is a commonly accepted set of rules of ethics governing journalism. The authors of the website TheMediaBriefing.com have summarized these rules as follows:

> While various existing [media] codes have some differences, most share common elements—including the principles of truthfulness, accuracy, objectivity, impartiality, fairness, and public accountability—as these apply to the acquisi-

tion of newsworthy information and its subsequent dissemination to the public.[4]

African Americans hold a long, long memory of the powerful influence of the press in their fight to receive equality as full citizens and democracy in full bloom. During the black migration to Chicago, the *Chicago Defender* and other black newspapers played a monumental role in former enslaved and free blacks' fight to escape Jim Crow and other forms of blatant racism. The black newspaper is second only to the black church in providing news and inspiration, as well as challenge, support, and optimism, to a people who are pursuing the right to seek and secure the American dream. An article in the *Chicago Defender* speaks passionately and persuasively to this pursuit: "Patrick Henry said: 'Give me liberty or give me death.' And his words have become one of America's great clarion calls down through the years. Suppose Patrick Henry had said, 'Give me half-liberty and let me live half-dead.' Nobody would have paid him any mind, nor would we remember his name today."[5]

The power and the role of the Negro press in shaping democratic values, framing arguments, and encouraging the civil action of people is again observed during World War II. Drake and Cayton state:

> With the outbreak of the Second World War, the Negro press emerged as one of the most powerful forces among Negroes in American. These weekly papers became the "racial watchdogs" and with a unanimity that surprised Negroes as much as it did the rest of the country their editors began a campaign for the complete integration of Negroes into all war-related activities. The Negro newspapers called conferences, and their representatives haunted the offices of the White House, the Congress, and the Pentagon with a set of clear-cut demands: No segregation in the armed forces; no discrimination in industry; the progressive abolition of exclusion and subordination in civilian life. The newspapers advised Negroes to support the war, commended the partial relaxation of discriminatory barriers here and there, but defined the primary function of the press as one of pressure and needling. The Negro papers drew heated denunciations from illiberal die-hards and words of caution from white liberals. (The FBI, completely off the track, sniffed about for traces of Japanese subsidies.) In spite of these attacks, most Negro papers continued to follow the policy that the *Pittsburg Courier* dubbed "Double V"—a fight for the victory of democracy at *home* as well as abroad.[6]

African Americans as a people are aware that the media is a powerful force in the shaping and framing of issues. They know that, just as it can work for and with them, it can also shape and frame arguments that work against them. Much of democracy's future depends upon the professionalism and values that journalists put into their work, which is increasingly challenged by other forms of communication and the corporation and many media outlets.

In a speech titled "Can Democracy Survive 21st Century Journalism?" Bill Kovach, founding chairman of the Committee of Concerned Journalists, asks, in a variation on the title of his speech, what he considers a more pressing question: whether or not journalism itself can survive the twenty-first century.[7] In his speech, Kovach discusses a set of values generated by the Committee of Concerned Journalists that they propose define their field: a commitment to truth as a primary purpose, loyalty to citizens first, verification as the essence of the discipline, independence from those they cover, serving as a monitor of people and institutions of power, providing a public forum for criticism and compromise, making the significant interesting and relevant, and keeping news comprehensive and proportional.[8] Kovach also highlights some current trends in journalism today as compared with the past, including increased immediacy through digital technologies, lack of investigative reporting, headlines versus depth, a rise in opinion and spin, and a belief that quality exists more in newspapers such as the *New York Times* and the *Washington Post* than in TV news.[9]

All of these concerns come into play as we consider the journalism associated with the Moment—that point in time when Barack Obama's views on black liberation theology became part of a national debate. How did issues of fairness, journalistic ethics, and investigative reporting play out in the media's coverage and the public's commentary? This is a particular concern when it comes to reporting on race. Gonzalez and Torres note the difficulty of fair reporting with regard to race.

> It is our contention that newspapers, radio, and television played a pivotal role in perpetuating racist views among the general population. They did so by routinely portraying non-white minorities as threats to white society and by reinforcing racial ignorance, group hatred, and discriminatory government policies. The news media thus assumed primary authorship of a deeply flawed national narrative: the creation myth of heroic European settlers battling an array of backward and violent non-white peoples to forge the world's greatest democratic republic. The first draft of America's racial history was not restricted to a particular geographical region or time . . . nor was it merely the product of the virulent prejudice of a few influential media barons or opinion writers or of a specific chain of newspapers or television stations. Rather, it has persisted as a constant theme of American news reporting from the days of *Publick Occurance*, the first colonial newspaper, to the age of the Internet.[10]

Thus, our interest is in the behavior and attitudes of the media while they are covering the actions and affairs at and in Trinity UCC during the Moment. How did the media contribute to the shaping and framing of people's response regarding the church and its pastor, Reverend Jeremiah Wright? We are reminded of legendary news reporter Walter Lippmann's observation regarding news reporting: "For the most part we do not first see, and then define, we define first and then see."[11]

## SEVEN EVENTS THAT CONSTITUTE THE MOMENT

We refer to the debate on Obama and Rev. Wright as the Moment, but it is actually composed of several events that occurred during a roughly two-and-a-half-month period of time, from March 13 to May 31, 2008. On March 13, ABC aired snippets of Wright's sermons, the media event that triggered the entire debate. Starting with this airing, we identified seven events in the Obama-Wright debate that we considered to be significant. Other media events may have occurred, but many were characteristic of hard-boiled politics or "Washington theater"—events of grandstanding but no real importance. Two examples are the March 15, 2008, media discussion of why *Rolling Stone* changed the title of an article from "Obama's Radical Roots" to "Destiny's Child," and the April 11, 2008, statement by Obama that some rural communities "cling to their guns."[12]

Putting aside these sideshow attractions, we identified the seven key events in the Moment as these:

March 13, 2008: ABC airs snippets of Rev. Wright's sermons.
March 14, 2008: Obama makes statements to the media about Rev. Wright and Trinity Church.
March 18, 2008: Obama gives his speech, "A More Perfect Union."
April 25, 2008: Rev. Wright is interviewed by Bill Moyers on PBS's *The Journal*.
April 27, 2008: Rev. Wright gives an address to the NAACP.
April 28, 2008: Rev. Wright speaks at the National Press Club.
May 31, 2008: Obama resigns from Trinity United Church of Christ.

Four of these events center on presidential contender Barack Obama and three events center on Rev. Wright.

In this chapter, we look back at the postings and comments on news media websites that accompanied these events. Our purpose is to provide a richer, more inclusive, less political, and more personal account of a historic happening in this country. We examine newspaper accounts, letters to the editors, TV programs, and, most important, the online media outlets, including the websites of established media like the *New York Times* and CNN as well as stand-alone sites. We present not only the views of the news producers of these websites but also the voice of the public expressed in the comments sections of these same sites.[13]

## EVENT 1: MARCH 13, 2008

The first event took place on March 13, 2008, when an ABC News article by Brian Ross and Rehab El-Buri was headlined, "Obama's Pastor: God Damn America, U.S. to Blame for 9/11" and "Sen. Barack Obama's Pastor Says Blacks Should Not Sing 'God Bless America' But 'God Damn America.'"[14]

The headline was followed with this statement: "The Rev. Jeremiah Wright, Obama's pastor for the last 20 years at the Trinity United Church of Christ on Chicago's south side, has a long history of what even Obama's campaign aides concede is 'inflammatory rhetoric,' including the assertion that the United States brought on the 9/11 attacks with its own 'terrorism.'"[15] ABC also played snippets of Wright's sermons.[16] One statement that grabbed the public's attention was from an April 13, 2003, sermon titled "God and Government":

> "God Bless America." No, no, no. Not "God Bless America"; God Damn America! That is in the Bible, for killing innocent people. God Damn America for treating her citizens as less than human. God Damn America as long as she keeps trying to act like she is god and she is supreme![17]

Another sermon, given shortly after the terrorist attacks of September 11, included this passage:

> We bombed Hiroshima! We bombed Nagasaki! And we nuked far more than the thousands in New York and the Pentagon, and we never batted an eye. We have supported state terrorism against the Palestinians and black South Africans and now we are *indignant* because the stuff we have done overseas is now right back to our own front yards. . . . America's chickens . . . are coming home . . . to roost.[18]

The ABC video compilation was first played during a week of reduced campaign coverage in the Democratic primary race between Barack Obama and Hillary Clinton. The way in which ABC presented these snippets framed how the subsequent discussion took place, focusing the debate on issues of patriotism. For the most part, the media left untroubled additional and deeper explorations into the points Wright argued in his sermons, including issues of racism, U.S. foreign policy, and social justice.

It is natural that people in a democracy should respond when they believe that Americans' values are being reproached or that someone is speaking negatively about their country; they can and should offer their criticism. Such criticism is fundamental to democracy and the American way of life: "The ways in which information passes through a society are the key to that society's culture and are inseparable from its understanding of how to preserve itself and its internal group relationships. It is the silence that controls a society and keep it 'stable' much more than the conscious noise it generates."[19] That said, democracy also requires listening to and hearing the "whole story," not only the snippets. The dangers of a narrowly defined view of an issue is one that African Americans as a people have learned over and over again during enslavement, reconstruction, the civil rights movement and presently in their everyday lives. A broad view and an openness to criticism are fundamental to America's well-being and health as a democracy. As James Baldwin said, "I love America more than any other country in the world, and, for exactly this reason, I insist on the right to criticize her perpetually."[20]

When ABC aired this segment on March 13, Obama had a substantial edge in news coverage over Clinton (67 percent to 51 percent).[21] Obama's edge in news coverage can presumably be attributed to his victory in the March 8 Wyoming caucus and the March 11 Mississippi primary by substantial margins. Obama's race had not yet become a major issue in the campaign coverage, and there had been only a few race-related controversies. Just the week before, former vice presidential candidate Geraldine Ferraro had implied that Obama's race and gender had given him an advantage in the primaries: "If Obama was a white man, he would not be in this position. And if he was a woman (of any color) he would not be in this position. He happens to be very lucky to be who he is. And the country is caught up in the concept." Both Ferraro and Clinton publicly apologized for these remarks. The combination of Ferraro's remarks and Wright's sermons accounted for heavy news coverage for Obama the week of March 10–16, these stories constituting 18 percent of the election news, notably more coverage than Republican candidate John McCain received during this same period.[22]

Once the videos had played on ABC, they soon came to dominate television and print media, leaving journalists scrambling to discover different angles to report on the effects of the videos on the Obama campaign. The public's reaction to the video snippets was swift, widespread, and accompanied by a great deal of punditry. The continuous replaying of the videos results in comments depicting anger, frustration, and dissatisfaction with Obama, Wright, and the media's actions. Many of the comments posted on media websites showed people engaged in dialogue with each other just as much as commenting on the main actors. This public outpouring covered a range of topics, but four main threads are clearly evident: patriotism/anti-Americanism, race and racism, Obama's decision-making, and the media.

## Patriotism/Anti-Americanism

One main theme was patriotism and anti-Americanism. Some comments on the various news websites described Rev. Wright as being anti-American or unpatriotic; some disagreed and argued that a patriot speaks the truth. A few comments questioned Michelle Obama's patriotism as well, referencing a statement she made in February 2008: "For the first time in my adult life I am proud of my country." Representative examples expressed all of these angles:

> I consider Wright an enemy of the USA. It is greatly ominous that for many years Obama has continued to attend Wright's anti-American and anti-Christian services.

> I have really had enough! There is NO way in the world a President should be elected who has chosen to align himself with a Pastor who holds so much apparent hate for the country he is in.

> The "audacity" of Obama running for Presidency and having a wife who is not proud to be an American? What kind of message does that send, and what kind of "first lady" will she be??

> I think that to put Reverend Wright in opposition to the US is wrong, surely one must recognize that the US has not always been on the side of right, and has committed some acts against humanity. If you are going to paint a portrait, use both sides of the brush.

> The LOVE we have for America is precisely the reason that many of us are ready to be honest about our wrongdoing. It is our patriotism that compels us to aspire toward the justice we claim to champion.

## Race and Racism

Race and racism were another major theme of the public reaction to Wright's sermons, perhaps even the central one. Race was often not addressed directly by the media; it is as if they walked to the door, knocked softly, but did not dare to enter. On the comment boards, however, race was discussed widely and openly. It was referenced in terms of the background of comment posters, in terms of the potential black racism of Obama and Wright, and in terms of its overly significant influence on the presidential election. Additionally, it was asserted that race and racism are something that people needed to "get over"; that Obama was picked on because of his race; and that what was at issue was that black and white people don't know true American history. The six examples below represent some of these different angles: concern with Obama's race, the argument that black racism is central in the Obama/Wright relationship, the argument that the United States needs to "get over" black versus white, the feeling that no other (white) candidate has undergone such scrutiny because of his faith, and the suggestion that both black and white people do not know American history:

As a white male, I'm starting to get really worried about the possibility of having an African-American as President of the United States.

The fact that Obama has been supportive of this Rev. for so many years proves he wasn't offended by the awful statements Wright made and that black racism is tolerable.

This will be sad if the election comes down to race, we need to get over the past in our country. The fighting and quarreling of events 50 years ago only hurt our progress.

People need to get over the black and white thing.

No white candidate has come under scrutiny because of his faith.

Many Americans both white and black do not know the true history and therefore when men like Jeremiah Wright and even Min. Louis Farrakhan hold up the mirror or our violent history on people of color, we try to portray them as militants promoting racial hatred. Nothing is further from the truth.

## Obama's Decision-Making and Judgment

The third theme of the news coverage and public reaction has to do with questions about Obama's judgment and decision-making—specifically, why he hadn't distanced himself from Wright. Some wondered why he maintained a relationship with Wright, and others why he hadn't disavowed Wright's statements. Commenters saw his continued relationship with Wright and Trinity as evidence of impaired judgment or foolish decision-making. The decision-making theme had many foci: whether Obama had the "courage and morals" to leave Trinity UCC, issues of procrastination, Wright's sermon as the "petri dish for Obama's views," and whether Obama was secretly in agreement with Wright.

If Senator Barack Obama does not have the courage and morals to not only distance himself from his own pastor's evil and divisive comments; yet demands that Senator Hillary Clinton fire her friend Geraldine Ferraro . . . he is nothing more than a hypocrite and the "typical politician" he insists not to be.

I am aware that Obama may not support all his positions but he has done nothing to disavow them or separate himself from Wright's overt condemnation of the U.S.

You can't say "he is like an old uncle that says things." This is not a "crazy" uncle, this is your pastor who clearly spurs hate for anyone other than Africans. If Obama worships there does he in fact have the same views?

This is the man Obama calls his "spiritual mentor," probably the most significant influence on his thinking. This is the guy Obama got to give up his pastorship for now, but Wright's sermon's are the petri dish where Obama's views were formed.

Obama selected and continued to go hear this man speak—preach—for 20 years! No one goes and listens to someone speak every week for 20 years if they did not agree with him or have his words strike a chord within as some truth.

Some comments minimized the significance of the influence of Reverend Wright on Obama:

I haven't agreed with everything my Pastor's said concerning social issues. Why? I am not a clone. Remember, Wright is Obama's "SPIRITUAL" leader. That's what a Pastor is. I think it's best to look at what Obama's actions have been instead of what his Pastor has said.

## The Media

Centuries ago, in 442 BC, Sophocles argued, "Don't blame the person who brings bad news." This "don't-kill-the-messenger" axiom is still relevant today and, more than ever, the media, broadly defined, is the messenger. This includes newspapers and television as well as social media and websites. Numerous comments in the website postings voiced opinions about the media's role in this controversy. The majority claimed the reporting of these events had been biased and viewed the continuous broadcasting of Wright's sermons as unnecessary. The examples of public comments below illustrate the theme of biased reporting: expressing frustration with the nonstop replays of the video snippets and grabbing headlines, suggesting that the media focus on more important issues, and lamenting the decreased reporting standards.

This is a great example of biased reporting! I've never been to the church or met the pastor, but I can tell you just by watching the story that a few sermons out of thousands were chosen to paint a picture of this man spending every Sunday morning on the pulpit preaching inflammatory anti-American sermons.

I know this story makes great headlines and will be another great story at appealing to people's fear.

Anybody else tired of all these distracting headlines besides me? Why isn't the media raising questions about the issues instead of looking for every potentially inflammatory remark? Oh, wait, I forgot, that's what political discourse has been reduced to in this country.

> I am outraged that Good Morning America would pick and choose excerpts from Pastor Jeremiah Wright and try to use it against Senator Obama. I used to have great respect for reporters but the days of the "Walter Cronkite Integrity Reporter" are gone.

Following ABC's airing of snippets from Wright's sermons, YouTube became a key circulation site for editing the sermon clips, creating mash-ups of other sermons, posting personal videos of reactions to the clips, and responding to others' posts.[23] According to Viral Video, a daily catalog of popular videos on major sites, by Sunday, two days after the first video clip aired, some three hundred videos on the topic had been posted, and an additional five hundred had been posted by Monday, the day before Obama's "A More Perfect Union" speech in Philadelphia; by the morning of the speech, the video tally was over nine hundred.[24]

## EVENT 2: MARCH 15, 2008

"Obama Disavows Pastor's Remarks" —*Washington Post*[25]

"Obama: Wright Wrong" —ABC News[26]

"Obama Condemns Pastor's Statements" —*New York Times*[27]

On March 15, 2008, Barack Obama made his official response to the Wright debate. Heated discussions about Obama and Wright had continued to dominate the news and daily discourse among the general public, and in response he issued a statement on the topic on the Huffington Post titled "On My Faith and My Church" and appeared on several major television networks. In these appearances, he showed respect for and support of the man who brought him to Christ, performed his marriage, and baptized his daughters, but at the same time he denounced the specific statements by Wright that were being played over and over again on TV and reported on in the print media.

Obama's essay began with an acknowledgment that Rev. Wright, the pastor of his church, was retiring and that some of the comments he made about our country, our politics, and his political opponents had caused a firestorm. About Wright's comments, Obama stated:

> Let me say at the outset that I vehemently disagree and strongly condemn the statements that have been the subject of this controversy. I categorically denounce any statement that disparages our great country or serves to divide us from our allies. I also believe that words that degrade individuals have no place in our public dialogue, whether it's on the campaign stump or in the pulpit. In sum, I reject outright the statements by Rev. Wright that are at issue.

> Because these particular statements by Rev. Wright are so contrary to my own life and beliefs, a number of people have legitimately raised questions about the nature of my relationship with Rev. Wright and my membership in the church.

From his rejection of Wright's comments, Obama went on to declare that the comments Wright made did not define who he is and what he stands for:

> I knew Rev. Wright as someone who served this nation with honor as a United States Marine, as a respected biblical scholar, and as someone, who taught or lectured at seminaries across the country, from Union Theological Seminary to the University of Chicago. He also led a diverse congregation that was and still is a pillar of the South Side and the entire city of Chicago. It's a congregation that does not merely preach social justice but acts it out each day, through ministries ranging from housing the homeless to reaching out to those with HIV/AIDS.

Next, Obama addressed the question that many in the media and general public were asking: "Was Obama present when Wright made the comment?"

> The statements that Rev. Wright made that are the cause of this controversy were not statements I personally heard him preach while I sat in the pews of Trinity or heard him utter in private conversation. When these statements first came to my attention, it was at the beginning of my presidential campaign. I made it clear at the time that I strongly condemned his comments. But because Rev. Wright was on the verge of retirement, and because of my strong links to the Trinity faith community, where I married my wife and where my daughters were baptized, I did not think it appropriate to leave the church.

To close his essay, Obama argued that he believed the American people would judge him not because of what someone else had said but on the basis of his beliefs, values, and experience to be the U.S. president.[28]

Obama followed up the print statement with a round of television interviews on MSNBC, Fox News, and CNN,[29] during which he pushed back against the growing outcries that were affecting his nomination bid.

Appearing on Keith Olbermann's show on MSNBC, Obama was asked a number of open-ended questions that permitted him to craft responses much the way he wished. He took a strong stand against Reverend Wright's remarks but stopped short of severing his relationship with Wright. Here, Obama presented the talking points that he would repeat throughout the day in the other interviews. Four to five times he vehemently condemned Reverend Wright's comments; he argued that he did not hear the comments circulating on almost every media outlet throughout the country; and he insisted that the statements are antithetical to him as a person and greatly conflict with his profound love of the United States. In these responses, Obama limited his responses to the issues raised by the handful of video snippets being broadcast and did not address the more general themes of Wright's sermons, such as poverty, the use of American power on the world stage, and social justice. Was Obama's response also conditioned by how the media frames the discussion, with the attention on patriotism? At one point Obama declared, "He [Rev. Wright] helped to bring me to Jesus and helped to bring me to church. He's like an uncle who talks to me, not about political things and social views, but faith and God and family."

Obama followed these same talking points when he appeared Fox News, but interviewer Major Garrett used a more direct interview style, asking for "yes or no" responses to his pointed questions. Garrett stated at the outset that he wanted to ask Obama "a set of basic, sort of threshold questions about your [his] faith experience at Trinity United Church of Christ," which he framed as yes/no questions regarding Obama's membership, regularity of attendance, and donations to Trinity UCC. Obama responded affirmatively or negatively, but added further context and qualifying commentary. When asked about the specific snippets from Rev. Wright's sermons, Obama emphasized that these sound bites did not represent "the tenor or tone [of Wright's sermons] on an ongoing basis." This response, however, did not transition into a deeper and wider discussions of the issues raised by the sermons. Garrett repeatedly asked—employing a prosecutorial style of questioning—whether Obama would have quit if he had heard the statements personally. Obama stressed he was not present when the statements are made and had previously only heard about one or two of them.

In these television interviews and his statement in the Huffington Post, Obama tried to put to rest the outcries that began with the showing of the snippets of Reverend Wright on ABC. But America was not done with this event. The narrow framing of the discussion held firm, not just because of the media's focus on those few inflammatory statements but because of Obama's focus on them as well. Obama's television appearance did very little to satisfy the questions about his relations with Wright. To some extent he acerbated the issue and vexed others who argued "enough already."

In many website comments, people spoke back to each other rather than to the media or the candidate. In some cases, they argued about the ideological stance taken, reasoning that *that* stance is costly both socially and historically to their "correct" view of America. For them, the Wright event is personal, with significant social, political, global, and historical implications. Other comments vent anger at the media, implying that the media is the power broker and major actor in this event. Many and varied, the comments argue with, sympathize with, and scream at Obama.

Argue with Obama:

> So Obama is attempting to tell us that the pastor who preached to him, married
> him, counseled him, baptized his children, and served as his personal mentor
> and spiritual adviser suddenly blindsided him right before his presidential bid
> with socialist, divisive, black liberation theology and hateful anti-American
> rhetoric that apparently had never ever been uttered in Obama's presence
> before (let along discussed in his general vicinity by even one fellow member
> of the congregation) in the last twenty three years?
>
> He should be ashamed of himself. He knew about this at the beginning of his
> campaign and still kept his mentor as one of his advisors in his campaign. He
> didn't remove him till it hit the media.

Sympathize with Obama:

> Before anyone criticizes you over Rev. Wright's comments, they ought to ask
> themselves: "Do I agree with everything my priest/minister/preacher/pastor/
> rabbi/imam says?" If not, they should ask, "Did a disagreement with my relig-
> ious leader cause me to leave my church/synagogue/temple/congregation?"
> That should make clear what a bogus issue this is.

Scream at Obama:

> You're a liar Barack Obama!! YOU SHOULD REJECT THIS CHURCH
> NOT JUST THE PASTORS WORDS.

Some chastised Obama, arguing that he displayed poor judgment or decision-
making:

> As a prospective candidate for the presidency, Senator Obama showed poor
> judgment in remaining in Trinity United.

Speaking truth to power is perhaps more clearly visibly in the statements
made by bloggers about the media. Some statements focus on the media's
power to shape potential voters' views:

> The media isn't letting this go, so therefore it's not over. If Obama didn't think
> it was an issue that could keep him out of the White House, he wouldn't have
> written on HuffPo.

Others consider the media's power to control the story:

> Consider WHO, primarily, is pushing this story: Fox, MSNBC, Limbaugh,
> Hannity, all the right wing talk shows. Who stands to benefit from this story?

> Certainly, not Obama. Hillary, the obvious beneficiary, is the candidate McCain and the GOP most want to run against!

Trinity United Church of Christ did not remain silent during this debate. The church and its new pastor, Reverend Otis Moss III, mounted a vigorous defense of Rev. Wright and the church. Rev. Moss posted a statement on Trinity's website: "It is an indictment on Dr. Wright's ministerial legacy to present his global ministry within a 15- or 30-second sound bite."[30] Moss added, "The African-American Church was born out of the crucible of slavery and the legacy of prophetic African-American preachers since slavery has been and continues to heal broken, marginalized victims of social and economic injustices."[31]

The *Washington Post* reported Moss's comments to his parishioners during the March 16 Sunday church service. Looking down at his congregants, upset and dismayed by the media reports on their beloved former pastor and the media's coverage and entrance into Trinity Church's worship space, Rev. Moss said, "The world is only seeing this tiny piece of him. Right now we are all being vilified. This isn't just about Trinity, isn't just about [Wright]. This is an attack on the African American church tradition, and that's the way we see it. This is an attempt to silence our voice."[32] Moss, as the minister following in the footsteps of Wright, was also being observed by the congregation to see how he handled the firestorm. Moss explained that there were two narratives about the controversy surrounding Wright: "There's the narrative of the African American church community that understands what has happened, that knows Wright's record and his legacy. And then there's the narrative of the wider community that doesn't understand."[33]

In a continuation of the narrative about the need to understand the African American church in order to understand Rev. Wright's sermon, Dwight Hopkins, a theologian and longtime Trinity member, stated, "Things that might mean one thing in the church take on a new meaning when you don't see the full sermon, or understand the full context."[34] (Chapter 3 attempts to provide that full context.)

## EVENT 3: MARCH 18, 2008

"We the people, in order to form a more perfect union" was the lead sentence following the headline in the *New York Times* on March 18, 2008, which read, "Barack Obama's Speech on Race."

Obama's TV interviews and his statement to the Huffington Post did not quell voters' concerns about his relationship with Wright, whether he heard or agreed with the statements on the snippets, and his patriotism. After nearly a week of continuous media attention, Obama's campaign realized that the short TV interviews and press statements were not sufficient to put the matter to rest. And the controversy brought to the fore the issue that Obama was most anxious to avoid: race. Knowing how fraught the notion of race is for many Americans, he strove to rise above an issue that he feared would narrowly define him. As a result, he avoided discussion of topics like the civil rights sit-ins and boycotts of the 1960s; the snarling dogs in Birmingham, Alabama; racial inequality in public schools; the economic difference between races; and the overrepresentation of African Americans in prisons. Instead, he wished to leap to Martin Luther King Jr.'s dream of "the sons and daughters of former slaves and the sons and daughters of former slave owners sitting down together at a table of brotherhood."[35]

Obama's campaign reasoned that concerns about patriotism and other social issues, while serious challenges, could be handled. Not so with race. Without a direct offensive strike to meet it head on, race was rapidly becoming the focus of the campaign, much to their chagrin. Obama and his advisors decided he should give a speech addressing the controversy through a larger frame of a national conversation about race in American society. At a town hall meeting in Monaca, Pennsylvania, Obama reiterated his criticism of Wright's statements but also previewed his upcoming speech: "I think the caricature that is being painted of him [Wright] is not accurate. And so part of what I'll do tomorrow is to talk a little bit about how some of these issues are perceived from within the black church community, for example, which I think views this very differently."[36]

Media speculation about this upcoming speech was heavy. The media played it up, hyping the anticipation. Comments on television and in the print media spoke of hopes and possibilities about what the speech would be able to accomplish. These comments included expectations that the speech would quell the Wright issue but also, perhaps more importantly, that it would help America to deal with the "race problem." Others argued about the limitations of any one speech. Still other comments spoke to people's anger and resentment toward Obama and Wright, and they had little hope that the speech would be able to quiet the controversy. Some anticipated the speech as one anticipates reading or hearing a good piece of literature. For instance, one person described it as "a speech that will be documented in history and on par with William Faulkner's Nobel Prize speech in Stockholm in 1955."

Would it be a good piece of literature? At this point we borrow from Gao Xingjian's 2000 Nobel Prize Lecture "The Case for Literature," delivered in Stockholm on December 7, 2000. During this lecture, Gao Xinjian made a statement that is useful for understanding Obama's speech: "What I want to do is to use this opportunity to speak as one writer in the voice of an individual [and] a writer as an ordinary person."[37] Gao Xingjian goes on to describe the tenets that good writers should follow. These tenets can help make sense of not only Obama's speech but also the wide range of comments in the media from journalists and the general public both before and after it. Gao Xingjian addresses several themes a writer should consider. He suggests a writer is both an ordinary person and an individual engaging in a process to preserve a human consciousness through the use of language. He asserts that the writer should not be controlled by the political ideology of those governing; instead, a writer's concern is to speak to and give voice to the everyday people. He states:

> In the century just ended literature . . . was more scarred by politics and power than in any previous period, and the writer too was subjected to unprecedented oppression. In order that literature safeguard the reason for its own existence and become the tool of politics it must return to the voice of the individual, for literature is primarily derived from the feelings of the individual and is the result of feeling.

Gao Xingjian continues, "This is not to say that literature must therefore be divorced from politics or that it must necessarily be involved in politics. . . . If ideology unites with power and is transformed into a real force then both literature and the individual will be destroyed."

Comparing Gao Xingjian's philosophy of literature to Obama's speech, we can see that Obama sought to use his individual story to raise the nation above politics about race. He wanted to use language—words, storytelling, metaphors, and narratives from history—to take the conversation to another place: a place where race is not the dominant theme. Gao Xingjian, however, issues a caution that is relevant for taking into account the potential and the limits of Obama's noble ambition to use a speech to quell the Wright controversy:

> Born at the start of human civilization, like life, language is full of wonders and its expressive capacity is limitless. It is the work of the writer to discover and develop the latent potential inherent in language. The writer is not the Creator and he cannot eradicate the world. . . . He cannot establish some new ideal world even if the present world is absurd and beyond human comprehension. However, he can certainly make innovative statements either by adding to what earlier people have said or else starting where earlier people stopped.

Could Obama's speech help the public to return to his vision of unity and transcendence of race?

## Anticipation of the Speech

How were potential voters anticipating Obama's speech? Some of the message boards and comments on news media websites argued that Obama was doing the nation a favor by addressing race because it has prevailed as a neglected and misunderstood issue in the United States: "Obama is doing the country a great service by addressing the issue. . . . We really do need to get beyond race." From the opposite end of the spectrum were claims that the speech would be nothing more than "damage control," that it would be "too late," and that people "don't need any more speeches from him . . . they didn't want to be preached to"; others argued that he was playing "the race card against his two racial groups: black and whites." Many contended that Obama had remained at Trinity Church too long, listening to Rev. Wright's sermons, suggesting that this showed "poor judgment" that cannot be ameliorated with a speech.

Still others wondered if the speech would contextualize the "real issues" of the economy and unemployment. Some hoped the speech would penetrate the layer of racism that impedes progress for all in the country: "As a nation we will never be able to transcend race until we are willing to confront openly its divisiveness in our politics, our communities, and yes, in our churches. . . . This is more important than politics; this is about who we are as a people." Some anticipated the speech itself: "I look forward to hearing it. Race and religion has been the elephant in the room long enough in this campaign."

Throughout the discussion about what the speech would or would not accomplish were comments about Obama, the man and candidate. In Obama's upcoming speech, people wondered if they would hear an ordinary, authentic person telling his own story, expressing feelings derived from his own life experiences and spoken based on those feelings. Or would the speech be conceptualized and written by a staff whose only interest was winning at any cost or regardless of who had to be sacrificed in order to achieve victory?

Some were not interested in Obama's speech at all. They had heard enough from Obama; he had become just another candidate: "It's too late Obama. We don't need no more speeches from you." Another asserts, "Sorry to say I lost all respect for Obama, to me his words are just words." Others thought that the speech would be patronizing: "I fully expect another patronizing speech to us all from Mr. Obama." And a few questioned Obama's moral "right" to give such a speech: "The speech will be called 'The Audacity of Obama, Giving a Speech on Race, after 20 Years on Wright's Pew.'"

Anticipation of the speech thus encompassed many disparate feelings: hopeful anticipation and expectations, so-what anticipation and expectations, and I-couldn't-care-less assertions. Obama had the audience hyped-up and all were highly aware of it, even those who derided the speech as just more Obama rhetoric. It was now up to him to convince those who listened that he was an ordinary, authentic person, who, because of his life experiences and vision of America, could best lead them at this critical time in the nation's history.

## The Speech

On March 18, 2008, standing in front of seven American flags, Obama delivered his speech at the National Constitution Center in Philadelphia to a small audience of local supporters, elected officials, and clergy members.[38] According to Obama's aides, the senator stayed up late the night before, writing and polishing much of the speech himself. One indication of his personal involvement in writing the speech is the familiar strains of his search for racial identity, found in his biography *Dreams from My Father*.[39]

Obama spoke for thirty-seven minutes. Billed as a "race speech" by his staff and the media, the title of the speech, "A More Perfect Union," was indicative of more far-reaching goals. In the speech, Obama reassured citizens that he was a loyal American and disagreed "vehemently" with Rev. Wright's statements, while stopping short of denouncing his former pastor. Obama reminded voters of his campaign messages of unity, hope, and change. He promised to address pressing economic, educational, and social issues. And Obama spoke directly to the black community, urging them to "understand the sources of the racial fears and resentments among whites." Likewise, he spoke to the white community, trying to explain "the anger and frustration behind Mr. Wright's words."[40] Speaking at length about race in ways that were unusual for an American politician, the speech had two goals: to refocus the public's attention away from the Wright controversy and to turn the conversation toward current social issues.

In his speech, race was contextualized and discussed in a more complicated and complex manner than it usually is by media pundits. It was not that the speech was exceedingly profound as much as that America had not heard a discussion of the differences in privileges and experiences of whites and blacks in America presented in such a direct manner. Furthermore, Obama did not hide race in the coded language often used through terms such as "welfare queens." He penetrated the surface of race and reached deep into the inner workings of its reality. He removed false illusions, spoke in a simple language, and provided examples that both black and white, young and old, could relate to. In so doing he tried to convey the insidious nature and pervasiveness of racism and how it operates throughout the country.

## Reaction to the Speech

After the speech, the web traffic was extremely heavy. A video of Obama's speech was viewed 2.5 million times on YouTube in the first seventy-two hours after its delivery, in addition to those who saw it live on cable or read excerpts.[41] Television pundits frantically searched for words and themes to comment on. They looked for these themes partly because of the need to meet deadlines but also because many journalists had a difficult time discussing issues of race in the manner that Obama had discussed them in the speech. The Project for Excellence in Journalism observed this discomfort: "Perhaps the most intriguing element was watching the media culture try to deal with a speech so complex it defied the TV panel debate, the skills of the veteran political writer or the parameters of a 90-second nightly news segment."[42] Is the challenge that many pundits lack the requisite skills and background knowledge to offer substantive commentary about matters of race and racism in the United States?

Jeff Zeleny of the *New York Times* described Obama's speech as "a sweeping assessment of race in America."[43] Zeleny suggested that the candidate gave two messages for two communities: "Mr. Obama went on to try to explain to white voters the anger and frustration behind Mr. Wright's words and to urge blacks to try to understand the sources of the racial fears and resentments among whites."[44] Zeleny also pointed out Obama's dual goals: the political goal to squelch voters' doubts about his relationship with Rev. Wright and the need to refocus attention toward his campaign messages of unity and concrete issues such as the economy.[45]

When asked for her immediate reaction to Obama's speech, Hillary Rodham Clinton stated she had not heard it or read the transcript yet, but noted that she was "very glad" Obama was making a speech about race, calling it a "complicated" and "difficult" issue.[46]

On Fox News, Sean Hannity interviewed pollster Frank Luntz about his reactions to Obama's speech. Hannity characterized Obama's speech as "political expediency."[47] While praising the speech as "Kennedy-esque," Luntz critiqued what he viewed as Obama's defense of Wright and his attention on race rather than on other pressing national issues.[48] Hannity hinted at the fact that Obama may "deep down in his heart think like Pastor Wright," suggesting that if he does that "would mean a racist and an anti-Semite would be president of the United States."[49]

For the most part, the speech produced the desired outcome for the Obama campaign: it shifted the focus away from Wright, allowed Obama to dominate the news in a positive way, and gave his supporters and those leaning in his direction a moment's peace. For the campaign, the fact that some supporters praised the speech's honesty and content and saw it as a teaching moment was an added value. Speaking to the Huffington Post, Obama supporter Reverend Jesse Jackson characterized Obama's speech as follows: "He was forthright and not evasive, and uses it as a teaching moment in American history: America's struggle to overcome its past and become a more perfect union."[50] Carole McDonnell, on the blog *African American Opinion*, stated, "Because they identify America as a white nation, they can't picture black Americans as loving a country and at the same time being upset at that country's history."[51] In the week of the speech, March 17–23, Obama dominated the media narrative as a significant figure in 72 percent of the week's campaign coverage.[52] Obama also succeeded in shifting the focus from Wright onto himself, reducing coverage of Wright as lead newsmaker to 7 percent, though their relationship and its fallout made up 37 percent of the week's coverage.[53]

## How Did Jane and Joe Public React to the Speech?

Many people were pleased with the success of the speech. As Gao Xingjian reminds us, "the impact of one's writing is determined by society and not determined by the wishes of the writer."[54] These comments reflected that success:

> That was the most incredible and gutsy speech I've ever seen from a U.S. politician.

> A historic speech—one that made me think again that this is why we need this man to be our next president. It was blunt, honest, straightforward and riveting—a breath of fresh air that is rare in this political climate!

> It is a truly great speech, a momentous response to critics and to supporters of Senator Obama, a speech written by the senator over the course of a day or two, eloquent, passionate, honest, heartfelt, patriotic, thoughtful, poetic, and fierce.

Gao Xingjian stated, "There is no greater consolation for a writer than to be able to leave a book in humankind's vast treasury of literature that will continue to be read in future times."[55] Some contended that Obama gave a speech "that will continue to be read in future times":

> Grand slam. Congratulations, Senator Obama. When the election has come and gone, the speech should be anthologized in all US history textbooks.

> This is a speech that will be talked about and studied in every school and in every corner of the world for decades to come. I taped it and will print the text for my children and ask that in the future they share it with their children.

> Absolutely the best speech on race since "I Have a Dream."

Other commentators reflected on whether the speech quelled the Wright controversy. To have a successful teachable moment that helps to transform and bring about reconciliation between whites and blacks, a moment that men have striven toward for decades, demands many elements, including "speaking and writing that allows for communication between individuals of different races and socio economic class." Such communication, in the case of Obama and "A More Perfect Union," also provided an opportunity for him to be judged by his audience to determine if he is achieved his goal. Some assessed his speech as having successfully quelled the controversy.

> We just witnessed a major change in racial discourse in this country, and it is rooted in the need for basic economic fairness for all races, genders and classes.

> Obama just gave an incredibly inspiring and moving speech that did a lot to put to rest this whole Rev. Wright thing. Let's all move on now, shall we?"

> No other politician in America today could deliver such an intelligent and thoughtful discourse about race and its role in American society and politics.

Others claimed the speech was weak and believed that Obama had not put an end to the issue:

> Once again with beautiful words, he said almost nothing.

> He is engaging in double speak and it is really cynical that he tries to have it both ways. This speech was given because the controversy has threatened to derail the central tenets of his candidacy. It's too little and it's too late.

> One nice speech after several days of political pressure cannot make his two-decade-long relation with Wright go away.

The speech did very little to improve some people's feelings and attitudes toward Obama. For them, it was a source of annoyance.

> I am so tired of this attention grabbing cult of personality. The country has real problems and racism is one of them but this is about Obama.

> This man is a black Bush. Lies, lies, lies and more lies. A written speech does not cover up the hatred and racism exposed in the tapes of Pastor Wright cursing America.

Many comments specifically addressed the literary qualities of the speech. Admirers argued that Obama used language that conveyed honesty and clarity, addressed inclusiveness, and looked beyond the controversy at hand.

> While the speech primarily addressed racial issues it maintained an overall sense of inclusion of all Americans for the challenges that lie ahead and the underlying recognition that in a country that has been so divided some more healing needs to be done for "us to become the change we can believe in."

> The most fair assessment of racial issues which I have ever heard.

Others saw Obama's rhetoric as overly smooth and superficial:

> He is certainly a smooth operator and has everyone feeling good again, except for the fact that he never touches on what people are worried about. It's the economy stupid!

> But the majority in America is not black and the race issue Obama has promoted does not impact non-black voters and on the contrary, has alienated many against this pro-Obama black pride movement.

Many comments conveyed whether the speech moved them to support Obama more or less, especially among undecided voters.

> NOTHING he could say today would appease his detractors, but for those of us like myself who were on the fence, this was the push I needed towards the Obama side.

> This resonates very strongly with Richard Nixon's Checkers speech. It tugs on the same emotions that Nixon used so expertly way back then. The critical piece for Obama is: are we as gullible now as America was back in the early 1950s.

## The Aftermath

In an interview with CNN's Anderson Cooper two days after the speech, Obama stated, "In some ways, this controversy has actually shaken me up a little bit and gotten me back into remembering the odds of me getting elected have always been lower than some of the other conventional candidates."[56] With this reflection, Obama and his campaign moved away from the discussion of race that the polls and pundits suggested might be threatening his run for the Democratic nomination. The war, the economy, other domestic issues, and an upcoming debate with Hillary Clinton quickly became the focus on the campaign trail. Obama's camp was anxiously waiting to find out if the controversy about Wright and the black church would affect him in the Pennsylvania state primary on April 22.

Obama received bad news. Not only did he lose the Pennsylvania primary, but Clinton also scored a major victory and reenergized her campaign. Pennsylvania's largely white, working-class electorate gave Clinton a 56.6 to 45.4 percent victory, with 60 percent of the white vote. After the loss in Pennsylvania, Obama's campaign tried to shake off the sting of defeat and prepare for the upcoming May 6 primaries in Indiana and North Carolina. They strove to put to rest the lingering stories about Wright still in the news cycle and faced a revitalized Clinton campaign. Meanwhile, unbeknownst to the Obama campaign, Wright was finalizing his itinerary for three major speaking engagements: an interview with Bill Moyers, the annual NAACP dinner, and a lecture and Q&A at the Washington Press Club. We discuss these events next.


## EVENT 4: APRIL 25, 2008


Online headlines from April 25, 2008, after Bill Moyers of PBS interviewed Jeremiah Wright read as follows:

"Rev. Wright, in PBS Interview, Defends Sermons and Calls Coverage 'Unfair'" —*Washington Post*

"Rev. Wright says 'devious' forces behind use of his words against Obama: People who heard entire sermons understood his message, he says in Moyers interview" —*Chicago Tribune*

On April 25, 2008, Bill Moyers interviewed Jeremiah Wright on his PBS program *Bill Moyers Journal*. Among the statements that Wright made was that Obama is "a politician." This term was picked up by many media outlets because it's a word that's a sting in the Obama world, where Obama had been campaigning for more than a year as a transformational, anti-Washington agent of change.

Media headlines took different approaches and developed diverse themes when they reported on the first phrase of Wright's three day (April 25–28) "rehabilitation tour." For some, Wright spoke with a passion and moral conviction reminiscent of Martin Luther King Jr. when he spoke out against the Vietnam War, with the defiance of Cassius Clay (Muhammad Ali) when he refused to be drafted into the U.S. military, and with the resolve of Tommie Smith and John Carlos when they gave the Black Power salute during the 1968 Olympics in Mexico City. In this same way, Wright set out to defend the black church, to inform the public of its history and traditions, and to personally push back against the public's impression of him heretofore defined solely by sermon snippets that many people viewed as anti-American, unpatriotic, and racist.

During this interview, Moyers asked Wright questions about the sermon snippets and statements circulating in the media that caused dismay, anger, and confusion among so many. How did he respond to the questions posed by Moyers that many Americans were anxious to hear his answers to?[57]

### On Trinity's Motto

When asked by the host if Trinity Church's motto, "Unashamedly black and Unapologetically Christian," embraces a race-based theology, Rev. Wright asserted that it does not; instead, it embraces Christianity "without giving up Africanity." In addition, he noted that missionaries were going to countries with the assumption that the U.S. culture is superior, that the other country has no culture, and that in order to be a Christian, one must adopt the U.S. way of life.

## On the Black Church

To Bill Moyers's questions about the black church in the black community, Wright quoted what Jesus said to Nicodemus: "God should love the world," not just the black community. Wright also stated that on Sunday morning, church service in the black community "means many things. . . . I think one of the things the church service means is hope . . . that life has meaning and that God is still in control."

## On the Most Talked-About Sermon

To Moyers's question "One of the most controversial sermons that you preach is the sermon you preach that ended up being that sound bite about Goddamn America. What did you mean when you said that?" Wright asserted the following: "When you start confusing God and government, your allegiances to government—a particular government and not to God—then you're in serious trouble because governments fail people. And governments change. And governments lie. And those [are the] three points of the sermon. And that is the context in which I was illustrating how the governments biblically and the governments since biblical times, up to our time, changed, how they failed, and how they lie. . . . [G]overnments that wanna kill innocents are not consistent with the will of God. And that you are made in the image of God, you're not made in the image of any particular government. We have the freedom here in this country to talk about that publicly, whereas some other places, you're dead if say the wrong thing about your government."

Moyers then asked about the sermon Wight preached on the Sunday after 9/11: "When people saw the sound bites from it this year, they were upset because you seemed to be blaming America. Did you somehow fail to communicate?" Wright explained, "The persons who have heard the entire sermon understand the communication perfectly. . . . [W]hen something is taken like a sound bite for a political purpose and put constantly over and over again, looped in the face of the public, that's not a failure to communicate. Those who are doing that are communicating exactly what they wanna do, which is to paint me as some sort of fanatic or as the learned journalist from the *New York Times* called me, a 'wack-a-doodle.' It's to paint me as something. Something's wrong with me. There's nothing wrong with this country. There's—its policies. We're perfect. We—our hands are free. Our hands have no blood on them. That's not a failure to communicate. The message that is being communicated by the sound bites is exactly what those pushing those sound bites want to communicate."

## On Wright's Media Image

When Moyers asked, "What do you think they [the media] wanted to communicate?" Rev. Wright asserted, "I think they wanted to communicate that I am unpatriotic, that I am un-American, that I am filled with hate speech, that I have a cult at Trinity United Church of Christ. And, by the way, guess who goes to his church, hint, hint, hint? That's what they wanted to communicate."

In addition, when asked about what he thought when he saw the snippets, Rev. Wright said he thought they were unfair, unjust, and untrue, and that those who did it were doing it for "very devious" reasons, "[t]o put an element of fear and hatred and to stir up the anxiety of Americans who still don't know the African American church, know nothing about the prophetic theology of the African American experience, who know nothing about the Black church, who don't even know how we got a Black church."[58]

EVENT 5: APRIL 27, 2008

Online headlines from the second phase of Wright rehabilitation tour, a keynote address at the NAACP Annual Conference in Detroit:

"Rev. Wright Delivers Fiery Address to NAACP" —ABC

"Rev. Wright: 'Different Does Not Mean Deficient'" —*Washington Post*

The second stop on Reverend Wright's speaking tour was the annual meeting of the NAACP in Detroit, on Sunday night, April 27, 2008. His introduction bought a standing ovation from the energetic, full-to-capacity house. He began by situating the NAACP's roots in the black church, but clarified that all races and faiths have supported its fight for justice and equality. Wright discussed the mis-education of African American children. The recurring theme in his speech was that different does not mean deficient. Wright stated, "I believe that a change is going to come because many of us are committing to changing how we see others who are different." In a call-and-response style characteristic of some African American preachers, he addressed African American learning styles, pointed out that we all speak different varieties of American, and noted the differences between music from European and African heritages. In response to claims that his language and views are divisive, Reverend Wright asserted, "I describe the conditions in this country. Conditions divide, not my descriptions." Reverend Wright described Trinity's prophetic theology, stating, "I come from a religious tradition where we shout in the sanctuary and march on the picket line."

## EVENT 6: APRIL 28, 2008

Online headlines from about Wright performance during the Q&A at the National Press Club in Washington, DC:

"Jeremiah Wright Goes to War" —*Time*

"Rev. Wright Strikes Back" —*Washington Post*

"Wright Assails Media, Cheney, Obama at National Press Club" —ABC

The opening of the ABC article states, "'This is not an attack on Jeremiah Wright,' said Rev. Jeremiah Wright this morning. . . . 'This is an attack on the Black church.'" The first line in the *Washington Post* further explained Reverend Wright's actions at the National Press Club: "Sen. Barack Obama's former pastor today defended the fiery sermons that have become a political liability for the Democratic presidential contender, charging that a furor over his remarks represents an 'attack on the Black church.'"

On April 28, 2008, Wright walked to the lectern at the National Press Club in Washington, DC, as the keynote speaker for the Samuel DeWitt Proctor Conference. He delivered a lecture, followed by a Q&A that was the third and final phrase of his press tour. This occasion became the most discussed and debated event since the emergence of the videos of Wright's sermons on ABC. Each of the headlines used war terminology to describe Wright's performance during the Q&A, and while such terminology may have been in order, what also should be acknowledged is that military phrases can evoke fear in the listener. Media responses to the speech tended to emphasize this war terminology and ignore his discussion of the history and legacy of the black church. He discussed the beginning of the black church as "invisible institutions" and the many streams "that make up this multilayered and rich tapestry of the black religious experience." Wright also discussed the mis-education of African American children and compared the black church to Ellison's Invisible Man.

In this speech at the National Press Club, Wright characterized his coverage in the media as an attack on the black church, not on himself. He stated that his hope for the lecture and the DeWitt Proctor Conference was to make the reality of the African American church visible to mainstream America. He told the audience that Obama's speech had initiated a dialogue on race, which he hoped would transform Sunday morning at 11:00 from being "the most segregated hour in America." He stated, "Maybe this dialogue on race, an honest dialogue that does not engage in denial or superficial platitudes, maybe this dialogue on race can move the people of faith in this country from various stages of alienation and marginalization to the exciting possibility of reconciliation."

Wright revisited the theme of his NAACP talk that "being different does not mean one is deficient." He used as an example the difference between Sunday church services at white and black churches, including Trinity UCC. He explained the origins and history of liberation theology, situating the prophetic theology of the black church within this tradition. He also enumerated three principles of this theological stance: liberation, transformation, and reconciliation. Wright explained that these principles are at the core of the United Church of Christ and the foci of Trinity UCC since its founding in 1961. He told his audience:

> The Black church's role in the fight for equality and justice, from the 1700s up until 2008, has always had as its core the nonnegotiable doctrine of reconciliation, children of God repenting for past sins against one another.
>
> To say "I am a Christian" is not enough. Why? Because the Christianity of the slaveholder is not the Christianity of the slave. The God to whom the slaveholders pray as the ride on the decks of the ship is not the God to whom the enslaved are praying as they ride beneath the decks on that slave ship.

The audience was focused and attentive, hanging on to the speaker's words, though not necessarily for the same reasons. We can imagine audience members who were supportive of Wright, others who were against him, and still others who were questioning his stances. Wright's lecture was the second teaching-and-learning opportunity on race and the black church that America was having within a one-month period.

Typically, the question-and-answer period (Q&A) after a speech, especially an engaging and informative lecture with a distinguished, articulate person, is a time when the speaker receives accolades for a job well done. A robust round of applause and perhaps a standing ovation is a precursor to extending the discussion, often in a less formal manner than the initial presentation. Q&As can be fun or serious, provide opportunity for retorts from the audience, allow the speaker to expand, amplify, or clarify points, and so on. Reverend Wright's Q&A at the National Press Club was all of the above and more. Barack Obama, the media, and members of Trinity UCC all had something to say about the Q&A. Arguably, it might go down as one of the Press Club's most memorable Q&As. Upcoming scholars and public personalities may look to it as a guide for what to do and what not to do.

At the Q&A following Wright's lecture, visible tension developed between the speaker and the National Press Club moderator and *USA Today* reporter Donna Leinwand as they interacted. The moderator's first question referred to the sermon in which Wright stated, "America's chickens are coming home to roost," to which Reverend Wright responded by asking the moderator repeatedly if she had heard the whole sermon. From that question and response, a tit-for-tat developed between the two. Wright had to once again respond to some of the more controversial questions that he had covered in his lecture, in his interview with Bill Moyers, and in his speech at the NAACP over the past few days. Topics covered during the Q&A included U.S. imperialism, Israel and Palestine, and Wright's relationship with Louis Farrakhan.

There were additional moments when things became personal between the speaker and the moderator. Some instances included when Reverend Wright asked the moderator about her church attendance, her question about whether it was God's will for Obama to become president, and the closing question in which she repeated Chris Rock's joke about Wright being "an angry 75-year-old black man," asking for Wright's reaction. Wright responded, "I think it's just like the media. I'm not 75."

Besides the tension between the speaker and moderator, there was joking back and forth between the speaker and the audience, sometimes at the moderator's expense. The audience booed, cheered, and called out questions. In response to the audience's participation, the moderator wielded a gavel to establish order. Wright's facial expressions and gestures added to the show. He sometimes smirked when he finished responding to a question, engaging with the audience through nonverbal communication like salutes and other hand signals.

As we stated above, a Q&A can be a tool for teaching. In doing so, consider the following adjectives that arguably describe Wright's behavior: *sassy, cocky, brassy,* and so forth. Each of these three adjectives has a double meaning, a meaning that is negative and a meaning that is positive. Some who saw Wright may say he was sassy—does that mean imprudent or assertive? He was cocky—does that mean self-assured or full of himself? He was brassy—does that mean assertive or arrogant? Perhaps the images that one sees of Wright in the Q&A are as much in the eye of the beholder, influenced by the continuous media coverage of the controversy, as in the nature of the event itself. Would people's opinions have been different if they had also had the opportunity to hear his lecture before the Q&A on national television?

The members of Trinity Church we interviewed had much to say about their pastor's appearance at the National Press Club, as detailed later in this book.

Obama and his campaign moved quickly to respond to Wright's comments at the National Press Club over the next three days. On April 29, 2008,

Obama gave a speech in Hickory, North Carolina, where he left no doubt about his disagreement with Wright's comments. Obama asserted, "The person I saw yesterday was not the person that I met 20 years ago. His comments were not only divisive and destructive, but I believe that they end up giving comfort to those who prey on hate, and I believe that they do not portray accurately the perspective of the black church."[59] Obama reiterated his vision of unity and racial transcendence: "I have spoken and written about the need for us all to recognize each other as Americans, regardless of race or religion or region of the country; that the only way we can deal with critical issues, like energy, and health care and education and the war on terrorism, is if we are joined together."[60]

## EVENT 7: MAY 31, 2008

Online headlines from May 31, 2008, on Obama's resignation from Trinity Church:

"Obama Quits Chicago Church" —NPR

"Obama Resigns from Trinity Church" —CBS

"Obama quits church, citing controversies" —CNN

The CNN article opened with this statement: "Sen. Barack Obama said Saturday that he has resigned from the church where controversial sermons by his former pastor and other ministers created political headaches for his campaign." The CBS article similarly opened with the line, "Barack Obama has formally resigned from his church, Trinity United Church of Christ in Chicago . . . a painful decision."

On May 31, 2008, Barack Obama resigned from Trinity Church. Obama stated that the reason for resigning at this time was because Rev. Michael Pfleger, a visiting Catholic priest, mocked Hillary Clinton, Obama's Democratic rival, during a sermon at Trinity Church: "In the sermon, Pfleger wipes his eyes with a handkerchief and suggests that Sen. Hillary Clinton wept because she thought that as a white person and the wife of a former president, she is entitled to the presidency."[61]

Speaking to a national audience about his family's decision to resign from Trinity Church, Obama says the Pfleger controversy made it clear that, as long as he remained a member of the congregation, remarks from the pulpit would be "imputed" to him, even if they conflicted with his personal views. Obama noted that he and Michelle began discussing their resignation from

Trinity after Wright's speech at the National Press Club on April 28. In response, the Clinton campaign chastised Obama for calling Pfleger's remarks "divisive" rather than condemning the remarks more forcefully.[62]

In his remarks Obama said, "I'm not denouncing the church and I'm not interested in people who want me to denounce the church." Obama also noted that Rev. Moss, Trinity's new pastor, and "the church have been suffering from the attention my campaign has focused on them."[63] Additionally, Obama told the press, "My faith is not contingent on the particular church I belong to and I do not believe that I am going through a religious test."[64]

Obama let Trinity UCC know of his decision in a letter of resignation he sent to the church on Sunday. Obama also explained that his plans were not to tell the press of his and Michelle's decision at the time, but that a leak to the press caused him to do so.[65]

Many comments from readers of various media outlets were sympathetic to Obama's decision:

> This is a sad day for America. The dark forces of superficial judgmentalism and denigration have won again.

> There are several ways to see this: depending on whether one is "fur or agin" the candidate Obama, including those who consider the entire situation overhyped or not their concern.

> Myself, I consider the meat of the matters underlying these sermons to be under-investigated and under-reported across the board. The roots of what causes the sermons to pour from this particular aperture have been given slapdash treatment. But that's a deeper, longer story for another time.

> It's a sad day when someone has to cut off the church that has meant so much to someone for so long. I hope it's worth it to him.

Others view Obama's decision as purely political:

> He joined the church for political reasons twenty years ago. He is leaving the church for political reasons now. He has no true spirituality or religious conviction.

> In quitting his church today, Obama has abandoned the black community, and proven that while he is a great speaker, he is all form and no substance or conviction. In other words, he is just another politician, and I for one, do not believe in his slogan, "Change We Can All Believe In"—what a bunch of baloney!

Still others criticized the "I'm not denouncing the church and I'm not interested in people who want me to denounce the church" comment.

In response to the Obamas' letter of resignation, Trinity United Church of Christ issued a response from the current pastor, Rev. Otis Moss:

> Trinity United Church of Christ was informed that Senator Barack Obama and his family will no longer be members of our church. Though we are saddened by the news, we understand that it is a personal decision. We will continue to lift them in prayer and wish them the best as former members of our Trinity community. As in the prayer for the Ephesians, our entire Trinity family asks that the nation entrust Barack, Michelle, Malia, and Sasha to God's care and guidance, so that Christ may continue to dwell in their lives, in their hearts, and in their work. We ask now for God's peace to be with them. "Now to him who is able to do immeasurably more and all we ask or imagine, according to his power that is at work within us." Ephesians 3:20. Rev. Otis Moss III[66]

Media attention on Reverend Wright and Trinity Church weakened considerably after Obama resigned from the church. Church members' opinions about Obama's resignation are fully discussed in chapter 5. That said, leaving after twenty years in an organization or institution (for example, a church) brings with it deep feelings for both parties involved. For Trinity Church to have had the possible future president and first African American president snatched from their midst leaves very powerful feelings about Obama and the parties who demanded, for multiple reasons, that he leave.

These seven events make up the Moment in which Barack Obama first dealt with race issues in a significant way. The purpose of this chapter was to recall not only the events themselves but also the political climate and the media and public's responses. In the next chapters, we look at the city of Chicago, discuss the black church as an institution, and finally consider these events from the point of view of the "unheard voices" within Trinity Church itself, the parishioners themselves.

## Chapter Two

# Race, Migration, and Politics in the Windy City

*By their actions, they did not dream the American Dream; they willed it into being by a definition of their own choosing. They did not ask to be accepted but declared themselves the Americans that perhaps few others recognized but that had always been deep within their hearts.*
  —Isabel Wilkerson, *The Warmth of Others Suns*

*The American Negro must remake his past in order to make his future. Though it is orthodox to think of America as the one country where it is unnecessary to have a past, what is a luxury for the nation as a whole becomes a prime social necessity for the Negro. For him, a group tradition must supply compensation for persecution, and pride of race the antidote for prejudice. History must restore what slavery took away, for it is the social damage of slavery that the present generations must repair and offset. So among the rising democratic millions we find the Negro thinking more collectively, more retrospectively than the rest, and apt out of the very pressure of the present to become the most enthusiastic antiquarian of them all.*
  —Arthur A. Schomburg, *The Negro Digs Up His Past*

Chicago is unique in that it offers strong political and social support for African Americans across social class lines and also because historically the concentration of blacks in defined areas of the city provided demographic significance that led to the development of an agency and critical consciousness about matters of race and citizenship. In addition, the concentration of blacks led to the development of institutions (e.g., church, art, leisure, medical) and businesses (e.g., restaurants, banks, insurance companies, clothing) for black people that promoted black pride and black people as central to America's declaration that diversity is its crown jewel.

The city of Chicago was a special place for Barack Obama's successful run for the presidency in 2008 in part because of its complex black-white relations, which range from amiability to indifference, antagonism and racism,[1] to post-racial beliefs and hopes. Not since the 1919 race riot has there been a complete disruption between the races, but since that time there continues to be a struggle and tension in black-white race relations as well as times when people come together to take action to benefit the everyday person, such was the case with the election of Harold Washington as mayor of Chicago and the overwhelming support given to Barack Obama to pursue a run for the presidency.

Obama's life experiences—including education at Columbia University in New York, attending Harvard University in Boston, and settling in Chicago's Hyde Park, a racially integrated upscale area—positioned him in a space where he could comfortably connect with and relate to both the black and white communities equally well. In addition, he was living in an area of Chicago that has seen many demographic changes from its past years of redlining real-estate practices and overt racial antagonism. The area has become recognized for its liberal bias and as a site where there existed a community of people that encouraged the development of a post-racial thesis and supported the notion that there was a lesser need for race as a central thesis to understand the problems and issues in the Black Belt. That said, the post-racial thesis, which argues that class is more a determinant of life chances than race, has overlooked the role that race still plays in society, and especially in Chicago; the intersection of race and class demands that both be dealt with equally and not separately. Such a point of view also dismisses the everyday effects of race and class of people living in Chicago and throughout the country.

Hyde Park, with its University of Chicago connection, sits only a stone's throw away from the Black Belt. (See the excerpt from Langston Hughes's "From the International House, Bronzeville Seems Far Away" at the conclusion of this chapter.) A number of the people—black and white—who live in Hyde Park easily see themselves as Americans who not only speak collectively about the "we" in "We the people," but whose ideology and daily actions also personify this behavior. These politically liberal and highly educated individuals, many of whom had money and friends with money, were a critical part of Obama's network. Furthermore, his University of Chicago faculty connection, along with his connection to Trinity Church and Rev. Wright and the tradition within the Black Belt of supporting the "race man," positioned Obama as an ideal candidate for the U.S. presidency.

Additionally, Chicago's geographical location, next door to the state of Iowa, where Senator Obama won the Iowa caucus that established him as a legitimate presidential candidate, was another piece of good fortune. Iowa has one of the largest numbers of United Church of Christ (UCC) congregations in the Midwest and Obama was a member of Trinity UCC. The day before the Iowa caucus, Douglas Burns noted, "One very much underappreciated dynamic in this race is that among the leading Democratic contenders Obama is the Midwesterner."[2] Following this line of reasoning, David Yepsen argued, "Given that lots of students in Iowa's colleges and universities are from Obama's neighboring home state of Illinois, the effort could net him thousands of additional votes on caucus night. It was not the first time that Obama profited from the fact he's from an adjacent state. Illinois residents routinely show up at the candidate's events in eastern Iowa."[3]

## THE HISTORY OF SEGREGATION IN CHICAGO

The history of the city of Chicago has played an important role in its current political culture. It was formed in 1837, with a population of 4,170. During the1840s, both free blacks and escaped enslaved people were reluctantly welcomed into the city. They were informed that they could remain in Chicago as long as they stayed in their part of the town and did not challenge social conventions.[4] Blacks were confined to the southern portion of the city, which soon came to be known as the Black Belt. At first the Black Belt was just a narrow strip of land about four blocks wide stretching from the downtown business district south to 39th Street. Because of their confinement to this area, black citizens put their mark on it, and in later years parts of it would become known as "Bronzeville." Some blacks—a much smaller number— settled on the west side of Chicago. By the late 1840s African American community life in the Windy City had become well established. Fugitive slaves from the South and free blacks from the East arrived, making Chicago a city of two races: black and white.

Early on whites were civil to moderately progressive in dealing with the matter of race. After the Civil War, the state of Illinois enacted progressive anti-discrimination legislation that influenced Chicago and other areas to which blacks from the South were migrating. The state of Illinois enacted fourteen anti-segregation statutes between 1865 and 1958, banning segregation in schools and public facilities and making the state's legislative record one of the more progressive in the nation.

School segregation was outlawed in 1874. However, from 1840 to 1914, Chicago offered few civil rights to blacks despite the legal statutes banning segregation. Whites resisted giving African Americans rights that came with citizenship. Schools that African American children attended were poor in almost every educational area: teaching, material resources, and physical plants. Much of the present-day ideology and arguments about the poor quality of schooling on Chicago's south and west sides where African

Americans live can be traced back to attitudes and policies of that time.[5] Schools in black neighborhoods to this day have yet to receive the financial and human resource transformation necessary to become high-quality, successful educational establishments.[6] For twenty-two years, from 1874 to 1896, the state statute that banned the exclusion of a child from school because of his or her race was not enforced. The lack of enforcement was in part due to the fact that the statute had no enforcement mechanism and also had loopholes that school officials could use to deny access to black students.

Between 1920 and 1930 the black population in Chicago increased from 109,458 to 233,903; the number of African American students in segregated schools doubled; and the number of segregated schools grew from six to twenty-six.[7] Throughout this period of school segregation, several factors were notable: Chicago Public School (CPS) officials were less directly responsible for the segregation of black students than of black teachers. This was so because both CPS officials and white parents had concerns about having white students taught by African American teachers. They questioned the black teachers' subject matter knowledge and teacher preparation.[8] And so teacher hiring by CPS officials accounted for racial segregation even more than restrictive housing policies. On the occasions when black and white students were in the same classroom, segregation still persisted in extracurricular activities, particularly social activities like school dances, from which black students were excluded.

The life of Gwendolyn Brooks, the first African American to receive a Pulitzer Prize for poetry, provides insight into race relations in Chicago in the twentieth century. Brooks attended three different schools and experienced major differences in the racial and socioeconomic make-up of the student population. She first went to Hyde Park High School, the leading white and wealthy high school on the city's southeast side at 6220 Stony Island. Brooks then transferred to the all-black Wendell Phillips High School with working-class and middle-class families at 39th and Pershing Road. She later transferred to Englewood High School, an integrated school with working-class and middle-class whites at 62nd and Stewart. The two-mile distance between these three high schools reflected the efforts of white neighborhoods to control the number of blacks who lived in the neighborhood or who were kept out because of race and socioeconomic status.

Schools in Chicago's black communities have had a history of overcrowding. To manage the overcrowding, the school district used such controversial methods as "double shifts," which had students attending school for only half a day. The *Chicago Defender* reported in 1939 that "78% of Negro children spend 40% less time in schools than do children outside of the colored communities in Chicago." And historian A. N. Knupfer notes that in 1941 Wendell Phillips High School enrolled 3,600 students, more than double its capacity. During this time, 20,000 empty seats were available for students in non-black schools, but "because of restrictive covenant associations (organizations established to restrict access to housing in white neighborhoods), black children could not transfer to these schools."[9]

It was not until 1957, almost three-quarters of a century after anti-segregation legislation was passed, that a state statute decreed that school officials could not bar black students from attendance and had to enforce the law. The progress on desegregation followed this track:

- 1874: "Boards of education prohibited from excluding any child on account of color from the public schools. Penalty: Those who excluded children based on race would be fined between $5 and $100. Those who threatened a child from attending a public school were subject to a fine up to $25."
- 1896: "Prohibited school officers from excluding children from public schools on the basis of color. Penalty: $5 to $100."
- 1957: "No exclusion or segregation in districts of fewer than 1,000 persons. Penalty: $5 to $100."[10]

The disjointed school integration practices of Chicago adversely affected African Americans living in the city to the extent that some students worried about their identity. Recalling her experiences as a student at the tip of the spear of a desegregation effort in Chicago, one member of Trinity UCC recalled her own education: "I was one of a hundred students that integrated a white school between 1964 and1968. So during my formative years, freshman through senior high school I was struggling with my identity. I was trying to figure out how I was going be in this white environment. We lived in the public housing on the east side of the city and I would have to take a bus and go to a school outside of my neighborhood a few miles west [from where I lived]. I [spent] four years trying to figure out whether I'm a little white girl, or . . . a little black girl; I struggled with my identity."

But the elimination of the statute on school segregation did not (and has not to this day) eliminated segregation in the Chicago Public Schools. In 1980, the U.S. federal government sued Chicago Public Schools for discriminating against black and Hispanic students. Gary Orfield, an education professor at UCLA who examined the consent decrees, stated that the Chicago Public Schools had "a history of really extreme segregation and discrimination."

This segregation and discrimination was obvious in the school curriculum: the readers did not includes stories about blacks, the history texts characterized enslaved people as happy and ignorant, and all other text materials portrayed whites as the superior race. CPS's biased curriculum still remains a concern today.[11] In our interviews with parishioners from Trinity UCC, many spoke passionately about this subject and argued that black children

needed to know "who they are and where they are from." They said that
learning about African American history and culture was a significant reason
for joining Trinity Church. The following three statements by Trinitarians are
representative of the congregants' views:

> What we learned at Trinity is that schools were not teaching us about our
> history or heritage. I wanted my children to know who they are and whose they
> are and that is what Pastor Wright always said, "Know who you are, know
> whose you are."

> We as black people have read and heard other people trying to define us and
> tell us about ourselves. At Trinity we have someone that really tells us where
> we came from and what we're about. Reverend Wright tells us about our
> background.

> At Trinity we learn so much about our history—not only spiritually enriching
> information, but we learn our history . . . it didn't begin in slavery. We just
> need to know who we are and where we come from. We need to live our lives
> that way.

Segregation in public accommodations was outlawed in 1885 but, much
like school segregation statutes, this ban did not eliminate segregation. It
took fourteen years to do away with segregation in public accommodation by
legal mandates. The statutes developed to eliminate discrimination in public
places read throughout Illinois history as follows:

- 1885: Made inns, restaurants, barbershops, public transportation, theaters,
  and places of public amusement available to all persons. Penalty: Viola-
  tors of the act would be fined between $25 and $500, paid to the victim,
  and would also be guilty of a misdemeanor, and subject to a fine of up to
  $500.
- 1897: 1885 law amended to include hotels, soda-fountains, saloons, bathrooms, theaters, skating-rinks, concerts, cafes, bicycle rinks, elevators, ice
  cream parlors, railroads, stages, streetcars, and boats.
- 1903: 1885 law extended to include funeral hearses as list of public services available to all persons.
- 1911: Amendment to 1885 Civil Rights law stating that cemeteries could
  not discriminate based on race the choice of burial plots. [12]

The truth that black-white relations range from "amiability to indifference
to antagonism and racism" is clear as we look across the history of the
education and public accommodation statutes. This is perfectly illustrated
when whites take legislative action to pass a public accommodation statute
that is intended to eliminate desegregation, which leads blacks to feel ami-

able toward the white power structure and to all whites by extension. The feelings change to antagonism when blacks realize that the statute thus enacted lacks the administrative structure required for enforcement.

## THE GREAT MIGRATION FROM THE SOUTH

The migration of thousands of poor, rural uneducated African Americans to Chicago after the turn of the twentieth century changed Chicago and changed the blacks who came seeking a new life. Blacks came to Chicago to escape brutal racism, inferior schooling, lynch mobs, Jane and Jim Crow, and all the political and social violence that came with being black and living in the South. Increasingly from 1910 onward, blacks came to Chicago in search of economic opportunities and for a dream they were hearing from friends and relatives and reading about in the *Chicago Defender*, Chicago's premier black newspaper. In 1919 *Defender* readers discovered that the daily wages in Chicago started in the $2.00–$2.50 range for men working in the packing house and about $2.00 per day for women working as domestics. These wages were as much as blacks earned in a week working in the South.[13] The North, as Richard Wright noted, retained a mythic quality in the hearts and minds of black southern sharecroppers who were in de facto enslavement.[14]

Escaping racism was not the only reason for African Americans to leave the South. The meager employment opportunities that had existed were disappearing as the boll weevil destroyed the cotton crops upon which so many in the South depended. While Chicago city living presented major challenges, the new arrivals adjusted, searched for work, located places of worship, and were pleased that their children had a better school to attend. It was far from ideal, however; life was hard and frightening at times. Migrants learned that although northern racism was usually not as violent as southern racism, it nevertheless took its toll on each and every black person living in the Windy City. That said, migrants' urban life was far better than what they left behind, in part because they had pride and hope that they might see better opportunities in the future for their children if not for themselves. One Trinitarian explains:

> People came from the South; they came from the small rural areas . . . and even though Chicago was a segregated city . . . people who came from South had more opportunity here than they had in the South. This gave them a sense of pride and with that pride they were happy; elated to have the freedom that . . . came [with being] here. To have opportunities to try [different] work and/or to have better jobs. Some of the jobs weren't as good as the jobs we have today, but they were not as bad as the jobs we had in the South.

The newly arriving blacks often arrived with friends or family members expecting them as well as providing them with a temporary place to live. In other cases, when blacks arrived they had to search out housing because promises made to them before they left the South were not kept for various reasons: agencies that they were told handled housing no longer existed; friends did not show up to meet them; no one had made them a promise to meet them and they arrived without funds, hoping that *luck* would be with them. The Chicago Urban League, Phyllis Wheatley Home, YMCA, and other places of lodging often became their port in the storm. Others were reduced to living in "attics and cellars, store-rooms and basements, churches, sheds and warehouses" with no room to store suitcases or trunks.[15] The common denominator for practically all blacks who arrived in Chicago was that they were directed, by anyone they sought help from, to go the South Side because that was where blacks lived.

African Americans who arrived in Chicago during the first two decades of the twentieth century were termed *new arrivals*. And they did not always receive a joyous welcome from blacks who had lived in Chicago for decades, residents known as *old settlers*. The old settlers had established a way of life that separated them from poorer, less educated blacks, which included the establishment of many institutions that heralded a middle-class way of life: businesses, churches, a bank, a hospital, lodges, clubs, and a YMCA. The old settlers held a strong belief in black solidarity and self-help. The new arrivals, many of them from the rural areas, were considered to be lacking culture and refinement. Tensions between old and new arrivals were the resulting outcome, but that was not all bad, as the new arrivals pushed the old settlers out of their comfort zone, told them that they were too satisfied in their middle- and upper-middle-class enclaves, and encouraged them to push for increased racial equality in all areas of city life: housing, shopping in the Loop, employment, schooling, and access to any all public spaces. The old settlers had become caught up in their middle-class lives: a good number had achieved a college education, some finished medical and dental school, and some earned a law degree. These settlers had acquired money, purchased nice homes with manicured lawns in the Black Belt, and established a European-style social life with debutante balls and other similar social events. Many new arrivals felt that in doing so, the old settlers were focusing energy away from combating the inequities and injustices black people faced outside the Black Belt. Many new arrivals viewed these actions as accepting and being satisfied with second-class citizenship; they were only "somebody" in the Black Belt, and once they left the seven-mile-long stretch of land on Chicago's South Side they became "boy," the "N" word, or worse. The new arrivals wanted and pushed for the old settlers to use some of their wealth and education to fight for equal rights in all areas of society for all black people.

Often the new arrivals would gather together and remain together because they had a common place of origin, were of the same religion, and held common customs. Out of this common adventure—coming to Chicago and pushing the old settlers to update their ways—some developed lasting friendships as they adapted to the northern reality and developed new customs. [16]

In Chicago the arriving migrants saw more blacks than they had ever seen before: thousands of others much like themselves. Some lived in apartment buildings where they were constantly in close proximity with people who looked like them, shared many of their beliefs and values, and had similar stories to tell about life in the South and coming to Chicago.

The apartments and houses where many had to live, although better than their dwellings in the South, for the most part were old, rundown, and overcrowded. The plumbing facilities in many residences were old and often didn't work properly, many apartment buildings had only one toilet or bathroom on a floor, and the rent was high. Many of the building had been converted into "kitchenettes." The kitchenette was a one-room apartment with a sink, stove, or hot plate. Residents of several kitchenettes would share a communal bathroom. The kitchenettes were small, dirty, and overcrowded, with many people living in a space barely suitable for one person. These cells of horror, with their filth, foul air, and poor sewage, were harbors for scarlet fever, dysentery, tuberculosis, pneumonia, and malnutrition and contributed especially to the death of black infants and the aged.

Living in cramped quarters made social life difficult. In the boiler room conditions, quarrels, accusations, vindictiveness, and the development of "warped personalities" became more frequent. [17] Incessant bedlam and unhealthy conditions caused some blacks "to give up the struggle, walk off and leave wives, husbands and even children to shift as best they can." [18] "The kitchenette . . . was a place where some black mother sat, deserted, with their children about their knees." [19] Gwendolyn Brooks lived in four such kitchenettes in her life, and her poem "Kitchenette Building" describes the realism of poverty and how the tenants' dreams of a better life were difficult to hold on to, let alone achieve. The migrants that the poem describes are trapped socially, psychologically, and physically.

*Kitchenette Building*

We are things of dry hours and the involuntary plan,
Grayed in, and gray. "Dream" makes a giddy sound, not strong
Like "rent," "feeding a wife," "satisfying a man."

But could a dream send up through onion fumes
Its white and violet, fight with fried potatoes
And yesterday's garbage ripening in the hall,
Flutter, or sing an aria down these rooms

Even if we were willing to let it in,
Had time to warm it, keep it very clean,
Anticipate a message, let it begin?

We wonder. But not well! not for a minute!
Since Number Five is out of the bathroom now,
We think of lukewarm water, hope to get in it. [20]

When the great-grandchildren of blacks who had arrived in Chicago at the turn of the twentieth century read about their odyssey in the school history books (where the story was sanitized and explained in a paragraph or two), their *real* understanding was that these were the family members whose names they had seen scrawled in the family Bible that Big Momma kept close to her. And on those occasions when her fingers ran down the page of the Bible, pausing at each and every name listed, they remembered hearing her step back into the past and recall the story her mother would tell, as in this passage by Richard Wright (1941):

LORD IN HEAVEN! Good God Almighty! Great Day in the Morning! It's here! Our time has come! We are leaving! We are angry no more: we are leaving! We are leaving our homes, pulling up stakes to move on. We look up at the high southern sky and remember all the sunshine and the rain and we feel a sense of loss, but we are leaving. We look out at the wide green fields which our eyes saw when we first came into the world and we feel full of regret, but we are leaving. We scan the kind black faces we have looked upon since we first saw the light of day, and, though pain is in our hearts, we are leaving. We take one last furtive look over our shoulders to the Big House— high upon the railroad tracks—where the Lord of the Land lives, and we feel glad, we are leaving. . . . When a man lives upon the land and is cold and hungry and hears word of the great factories going up in the cities, he begins to hope and dream of a new life, and he leaves. [21]

The Black Belt slowly expanded to accommodate the growing population, which between 1920 and 1930 increased by more than 125,000. As the population grew, African Americans nevertheless were still confined to this designated area, instead of being able to spread out throughout the city. If blacks moved into white neighborhoods, white hostility became an issue. In some cases whites left because they did not wish to live next door to blacks. This action on the part of whites was one of the major reasons that the Black Belt developed.

# JIM CROW LAWS AFTER MIGRATION

Whites did not like giving in to blacks. The thought of fleeing their neighbor-hoods was antithetical to them. In the 1920s, whites in Chicago and through-out Illinois struck back against blacks moving into their neighborhoods. Illi-nois led the nation in the use of restrictive covenants to maintain residential segregation. In 1927 Chicago adopted a housing covenant that restricted where black people could live. Racist behavior that paved the way for legis-lating residential segregation is recorded by Mary Pattillo in *Black on the Block*. Pattillo reports that race riots and house bombings (in 1919) were a fiery prelude to decades of white organizing against black settlement on the South Side of Chicago. Pattillo argued that the property owners' association organized efforts to control where blacks could and could not live. The most notorious organization, she contended, was the Kenwood and Hyde Park Property Owners' Association, formed in 1918. The association restricted blacks from moving into the area from 39th to 55th Streets (roughly two miles) and Lake Michigan to State Street (roughly three miles), and it vowed to make and keep Hyde Park white. Ironically, Barack Obama's Chicago residence is in Hyde Park.

In 1919, the organization minced no words in the *Property Owner's Jour-nal* in declaring that Hyde Park was for whites only: "Keep the Negro in his place, among his people, and he is healthy and loyal. Remove him, or allow his newly discovered importance to remove him from his proper environment and the Negro becomes a nuisance." Pattillo's research was not the only report of efforts to "Keep the Negro in his place." Michael Homel argued that if blacks attempted to settle outside the ghetto, whites threatened them, tried to buy their property, and vandalized or bombed their homes. Realtors either refused to deal with blacks or steered them to areas that were already pre-dominately black or designated for black occupancy. Banks and savings associations supported this practice of "redlining" by financing homes in a racially discriminatory fashion.[22]

Some of the Trinity Church congregants whom we interviewed for this book were alive during this time or had relatives—mothers, fathers, aunts, uncles—who lived through this experience. One Trinitarian describes how Jane and Jim Crow practices and their perceived legacy influenced the daily action of blacks, including demanding that blacks conduct their life activities in a particular geographic area of Chicago:

> I was born and raised (1950s–1960s) on the South Side. . . . Everything (e.g., school, family eating out) was done right there in your neighborhood. You shopped on 47th Street because you weren't welcomed in the Loop. From older family members and neighbors you heard stories about violence being heaped upon blacks who strayed too far out of neighborhoods; even to walk

through a white neighborhood was a no-no; to stop at a gas station brought
stares and made you feel uncomfortable.

In 1924, Nathan MacChesney, a prominent Chicago attorney and a member of the Chicago Planning Commission, drafted an addition to the Code of
Ethics of the National Association of Real Estate Boards that "forbade realtors to introduce members of any race or nationality" into neighborhoods
where their presence would damage property values. In 1927, MacChesney
drafted a model racial restrictive covenant for the Chicago Real Estate Board,
solely targeting African Americans.

The Chicago Real Estate Board promoted the racial covenant to YMCAs,
churches, women's clubs, PTAs, Kiwanis clubs, chambers of commerce, and
property owners' associations. Hyde Park, Woodlawn, Park Manor, South
Shore, and other neighborhoods on Chicago's South Side adjacent to the so-
called Black Belt responded, as did outlying Chicago neighborhoods and
suburbs. Additionally, the University of Chicago was a strong supporter of
the covenant campaign in Washington Park, although they denied their affiliation for many years. In 1948, the United States Supreme Court ruled that
enforcement of racial restrictive covenants was unconstitutional. The Supreme Court's ruling, however, did not put an end to the problem of blacks
finding adequate housing.[23] Homeowner associations continued to push for
segregation. Shortly after the court decision, the Woodlawn Property Owners
Association wrote, "If the colored people are convinced that life in Woodlawn would be unbearable, they would not want to come in. There must be
ways and means to keep whites from selling, causing colored not to want to
come in because life here would be unbearable. We are going to save Woodlawn for ourselves and our children!"[24]

In the 1940s and 1950s, blacks who migrated from the South pushed into
some white-only areas and broke up residential conclaves. However, their
entry into white residential conclaves was short lived, thanks in part to a
grand housing scheme carried out by Mayor Richard J. Daley. Many admirers of Daley, including his sons, argued that when his tenure began in 1955
plans for major housing construction in the Black Belt were already under
way, and therefore he should not be criticized for constructions that helped to
further develop and maintain a black ghetto on Chicago's south and west
sides. Daley critics, however, strongly disagreed with that thesis and argued
that Daley did very little to stop the building of the massive high-rise structures that warehoused poor African American families.

Between 1955 and 1971, the Chicago Housing Authorities "built 10,256
apartments—all but 63 in black neighborhoods."[25] "Old Man Daley saw the
value of the high-rises being able to keep blacks hemmed in, while at the
same time they would be easy to control politically by controlling the vote in
all of the buildings."[26] Lois Wille writes, "If you look at where the Robert

Taylor Homes were placed, where Cabrini-Green was placed, and where some of the other huge high-rises were, they did, ultimately, form a wall between black and white, between poor communities and affluent communities."[27] Tristram Hunt supports this observation: Chicago "is a city of racial polarities, thanks in part to Mayor Daley's 1960 zoning strategies that cordoned off the African-American community into vast 'projects' to the south of downtown. . . . It was these wretched, ignored, unfunded ghettoes that provided the political base for Jesse Jackson . . . and a young community organizer called Barack Obama."[28]

With 75 percent of the black population living in one section of Chicago,[29] the section developed into a powerful voting bloc. Some argued that this voting bloc played a major role in John F. Kennedy's presidential victory in 1960 (especially the Second Congregational District).[30] Our interviews with members of Trinity UCC included a real-estate agent, a retiree who had worked in the lending department of a large established Chicago Bank, and an appraiser of houses. They all had something to say about the Black Belt, and the following statement captures the sentiments of all three:

> [The Black Belt] still exists, but what I say to everybody [is that] it was called redlining when I was very active [in real estate]. It's how the lenders would not loan [to black people] and would not allow them to buy years ago in certain areas of Chicago; and not too long ago in Oak Park and River Forest. [Whites] didn't want us in there.

The racist conditions under which blacks lived in Chicago had a dual impact on the African Americans and their institutions.[31] These conditions shaped black political thought, identity, and behavior and put in place the intertwining dynamics of race, politics, and identity that over the years served as a causal force in Chicago politics. These dynamics motivated efforts of African Americans to improve their life conditions. The racist arrangement also influenced whites, giving them a sense of entitlement and privilege in all aspects of Chicago civic, political, educational, and social affairs.

A significant example of how racism impacted African Americans was in their inability to find employment. Jim and Jane Crow, the culprit—a calculating, invidious social policy—was kept in place and nuanced when necessary to exclude African Americans not only from employment but also from interracial contact in public places.[32] Industrial employers refused to hire African Americans; often they used stereotypical claims about blacks' mental aptitude as justification. Claims were fueled by the eugenics movement that was increasingly influential during that time and was spurred on by the publication of *The Passing of the Great Race* (1916) by eugenicist Madison Grant. The prestige of the book was enhanced by former president Theodore

Roosevelt, who wrote, "The book is a capital book: in purpose, in vision, in grasp of the facts that our people must need to realize. . . . It is the work of an American scholar and gentleman, and all Americans should be grateful to you for writing it."[33] That the book offered a very negative statement about blacks and others is clear. Professor Jonathan Mark reported that *The Passing of the Great Race* was translated into German in 1925, and Grant received a fan letter from aspiring politician Adolf Hitler as well ("The book is my Bible," wrote Hitler to Grant). When a few blacks did break through the employment barriers, they were given the lowest-level jobs requiring the least amount of skills, as pointed out in the following statement:

> The gigantic American companies will not employ our daughters in their offices as clerks, bookkeepers or stenographers; huge department stores will not employ our young women, fresh from schools, as saleswomen. The engineering, aviation, mechanical, and chemical schools close their doors to our sons, just as the great corporations, which make thousands of commodities, refuse to employ them. The Bosses of the Buildings decree that we must be maids, porters, janitors, cooks and general servants.[34]

Black women, who migrated in greater numbers than black men, experienced dual oppressions in both racism and sexism. Yet many black women tenaciously confronted the challenge of finding work to support their families. Cannon states, "The black woman began her life of freedom with no vote, no protection, and no equity of any sort. Black women young and old were basically on their own."[35] The job opportunities open to them were mostly as domestics, and when they were able to locate a job in industry or a meat-packing plant, it was usually a dangerous, low-paying position. Another force pushing against the employment opportunities of black women were "white women [who] had no intention of working alongside black women; even if some of them did speak of sexual equality, most did not favor racial equality. . . . Fear of competing with blacks as well as the possible loss of job status associated with working with blacks caused white workers to oppose any effort to have blacks as fellow workers."[36]

Over the years employment opportunities increased for blacks, but Jane and Jim Crow constantly and continually made certain that progress came in small steps. A Trinitarian explains:

> I started at Continental Bank in 1967. At that time there were very few blacks working there. Plastics (credit cards) were just beginning to come in circulation. They opened up a lot of jobs. . . . I was a keypunch operator. I was put on the third shift in another building where I would not be observed or seen as a black person. Not being aware of [why I was put to work in a different building] I said, "Oh, I am lucky I got a job"; being a single parent, it was my goal to get a job and support my family.

Knupfer noted that besides their efforts to find work to support the family and care for children, black women played a major role in the fight against racism. They were a force behind three types of activism used in Chicago from the 1930s to 1950s: pan-African intellectualism, the expressive arts, and social protest. Knupfer contends that the expressive arts were a powerful site of social protest. She cites the works of Katherine Durham, Margaret Burroughs, Margaret Walker, and Gwendolyn Brooks, and she uses pan-African intellectualism to refer to the intellectual movement that "emphasized the larger politics of the 'colored' races of the world." The "Free South Africa" sign posted in front of Trinity UCC speaks to the "larger politics of the 'colored' races of the world." Some Trinitarians spoke of Trinity's and Rev. Wright's pan-African position as a reason for their involvement with the church.

> I started to find out about Reverend Wright's connection with Africa; and how he would go over there once, twice, [sometimes] three times a year. He would not just to go over there, but he helped build up Africa. I started to think this is a pretty interesting guy. I also heard that Reverend Wright was among the first to speak out against apartheid in Africa in the '70s.

The social freedoms that initially attracted blacks to Chicago were either denied or fewer in number than they had hoped. They recognized how the impact of black-white relations and living as second-class citizens was affecting them and impeding their cultural hopes. But, although they understood they had to accede to what outside employment dictated, they were nevertheless motivated to become *subjects* making history, rather than being the *objects* of policy decisions enacted by others: "By their actions, they did not dream the American Dream; they willed it into being by a definition of their own choosing."[37] They increasingly developed a connection between black political thought, identity, and behavior that permeates Chicago's African American community to this day. Increasingly, blacks recognized that the Black Belt possessed economic and social power, and they began to develop independent institutions such as a hospital (Provident), a YMCA, local branches of the NAACP and Urban League, and newspapers such as the *Chicago Defender*, which started publishing in 1905, and *Chicago Sunday Bee*, which started in 1925 and lasted until 1947.

Though sometimes it seems to be forgotten, African Americans were not blank slates or empty vessels when they arrived in Chicago. Although they were poor, lacked formal education, and were eager to experience the freedoms they had heard about, they were not without experience, knowledge, or the ability to be perceptive and prepared to adjust to their new circumstances. As Grossman contends, "Many migrants viewed migration as an opportunity to share—as black people—the perquisites of American citizenship. These included not only participation in what seemed to be an open industrial economy from which they had previously been excluded, but also good schools, the right to vote, the right to be left alone or to share public accommodations with other Americans, and in general the right to live free from fears and daily indignities that characterized southern race relations."[38] Blacks came north with ideas about race relations, understandings about job prospects, dreams of better schools for their children, and visions of a different and far better social life. In other words they came, as Alain Locke noted, "with a new vision of opportunity."[39] Living in the South, under Jim and Jane Crow, did not stop them from envisioning a different role for black people in America as they studied the racist behavior of white individuals and the white power structure. In addition, thoughts about "opportunities" taught them the significance of building networks and establishing working relationships with other blacks who had a range of political and social outlooks about the future of the black race.

It would be a false illusion to imagine that blacks simply went to the railroad station, bought a ticket, boarded a train, and headed north. There were many obstacles to their migration.[40] Blacks' decision to leave the South was seen by many white southerners as an aggressive statement of dissatisfaction, one that constituted a "direct threat to the fiber of social and economic relations in the South."[41] Such action disrupted the assumption that blacks were docile, dependent, and unambitious. Also, since blacks were the South's labor force, their leaving was a loss to the labor supply. Aware of their dependence on blacks, whites became enraged. They tried numerous strategies to attract a new labor force, such as inserting pleas in southern newspapers for white immigration. In addition, they employed strategies to keep blacks in the South, which included everything from lobbying the federal government to interdict labor agents from the North from "enticing away" black workers to lobbying senators, congresspersons, and other government officials for aid in preventing blacks from going north.[42] On some occasions more direct and violent measures were used, such as forcibly evicting Chicago-bound blacks from the railway station, refusing to honor prepaid tickets, refusing to pay blacks for work they had completed, and making threats of lynching, raping of black women, and other forms of brutality.[43] Anger and resistance were not the only white responses, however. Some whites argued that the South would be better off without its black population. Others argued that blacks should be provided with better schools and higher wages to encourage them to remain in the South. Furthermore, some black leaders urged blacks to remain in the South, declaring that the North was not the promised land they heard and read about from friends and in the *Chicago Defender*.[44] Thus to board a train, bus, car, or to travel on foot to Chicago and other places in the North was a struggle that demanded both perseverance and resiliency. Arguably, no white southerner understood the extent of black people's ambition and desire for freedom. From these experiences African Americans who migrated to Chicago brought attitudes, character, values, and habits that reflected their experiences of life under bondage on plantations, farms, and villages in the South and the border states and their struggle to come north.[45] That said, the newcomers arrived with "courage, a willingness to face the unknown, curiosity about the differences, and confidence in the inevitability of individual and group triumph."[46] Richard Wright describes the hope of black migrants in the following quote: "I was leaving the South to fling myself into the unknown. . . . I was not leaving the South to forget the South. . . . I was taking a part of the South to transplant in alien soil, to see if it could grow differently, to see if it could drink of new and cool rains, bend in strange winds, respond to the warmth of other suns and, perhaps, to bloom."[47]

African Americans' attitudes, beliefs, values, and habits—in other words, *their agency and resiliency*—served as foundational structures for the development of black political thought, identity, behavior, and confidence as they pursued social freedom. True, some black migrants were hesitant about leaving the South and traveling to Chicago. But many did so with courage and optimism. O. S. Muelder in *The Underground Railroad in Western Illinois* tells about such a person who was determined to make it to Chicago:[48]

> John Anderson was born in the year 1831, in Howard County, state of Missouri. His mother was the slave of one Burton, a carpenter, who lived on a small farm near Fayette. His father, who was almost white, served as a steward on board a steamer, which sailed on the Missouri, but made his escape to South America while Anderson was young. . . .
>
> Anderson acquired great proficiency in running, jumping and other athletic amusements, usually practiced by slaves in the evening, which afterwards proved of great service to him. . . .
>
> In September, 1853, when he had been about two months with McDonald [his owner] he made his escape. . . . He usually traveled by night, and got what rest he could during the day. He suffered much from want of food, sometimes not tasting any for several days, and often he had to content himself with corn, hazel nuts, pawpaws and raw potatoes. A dollar and a half was all the money he had when he started on his perilous journey, and of this he never spent any except when compelled to do so by extreme hunger.
>
> One day, while resting himself by the wayside, a man on horseback rode up and attempted to capture him, but Anderson fled to a neighboring field and found protection among the stalks of corn. . . . Near a Mississippi [River] village he met with a colored man, and gave him ten cents to buy some crackers for him. This man, in whom Anderson placed little confidence, after some delay brought him the crackers, which he greedily devoured. He crossed the Mississippi by night, using for that purpose a boat which he found near the river, and keeping clear of the ferry for fear of detection. It was now Saturday night, and about two weeks since he had left McDonald, and he had reached the free State of Illinois; but from the attempts made to capture him in this

State, he was convinced that he was almost in as much danger there as he had been in Missouri.

On Sunday night he went into the house of a white man, an Englishman, who gave him a good supper and a bed. . . . His entertainer lent him a razor, by which he was enabled to indulge in the luxury of a shave. Having got breakfast, and after the good-hearted Englishman had prevailed on him to take some bread and apples in his pocket, John again set out with renewed strength and spirits. . . .

After two days, he struck a branch of the Illinois River, which he crossed, and after proceeding some distance, he came to a railway track, with the use of which he was acquainted. He next came to Bloomington, where he obtained some provisions. He availed himself of the railway track for a short distance north of Bloomington. Confused and bewildered, he met a man who promised him a ride if he would help him with his cow. Anderson consented to do so, and rode with the man to a certain village, where he was requested to leave. After leaving the village, Anderson again encountered him and accompanied him, notwithstanding his attempts to shun him. At this man's house he got his supper and a bed, and started early next morning before breakfast. . . . Overtaking some teams that were on the road to Rock Island, he got on one of them and reached that city by daylight. Here he hired himself as a barber, though he was quite uninstructed in the art of shaving. Remaining in that city for two days, he went to Chicago, the Abolition Society paying his fare.

## THE MIGRATION AND BLACK THOUGHT

Black social identity in the United States has always been diverse. Years ago some blacks defined themselves with a low self-concept; others defined themselves as proud and positive within their own skin: "Black is Beautiful." Some blacks, as Daniel J. Sharfstein noted in *The Invisible Line*, have crossed the color line and faded into the white world around them since the colonial era to the present.[49] Others—for example, Anna Julia Cooper, writer and future principal of M Street School in Washington, DC—defined themselves proudly within the context of their race. Cooper told a crowd of five hundred white women in 1893 at the International Congress of Women in Chicago the following about the wonders of the black woman:

The higher fruits of civilization cannot be extemporized, neither can they be developed normally, in the brief space of thirty years [after the Emancipation Proclamation]. It requires the long and painful growth of generations. Yet all through the darkest period of the colored women's oppression in this country her yet unwritten history is full of heroic struggle, a struggle against fearful and overwhelming odds, that often ended in a horrible death, to maintain and protect that which woman holds dearer than life. The painful, patient, and silent toil of mothers to gain a free simple title to the bodies of their daughters, the despairing fight, as of an entrapped tigress, to keep hallowed their own persons, would furnish material for epics. That more went down under the flood than stemmed the current is not extraordinary. The majority of our women are not heroines but I do not know that a majority of any race of women are heroines. It is enough for me to know that while in the eyes of the highest tribunal in America she was deemed no more than a chattel, an irresponsible thing, a dull block, to be drawn hither or thither at the volition of an owner, the Afro American woman maintained ideals of womanhood unashamed by any ever conceived. Resting or fermenting in untutored minds, such ideals could not claim a hearing at the bar of the nation. The white woman could at least plead for her own emancipation; the black woman, doubly enslaved, could but suffer and struggle and be silent. I speak for the colored women of the South, because it is there that the millions of blacks in this country have watered the soil with blood and tears, and it is there too that the colored woman of America has made her characteristic history, and there her destiny evolving. [50]

Some blacks saw their social identity in ideological terms. During migration, the ideological position of some blacks was to remain in the South. Booker T. Washington said that he had "never seen any part of the world where it seemed to me the masses of the Negro people would be better off than right here in these southern states."[51] He and some other blacks—for example, doctors, lawyers, newspapers editors, and ministers—presented a self-interest argument that blacks would be better off in the South. They contended that blacks moving to the North would be taking their business across the Mason-Dixon line and wanted to discourage that from happening. Other blacks, such as Robert Abbott, founder and publisher of the *Chicago Defender*, favored migration. W. E. B. Du Bois stated, "The North is no paradise, but the South is at best a system of caste and insult and at worst a Hell."[52] And W. Allison Sweeney, a *Defender* columnist, called a black opponent of migration "an unsightly wart."[53]

African Americans never engaged in lockstep thinking on the issue of migration. Reed's research for *Black Chicago's First Century* puts to rest any lingering notion of homogeneity among blacks. He explains that demographic analysis affords recognition of social segmentation and provides insight into composition, attitudes, and motivations within the African American community. Reed argues that, starting with the American Revolution, differences developed among black people as they thought about and longed for freedom.[54] He contends, "As distinctions between Africans and African Americans disappeared, new differences—between free and slave—emerged, creating new fissures within the black community along new points of alliance."[55] These fissures became solidified as some African Americans were legally "free" and others enslaved. Reed continues: "By the beginning of the nineteenth century, legal distinctions between slave and free had become an important basis of social standing in black society. With such distinctions, a new politics emerged, for free and slave had different aspirations and strategies for achieving their goals."[56] There were ideological differences about race relations (e.g., nationalism, integration), education (e.g., accommodation, Afrocentric), and politics (e.g., Democratic, Republican). These competing agendas complicated alliances and divisions within black society.[57]

## POSTMIGRATION DEVELOPMENTS INSIDE AND OUTSIDE THE BLACK BELT

That said, in Chicago before the 1960s, diverse groups of African Americans, differing along economic, social, and professional lines, lived together on the seven-mile-long and one-half-mile-wide strip of land that comprised the Black Belt. Pattillo notes that "Bronzeville was a wellspring of black businesses, vice, politics, religion, scholarship and music."[58] Within one block you could find the doctor, the dentist, the teachers, the postal worker, the piano teacher, and the sheriffs—the women with watchful eyes and powerful voices who refereed kids' behavior when needed and monitored who was coming in and out of the neighborhood. Whites were welcome if they were there for good reasons. Within these neighborhoods people of all kinds socialized and worked together. The formally educated blacks advised the children of the uneducated blacks about the social and economic significance of completing high school and attending college, including how to apply and fill out college applications. Similarly, the less educated blacks, who usually had certain types of mechanical skills or some other asset, would return the favor by doing repairs or other tasks or would work to beautify the neighborhood. Such engagements brought these neighbors together for a social education that included serendipitously establishing a code of conduct and standards for the neighborhood.

One knock on the outcome of the civil rights movement was that it shattered these social alliances; educated middle-class blacks and blacks who began earning decent incomes were able to leave their cramped living quarters and move into better homes and neighborhoods, thereby leaving poorer and less educated blacks to fend for themselves. In addition, for the blacks—often poor—who moved in to take the place of those leaving, the benefits of living in a community where your next-door neighbor was educated and possessed social and civic capital that might accrue in part to you ceased to exist.

A forerunner of the civil rights movement and a vital ally to African American social progress and social mobility was the GI Bill, which made it possible for soldiers returning home from World War II to attend college. The GI Bill, a federal program signed into law in 1944 by President Franklin

Delano Roosevelt and formally known as the Serviceman's Readjustment Act, provided among its benefits financial assistance for higher education and training for returning veterans.[59] Although present and past reviews of the implementation of the GI Bill show the ever-present influence of Jane and Jim Crow, the bill is noted for providing "a crack in the wall of racism that had surrounded the American university system."[60] Because of the civil rights movement, there was a substantial increase in the number of blacks who earned a college education. The college degree brought with it better economic benefits, the opening up of employment opportunities, and greater social mobility, including moving out of the Black Belt. This push for greater social mobility inspired blacks earning a poor to moderate income to secure second jobs in order to accumulate a down payment on the American dream—a home of their own with a yard and a wee bit of space between them and their next-door neighbor beyond the congested Black Belt. A Trinitarian explains, "My husband worked two jobs for many years. He taught school during the day and worked at the post office after school. We wanted a better life for our children and ourselves. When I would ask him 'Isn't it too much, for you?' he would say, 'Several of the people working with him including women are holding down two jobs.'"

Several Trinitarians in their late eighties spoke about life in and out of the Black Belt and African Americans' social progress. One led us to the following book as she spoke about how far we have come and how we have overcome the negative socialization of self that blacks received living in the South and among the blatant racism in the North. She adds that although "Shadrach Minkins" no longer exists, the legacy of his way of thinking, and the thoughts and images in society about black people that created such feelings, have not been completely eliminated, as racism and its effects on identity still plague our society. Minkins, in Collison's book *Shadrach Minkins: From Fugitive Slave to Citizen*, was an African American man who said in a matter-of-fact manner, "Han't got no self."[61]

> "Halloo, there! Where are you going?" I called to him.
> "Gwine chopping in de woods!"
> "Chopping for yourself?"
> *"Han't got no self."*
> "Slave, are you?"
> "Dat's what I is."

During her walks through Harlem, bell hooks noted this historical legacy: "At times when I wander around my neighborhood staring at the dark-skinned nannies, hearing the accents that identify them as immigrants still, I remember this is the world a plantation economy produces—a world where some are bound and others are free, a world of extremes."[62] The lingering legacy of Shadrach Minkins as an image, while a part of history and with its place, is nevertheless one that, like the depiction of Rev. Wright in the video snippets, is narrowly conceived and does not offer fair representation of the black man. Richard Wright gave voice to other blacks, men and women who present a different perspective and argue that they have "self" as they speak about a tremendous opportunity that America for decades missed out on with the caricaturized black man and women: "If we had been allowed to participate in the vital processes of America's national growth, what would have been the texture of our lives, the pattern of our traditions, the routine of our customs, the state of our arts, the code of our laws, the functions of our government! Whatever others may say, black folk say that America would have been stronger and greater!"[63]

In *Chicago's New Negro*, Davarian L. Baldwin describes the conditions and experiences that were significant in shaping black social and political consciousness between 1910 and 1935.[64] He writes about the arrival of migrants searching for and expecting the freedom that was said to exist in the North. These new migrants, who were poor but filled with optimism, brought changes to the black section of the city. Older, more stable, and somewhat more financially successful black residents were forced to search for homes in other areas of the Black Belt. An article in the *Chicago Defender* written during this time provides a sense of the pride that some African Americans felt regarding their financial accruement: "No one ever dreamed that a member of our Race would be wealthy, but today there are several in the $500,000 class and hundreds whose bank accounts or holdings reach the five figure proportions."[65] The same article gives a progress report on the history of the black race in Chicago since the turn of the century: "The race has advanced steadily and substantially ever since the first Black man set foot on Chicago soil, yet the progress made in the direction of securing a comfortable and sanitary home; educational advancement; and advancement in professional fields and politics, are the four outstanding general accomplishments made by our people during the past 25 years."[66] The article continues, noting how the *Chicago Defender* played a major role in these advancements: "The influence of the *Chicago Defender* in the promotion all of these, makes its inception by far the greatest single advent in the history of the city, so far as our Race is concerned."[67]

The streams of new residents also helped to reinvigorate blacks who had figured out how to earn money and navigate Jane and Jim Crow and thereby achieve a more comfortable life and style of living. The new arrivals to Chicago pushed to move into their well-groomed neighborhoods, the few that existed in the Black Belt, and argued that their efforts of fighting racism had become weak. This disruption of lifestyle reawakened blacks who had become too comfortable to take actions to eliminate racism. One action of significance at this time took place in the courts and resulted in the winning of a landmark anti-discrimination suit against a downtown theater, a suit that was led by those who were already established in the area and who had the credentials to carry it forward. The activism of the reawakened black middle class, in part inspired by the new migrants, led to the hiring of the first black teacher at Wendell Phillips High School, the high school that Gwendolyn Books and the authors of this book attended years later.

Agency and social action in the Black Belt came from numerous sources. One of the most exciting moments was when blacks bested whites in boxing. In 1910, black heavyweight champion Jack Johnson defeated Jim Jeffries for the heavyweight title of the world, causing a mass celebration in the Black Belt. People came out of their homes shouting, crying, and banging on pots and pans to joyously celebrate an occasion that rarely came to black people. Johnson's victory was not only a pugilistic win of a black man over a white man but also an opportunity for the black man to compete against the white man on equal footing. In addition, Jeffries, the former undefeated heavy-weight champion who came out of retirement for the fight, is claimed to have boasted, "I feel obligated to the sporting public at least to make an effort to reclaim the heavyweight championship for the white race. . . . I should step into the ring again and demonstrate that a white man is king of them all."[68] Here, for a fleeting moment, equality and equity became not a fleeting dream but a reality: equity in the context of fairness where each man received the human and material resources needed to prepare for the event, and equality in the context that the fight would be judged fairly, without racial bias.

Sports victories of blacks over whites, such as Joe Louis over James J. Braddock in 1937, Joe Louis over Max Schmeling in the return match, and Jessie Owens's outstanding four gold medals for track and field victories in the 1936 Summer Olympics, marked some of the few occasions of black pride at the national and international level during this time period. The black community celebrated these victories as very special occasions.

Other actions that stirred black pride and generated positive black identity at the local and national levels during the Jim and Jane Crow era included the barnstorming baseball team Chicago American Giants. Photographs were circulated of these ball players riding on a train as first-class passengers, not as porters or red-caps who handled the luggage. This was an image of equal-ity—one that blacks hoped would soon be a regular occurrence. But they regarded these images with both pleasure and anger because a "new vision of opportunity" was still not in clear focus.

Essays in black newspapers directly addressed racial pride, what it meant ("equality of rights") and did not mean ("Han't got no self"). Samuel Barrett, in a September 30, 1939, newspaper article, told the black community, "No race can achieve its highest in human advancement that lacks race pride or race consciousness. By race pride, I do not mean race arrogance, or an idea that one race is better than some other race, just because it happens to be the race with which we are identified and associated. It simply means that since different races exist, we must strive to make our race equal to the best in all those things which go to make up human progress. This spirit draws out of a race its highest quality."[69]

Barrett's statement provides an understanding of how and why Trinity UCC's motto ("Unashamedly Black and Unapologetically Christian") is held in such high esteem by its congregation. A Trinitarian speaks of the pride that came with living in the Black Belt and having successfully accomplished the migration to Chicago: "I think the experiences [gained from living] in the Black Belt gave people, especially blacks who moved here from the South, a sense of pride, different from that which they could have achieved in the South. The accomplishment achieved from their successful migration North brought them a lot of pride [but it is] much different than the pride they hold now."

Barrett also advised African Americans that they should welcome contact with people from other races, that they should reach out and develop relationships with other groups, but, in so doing, cultivate black pride: "While it is true that pride will force a people to develop largely among themselves, which should be, and is, natural, it is not, nor does it advocate, narrowness. We learn by coming in contact with others. But if we are going to take our place alongside of the worthwhile races and nations of the world, we must never cease to cultivate pride of race."[70]

The circulation of positive black images grew during this time. A positive black consciousness was marketed in locally produced records and films. Black race consciousness became especially popular during the 1960s, when the "Black is Beautiful" motto became known throughout the world.[71] Across the nation, D. Baldwin wrote,[72] "the Great Migration and its aftermath signaled a time of ideological, political, and cultural contestation between an emergent black middle class and an emerging working class." In Chicago, this was a time of structural and cultural contact and transformation between the self-described "better class" and the masses, giving life to competing "old" and "new" settler ideologies. Although blacks shared positions of marginality within Chicago's socioeconomic structure, community members drew lines of distinction around markers of refinement and, most importantly, respectability.[73] This distinction remains in place, shifting somewhat but never fully eliminated.[74] Today social class division remains in the black community. Trinity UCC recognized and had to deal with the socioeconomic divide from the time the vision of the church was announced, including throughout the tenure of Rev. Wright. As one parishioner said, "Trinity stresses so much about education. You know, going to school, not speaking so much and acting middle class or high class, or looking down your nose at other people. If you are middle class or high class it's your obligation to use your resources and what you know to help others."

The agency of the new migrants, the harshness of life experience, and the oppressed conditions under which many of them were forced to live provided the grist for the different literary and artistic expressions about urban life and living that soon emerged. Richard Wright observed that "Chicago is the city from which the most incisive and radical Negro thought has come; there is an open and raw beauty about that city that seems either to kill or *endow one with the spirit of life*" (authors' emphasis).[75]

It is not surprising, then, that it was from this city that Barack Obama was launched onto the national political stage. Chicago's history of political firsts for African Americans, forged within a crucible of black political thought, identity, and behavior in which race, politics and personal identity are ever present, shaped the circumstances that made Chicago a very special place for such "audacity of hope."

Chicago, nicknamed the "Windy City" as much for its politics as the icy blast that blows off Lake Michigan, has long been a crucible of social and political activism. Tristram Hunt, a historian writing in the *London Times*, argued that Chicago, along with Philadelphia and Baltimore, was the premier city of organized labor and radical activism in the late nineteenth century.[76] Often forgotten, but with a degree of relevance in today's political climate of civil actions by organized labor, is the fact that in 1886 Chicago was the location of the Haymarket affair (also known as the Haymarket massacre or Haymarket riot). Haymarket began as a rally in support of striking workers that came to a tragic end when an unknown person threw a bomb at police while they were attempting to disperse the rally. The blast from the bomb, along with ensuing gunfire, resulted in the deaths of eight police officers and an unknown number of rally participants. The Haymarket affair marks the origin of international May Day observances for workers.[77]

Chicago is also significant in the history of African American life because a black man, Jean Baptiste Pointe DeSaible, built Chicago's first settlement around 1790 on the current site of the Tribune Tower at 435 N. Michigan Avenue. The high school that bears his name as well as the community in which it sits served as one of the early sites of pride for a people whose history and culture was constantly denied or marginalized throughout society.

## THE CHICAGO BLACK RENAISSANCE

Chicago was also the source of a strand of artistic realism in the 1930s Depression era. This urban realism, while explicating the remorse and grit of life for people living in the Black Belt of Chicago, also brought a message of hope and change. It was expressed in literature, painting, theater, dance, lectures, music, and poetry and continued to highlight both the overt and nuanced racial and social injustices and the economic hardship that existed throughout urban society. This art also expressed the many ways that the black community could resist acts of oppression, and it supported the belief that "even if one has to be twice as good," success can and must be achieved. This artistic movement offered unvarnished pictures of the life struggles of African Americans, as well as heroic depictions of them working to achieve social freedom and well-being. Richard Wright, who was the leader of this movement, beseeched fellow black artists to write about their Chicago-based experiences with race, racism, and Jim Crow. In *Blueprint for Negro Writing*, he said, "Negro writers must accept the nationalist implications of their lives, not in order to encourage them, but in order to change and transcend them. They must accept the concept of nationalism in order to transcend it. They must *possess* and *understand* it."[78] Accepting America for what it was and is—in race relations—and then striving to change and transcend its "ordinary way" of doing things is a mode of thinking and acting that is surely reflected in the trajectory of Barack Obama's political life.

From 1925 to 1950 the black political and social thought that emerged from the Black Belt, "a city within a city," was second to none. Many literary scholars put forth ideas about black "plight and protest." Richard Wright, Arna Bontemps, Willard Motley, William Attaway, Gwendolyn Brooks, Frank Marshal Davis, Richard Durham, Langston Hughes, Fenton Johnson, St. Clair Drake, Horace R. Clayton, Charlemae Rollins, Margaret Walker, and others tell African Americans' stories of the grime and grit of urban life. These intellectuals and artists delivered messages about inequality and calls for political and social action. They wrote about black and white relations and described how the Jim Crow–like circumstances under which African Americans were living affected their identity and behavior and shaped race, racism, and politics in the Windy City and other urban areas.

*Black Boy/American Hunger* and *Native Son* by Richard Wright are riveting protest stories that address black identity, race, and racism. The two publications tell the story of what it was like to be a young black man shackled by the many manifestations of Jane and Jim Crow, including the frequency of black men being charged with the rape of white women and black men being described as animalistic and of very low intelligence. In *Black on the Block*, Pattillo explains that Richard Wright used the *Chicago Tribune* stories about Robert Nixon—an eighteen-year-old black man who was accused, convicted, and executed for the murder of a white woman, Florence Johnson—to fashion his character of Bigger Thomas in his novel *Native Son*. The brutal murder of Johnson set off racist reactions in the newspapers reporting on the incident, which created a public outcry: "Why don't they lynch them!" (*them* referenced a co-defendant). The horrible and tragic death of Florence Johnson was compounded by the media and prosecutors' treatment of Nixon, for he was portrayed in an animalistic manner, denied due process, forced to reenact the murder, and accused of raping the woman, although this was not the case. Pattillo suggests that this murder case fueled the fears of white neighbors in areas bordering the growing Black Belt: "It solidified the mental connections white residents made between crime, sexual perversity, and blackness, especially black men."[79]

Gwendolyn Brooks lived much of her life in Chicago and did a good deal of her writing about life in Bronzeville. She, along with writers like Richard Wright and Langston Hughes, used the urban landscape to frame her work. While women were not absent from Wright's and Hughes's work, Brooks put them at the center of her writing. As Beverly Guy-Sheftall notes, "Her poems present a more realistic view of the diversity and complexity of black women than the stereotypes (matriarch, whore, bitch, for example) which have persisted in other literary works by black and white artist alike."[80] Even short selections from different poems by Brooks give a snapshot view of the life experiences of women living in Bronzeville. What comes through in the readings supports what was said about her: "There is a general way in which women do tend to know women and also a general way in which they tend to know men, largely because our culture makes it so. Miss Brooks, whether she is talking of women or men . . . constantly speaks as a woman."[81]

In her work, Brooks speaks insightfully about women living in Bronzeville. In one case she tells of a woman staring solemnly down the long street where she lives, hanging on to thoughts of hope couched in uncertainty, who finds a moment of contentment and gives thanks that she is alive, although "yesterday's garbage ripens in the hall."[82] Life in urban areas for women, Brooks argues, follows a similar order of events that is also followed in the wealthy suburbs of Chicago: for some women, kids grow up and leave home, and kisses in moonlight become increasingly rare. As they age, Brooks's narratives tell us, daughters and sons put their mothers away the same as they do marbles and dolls, and men, be they husbands or lovers, are mostly just polite and caring and no longer look upon women with "lechery or love."[83]

African American people, Brooks contends, whether young or old, women or men, like most people, don't give up. They, too, are like Tom, Ma, and Pa Joad in *The Grapes of Wrath*: resilient. They don't give up and instead push forward seeking the next opportunity. Such resiliency, while perhaps expected from the younger generation of African Americans who migrated from the South or black soldiers returning from a war, was eloquently but simply captured in the poem "Two who are Most Good," which features an elderly couple, ordinary people, who continue to live their lives as best they could in spite of oppressive living conditions. Brooks' description of those two people seems to correspond to the lives of some the Trinitarians we interviewed and further resonates with the words in Curtis Mayfield's or Jo Jo's song, "Keep on Keeping On."[84]

Children, the little ones, suffered the most living in the kitchenettes in Chicago, many not knowing when and where their next meal would come from. Such harshness is described by Brooks in "John, Who Is Poor":

> Oh, little children, be good to John!—
> Who lives so lone and alone.
> Whose Mama must hurry and toil all day.
> Whose Papa is dead and done.
>
> Give him a berry, when you may.
> And girls, some mint when you can.
> And do not ask when his hunger will end.
> Nor yet when it began. [85]

Langston Hughes's weekly column in the *Chicago Defender* was a primer for the everyday black man and woman. Hughes tackled numerous topics, writing about segregation, Jim Crow laws, World War II, the treatment of black soldiers, and so on. The essays on race, politics, and culture were written to inform and assist black people thinking about their life in urban America and their lives as African American with its hopes, disappointments, Jim Crow laws, and eternal optimism for a real "AMERICAN America." An excerpt from Langston Hughes's column in the *Chicago Defender* on January 16, 1943, reads as follows:

*An American America*

The Negro people of America today are not threatening to fight and kill white Americans in order to get their rights. It was Mark Ethridge who said that all the armies of Hitler and the democracies together could not make the south change. We did not speak of armies. We did not mention violence. The most Negroes have threatened to do is stage a peaceful march on Washington to petition legal redress of grievances. The most we are doing is writing and speaking about—and working for—freedom and democracy as a reality— not as a shadow. The direst thought we are holding in our deep hearts is a dream of a real AMERICAN America. To shackle and muzzle this expression of that dream from Negro pulpits, Negro platforms, and from the pages of the Negro press would be to shackle the heart and to deny it hope.

Shall those of us who are colored in America ask for half-democracy? And shall we compromise with the poll-tax, with the segregation, with the Jim Crow car, with the Southern senators who are not elected by the people's vote, with the politicians who speak of liberty for the whole world and forget us, with the cheatery of the sharecropping system of the South, with the cheatery of the unequal distribution of public monies and the poor schools, poor parks, poor public services that we get? Shall we dilute the Four Freedoms to the strength of near-beer? Shall we, who are the Negro people of America, have no great dreams? Shall we ask only for the half-freedoms that move nobody to action for the great freedoms that this war is supposed to be about? Or shall we, with all other Americans of foresight and good will, seek to create a world where even Alabama will respect human decency?[86]

Lorraine Hansberry richly contributed to the "plight and protest" narrative with her acclaimed play *A Raisin in the Sun*. The play tells of black pride expressed though home ownership and how through struggle, steadfastness, and belief in a brighter day it came to be. In the play Hansberry spoke directly to black Chicagoans about the oppressive conditions they lived under because restrictive convents curtailed their progress, created black enclaves, and kept them in the Black Belt. The title *A Raisin in the Sun* was taken from a line in the poem "A Dream Deferred" by Langston Hughes. Hansberry's play was a retelling of the lawsuit *Hansberry v. Lee*,[87] which her father won in his battle against the restrictive covenants (*Burke v. Kleiman*).[88] The Hansberry family had been prevented from moving into a neighborhood and community of their choice. The property in the lawsuit was in the Chicago Woodlawn area, a school district that at times was the attendance area for Englewood High School, a high school that Gwendolyn Brooks attended.

Such protest writings were ongoing reminders of the racist circumstances under which blacks were compelled to live as well as a source for instilling hope and encouraging black people to strive until first-class citizenship was a reality for one and all. Writers such as Hansberry helped African Americans develop a critical consciousness response to the challenges of Jim and Jane Crow. In addition, since black intellectuals, artists, and teachers were forced to live in the Black Belt because of restrictive convents, their activism through book clubs, lectures, plays, and dance performances kept multiple and varied protest themes in constant motion. One theme in the plight and protest literature speaks of determination in the presence of the unknown. This theme had major significance to the new arrivals as they disembarked from the train tired and afraid in Chicago, as seen in Richard Wright's *12 Million Black Voices*:

> Timidly, we get off the train. We hug our suitcases, fearful of pickpockets. . . . We are very reserved, for we have been warned not to act "green." . . . Then we board our first Yankee street car to go to a cousin's home. . . . We have been told that we can sit where we please, but we are still scared. We cannot shake off three hundred years of fear in three hours.[89]

## AFRICAN AMERICAN POLITICS IN CHICAGO

Much of the development of black thought and identity over the decades from the 1920s to the 1960s came from the literary movement and from living in racially oppressed circumstances while the privileges of whites increased; this gave rise to the emergence of African American politicians in Chicago. Oscar De Priest's election as the first African American on the Chicago City Council in 1915 was an early story of that development. The opportunity for victory came as the African American population of the Second Ward reached 50 percent; in order to keep control of the Chicago City Council, white Republican leaders decided to run a black candidate to defeat a popular white Democrat in the election. De Priest's victory demonstrated how the convergence of interests between blacks and whites sometimes played a role in Chicago politics.

De Priest's surprising victory came after determination, struggle, and hard-boiled politics against two opponents, including Louis B. Anderson, another African American candidate who, it was predicted, would defeat De Priest. An article written by George Woodson, who was the Sixth Ward Precinct Committeeman and a strong advocate for Anderson, gave insight into the fierce political infighting and tough rhetoric at a critical moment in the black community, when it was reasoned and hoped that an African American would win a seat on the Chicago City Council. In addition, Woodson's article provided insight into the early development of racial unity around a political first. Woodson wrote that each and every black person in the community has a responsibility in the upcoming election:

> At this time and in this political crisis, the one question which is on the mind of every Afro-American citizen in the Second Ward is "Will we have an alderman?" . . . "Do we want an Afro-American alderman?" "Are we willing to adopt the best methods of getting one?" "Are the race voters of the Second Ward willing to do their individual share and work to remove the present existing obstacles?" Let us not, however, forget that success depends upon the individual voter, man and women, alike doing his and her duty by voting.

The energetic efforts of black women were critical to De Priest's election. African American women rigorously canvassed the neighborhoods, identifying voters who would support the "race man" (black candidate).[90] Women's suffrage clubs (such as the Alpha Suffrage Club) pledged "to leave no stone unturned" in their efforts to get a black man elected. The Club argued, "We realize that in no other way can we safeguard our own rights than by holding up the hands of those who fight our battles."[91] Black women also supported white candidates whom they believed would facilitate the goal of racial equality.[92] However, Dianne Pinderhughes argues that there were few elections that divided the African American vote in spite of intense debate within the Black Belt that allowed white candidates to win.[93]

During his one term on the Chicago City Council, De Priest pushed civil rights issues and argued for greater patronage for the African American community. In 1928 De Priest became the first African American to go to Congress since Reconstruction. He was initially selected to fill a vacancy in

Congress after the death of Congressman Madden and then elected to the House of Representatives. William Douglass Brainbridge for the *Chicago Defender* wrote:

> Under the state of Illinois it became the duty of the congressional committee of the [First] district to fill the vacancy. . . . The committee lost no time in performing its duty, and on April 20 [1929] Oscar De Priest was selected to fill the vacancy. The Associate Press carried the news to all parts of the country and reached points in other parts of the world. No sooner had the news been released that telegrams, telephone calls and letter began pouring in to Mr. De Priest. Whites and blacks, high and low, rich and poor, Jews and Gentiles seemed to respond with one accord in appreciation and approval of the selection of the committee. [94]

A picture on the front page of the *Chicago Defender* on April 20, 1929, has Oscar De Priest standing center stage in front of an artistic rendition of the US Capitol with the caption "In the Center of the Nation's Affairs." Articles abounded in Chicago's newspapers and other national dailies about this historic event—a black man goes to Congress. For its excellent coverage of the story, the *Chicago Defender* was singled out.

*Defender Is Praised for De Priest Story*

> Robert S. Abbott, editor and publisher of the *Chicago Defender*, is the recipient of hundreds of letters and telegrams from men and women of both races who have sent congratulations upon the splendid way the *Defender* handled the complete story of the life of Congressman Oscar De Priest. Outstanding among those received was a letter from former Congressman Joseph C. Manning, 516 Manhattan Avenue, New York City.
> Mr. Manning was a former congressman from Alabama and the first white man to advocate a federal law to stop lynching. His letter reads:
> My dear Mr. Abbot: The handling of the Congressman De Priest matter in this week's *Chicago Defender* is as fine a piece of journalism, if not better, than I have seen. Nothing could be more helpful and inspiring to your [readers]. I so much appreciate the genius and gift behind the *Defender*.
> Sincerely,
> JOSEPH C. MANNING

As a congressperson, De Priest became a national voice for civil rights. He argued that blacks should not have to live in segregated communities that negatively impact their social and cultural hopes. [95] De Priest participated in another first when he challenged First Lady Louann Hoover for refusing to invite his wife Jessie Williams De Priest to the White House to have tea along with the spouses of other Republican congressmen. When De Priest went public about the snubbing, Mrs. Hoover invited Mrs. De Priest to the White House. This became a highly symbolic event, marking the first time that an African American woman had ever been entertained by a First Lady in the official resident of the president. [96]

However, De Priest was not loved by all of the black community. Blacks who had been forced to live in the deplorable conditions of the kitchenette apartments vehemently despised De Priest. They accused him of buying large buildings, cutting them up into kitchenettes, and charging African Americans very high rent. Such practices were not consistent with the ideals of solidarity and social justice within the black community.

When De Priest died on May 19, 1951, the *Chicago Defender* published this statement: "The end of a career, and perhaps the end of an era, was signaled at 12:06 Saturday afternoon with the death of Oscar Stanton De Priest. He was the last of those men, big in stature, big in thought and big in heart, who had shaped the destiny of Negroes in Chicago, in Illinois, and to a large extent to entire U.S. for nearly half a century."

Another major political figure whose actions influenced the lives of old and new settlers in the Black Belt was William Dawson, "the Boss." Dawson did not have a special "first," other than being the first black member to chair a standing committee in Congress and one of the first African Americans to have considerable power during many of the thirteen consecutive Congresses in which he served. Dawson was a member of Congress from January 3, 1943, until his death in September 1970. He was considered "America's most powerful black politician." He gained political muscle by becoming a valued member of Mayor Richard J. Daley's political machine. However, Dawson's critics argue that he did not possess a strong black-centered political thought and identity, citing his overwhelming support of Mayor Daley's political machine as evidence. The sentiment in the black community was that Dawson was more concerned with being loved by the Chicago mayor than he was with providing opportunities for African Americans in the Black Belt.

The intersection of race, politics, and personal identity are visible because of who Dawson was as a person. However, the congressional wards that elected him and the fact that he lived in a segregated community did not seem to inspire him to be a "race man." Assessing Dawson's complete body of work as a member of Congress may lead his supporters to argue differently. One interpretation is that black political and social thought, behavior, and personal identity within the context of black-white relations and life in a segregated community do not produce uniform experiences or values. But for the most part, black men and women who experience discriminatory social configurations do take a stand against segregation and work to unmask oppression and white privilege.

Recognizing the power that can be derived from the growing African American community, black leaders developed independent institutions for racial progress. Between 1890 and 1916, black Chicagoans established a hospital, the Wabash Avenue YMCA, several black newspapers (including the *Chicago Defender*), and local branches of the NAACP and Urban League. The development of each and every one of these institutions carried with it stories of everyday African Americans engaging in some form of race struggle (e.g., segregation, resistance to equality) and politics (e.g., negotiations with the Republican or Democratic parties, negotiations with other blacks who had a different point of view) as these two configurations intertwine. When one closely scrutinizes the manner in which race is addressed in writings and discussions about politics with regard to almost any endeavor, including housing, education, city governance, and finances within the institutional structures in Chicago and other urban areas, one is struck by the lack of attention to race and racism as a major causal force in urban political outcomes.[97]

Today, race-neutral and race-evading language and the transcendence of race are used in discussions of governance, finance, and other social and civil contexts. Many people view the use of this language as "politically correct" or "color blind" and see it in a positive light. However, the use of race-neutral and race-evading language does not allow us to address race as an underlying social issue and thus allows racism to be perpetuated. Present-day racial dynamics remind us of the statement by Richard Wright that we placed at the beginning of the book. Though written more than fifty years ago, Wright's words have not lost their currency:

> An honest question merits an honest answer, and that answer lies in the hearts of the white and black readers of this book. The answer is, directly and bluntly: American whites and blacks both possess deep-seated resistances against the Negro problem being presented, even verbally, in all of its hideous fullness, in all of the totality of its meaning. The many and various groups, commissions, councils, leagues, committees, and organizations of an interracial nature have consistently diluted the problem, blurred it, and injected foggy moral or sentimental notions into it. This fact is as true of the churches as of the trade unions; as true of Negro organizations as of white; as true of the political Left as of the political Right; as true of white individuals as of black.

With that said, we offer the following observation: Though known as the second (or third) city, Chicago is not the second city, but rather the first city, when it comes to African Americans and national politics. Chicago (and the state of Illinois) has placed more African Americans in the U.S. Senate than any other state: Carol Moseley Braun, Barack Obama, and Ronald Burris. Chicago is also the city from which three African Americans (Jessie Jackson, Carol Moseley Braun, and Barack Obama) made viable runs for the presidency, with Barack Obama achieving success in 2008. Chicago is the city that elected the first African American to Congress, Oscar De Priest, and Chicago is the city where novelists and poets were the first to put the black urban experience of both men and women into the American literary canon. Chicago provided the rich soil where the African Americans' seeds of exceptionalism have flourished.

In concluding this chapter, where race and politics are center stage in the Black Belt, we provide an extended excerpt written by Langston Hughes in the June 11, 1949, issue of the *Chicago Defender*.[98] Hughes's essay "From the International House, Bronzeville Seems Far Away" provides illuminating insights into race and culture in the Black Belt/Bronzeville. He seeks to push past the tendency of people situated at the University of Chicago to "look past" and "distance" the Black Belt, despite its close physical proximity. Hughes uses his dual understanding of life both in and out of the Black Belt; Hughes had lived in the Black Belt and at the time resided at the University of Chicago and was thus able to look at Bronzeville from multiple perspectives, as an insider and an outsider, to make note of the weakness of "book study . . . ivory tower" in comparison to lived experiences and up-close investigation for understanding a problem or a people:

> Almost up to the sky, my room at the International House is the nearest thing to an ivory tower I have ever had. It faces North toward the downtown Chicago skyline and the horizon-blue of the lake off at the right. The eternal Chicago wind whistles by bringing long months of snow, sleet, rain, and recently a breath of delayed spring. When the window is open even a crack, the wind blows all the papers off my table.
>
> Chicago's wind goes well with the town because it is a big rough-neck city, a kind of American Shanghai, dramatic and dangerous, one of the cradles of the atom bomb, Carl Sandburg's "hog-butcher to the world" perfumed with stock-yard scents. It is a "Baby" Bell town (whose death by suicide sold out a whole issue of the Chicago Defender as soon as it appeared on the newsstands). It is a Joe Louis town with a knockout punch in its steel mills and stock yards. It is a Katherine Dunham town, seductive, determined, theatrical and clever. It's a Yancey town with a heart-throb like boogie-woogie.
>
> Heretofore I have always looked at Chicago from the Negro Southside. When I first came to the city as a kid just before the riots, my mother, my brother and I lived on Wabash in a one room level with the elevated trains that roared outside our windows. Later, writing some of my early plays, I lived where the el curves to cross Indiana. When I wrote The Big Sea I had a room back of the Grand Hotel not far from the elevated's rumble.
>
> So to be living this spring high in a quiet room in International House on the University of Chicago's Midway with green trees and grass below, is like living in another world far away from Horace Cayton—"Baby" Bell—Etta Moten—Bigger Thomas—Gwendolyn Brooks—Joe Louis—world of Bronzeville. Yet the "Black Belt" is only a few blocks off. But here one cannot hear it. No el trains cut the quiet. No winos mother-foul the evening air. No jitneys blow their horns. No big cards dispensing policy slips speed around the corners. No Bigger Thomases come home to kitchenette confusions. Here in the

University's sociology classes students only study about such things but do not live them. The "Black Metropolis" is a book in the library.

I understand better now what the words "ivory tower" mean. I understand better how people can live within a few blocks of daily melodrama, yet be as far away from it as one usually is from the news in the daily papers. I understand better how trees, yards, decent housing, cultured neighbors, clean bathrooms and ever-hot water can make people who live clean, quiet, library lives scornful of those whose lives are shattered by the roar of the el trains and chilled by the cold water that comes out of the faucet marked HOT in the kitchenette taps.

When I came to Chicago in February to be a "Poet In Residence" on the campus, I stayed at the Grand on South Parkway, my favorite little hotel. Then, to be nearer to my students, a room was secured for me at International House—with the rest of the foreigners. In the "Black Belt" I, too, am a foreigner. In the recent pre-Supreme-Court-decision days, Cottage Grove Avenue was the dividing line between Bronzeville and the restricted covenant areas. Japanese-Americans could live scattered among the whites, but not ourselves. Housing in Chicago is still difficult to find for colored persons outside the predominantly Negro section. But, fortunately, International House—being truly international—is open to both foreigners and Negroes, Jews and Gentiles of all nationalities. That is how I came to my quiet room high up in the wind and the nearest thing to an ivory tower I have ever had—since ivory towers do not exist in colored neighborhoods.

International House is a pleasant place to live, to practice one's languages, and to meet students and teachers from all around the world—including Dixie. There are International Houses only in Chicago, New York, Berkeley, and Paris, gifts of the Rockefeller Foundation to international friendship and understanding. It would be nice if every major university center had such a house for it is helpful and good to be able to live for a while with folks from China, Georgia, France, Mississippi, India, Germany, Tennessee, Sweden, Texas, Egypt, and Alabama. For white American and Negro American students from the South, it seems to me especially good that there is a house such as International House where they may be together and get acquainted in a friendly fashion—because they cannot share the same dormitories at home nor study together behind the Iron Curtains of Dixie.

## Chapter Three

# The Black Church and the African American Church in Chicago

*I . . . believe that many of our folks have learned from the church that big things can only be accomplished by the joining of a large group.*

—St. Clair Drake and Horace R. Cayton

*One of the continuing paradoxes of the Black church as the custodian of a great portion of Black culture and religion is that it is at once the most reactionary and the most radical of Black institutions, the most imbued with the mythology and values of white America, and yet the most proud, the most independent and indigenous collectivity in the Black community.*

—Gayraud S. Wilmore

Harsh criticism of the African American church was voiced during the presidential campaign of 2008. Most of the criticism was specifically directed at Trinity United Church of Christ because of the snippets of Reverend Wright's sermons aired by the media. The notion that "Trinity is racist" was repeated and repeated. Being thought of as racist caused great consternation among the membership. The accusations riled Trinitarians:

I say to [white Americans] that Trinity is a church that is pro-black and being pro-black does not mean that you are anti-white or anti-anything. We are definitely pro-black but we are not racist, not even a little bit.

It would never happen . . . no one would investigate a synagogue. No one would investigate any particular other religious entity. But because the African American community and specifically African American church is mysterious and exotic to those who are non–African American, it's easy to create any type of perception that you want; and it becomes believable because you are so

disconnected. You already see a group of people as exotic, mysterious, dangerous—all of the particular metaphors.

The bias and narrow framing of Trinity, congregants argued, is based
upon a single story of the black church in America, a story that frames the
black church as alien, exotic, and out of the mainstream. This framing is
situated within the history and the historical legacy of efforts to "make an
abstraction of the Negro"—to diminish black people's humanity and their
rights as human beings.[1] While this has had a powerful negative effect on
black people, it has not been successful in making black people an abstraction. On the contrary, it has substantiated the tremendous effect that African
Americans continue to have on the American character, which whites often
struggle to control; the black person is characterized as an exotic rarity,
different and deficient. The black church (and all that is embodied therein,
including its historical prominence) is made out to be comical, foreign, and
increasingly a site for cultural tourism; it is not a place to get to know, in
order to examine your current way of thinking about black people, their
history, and their culture.

Almost three years ago, Jan Benzel, an editor for the *New York Times*,
informed her readers that she was being reassigned to Paris. Before leaving
New York, she wanted to keep a promise that she had made to herself. The
promise was to attend the eleven o'clock Sunday church service at Abyssinian Baptist Church in Harlem. Ms. Benzel writes, "In this city of churches, I
headed for one I'd always meant to attend, at least once, out of curiosity."[2]
She continues: "The church . . . is a highlight on the tourist circuit. The very
notion of a church service as a sight to check off, a spot where busloads of
white people arrive to peer in on black Baptist worship service, is uneasy-
making."[3]

Visits to black churches to observe the Sunday service have become a
regular tourist attraction. Tourists come not to worship "but to record black
parishioners worshipping," states Fiqah.[4] Quoting Reverend Calvin Butts,
the pastor of Abyssinian Baptist Church, who stated in response to tourists
gawking and looking upon Sunday service as a spectacle, alien ritual, and
eye and ear candy, "This is not a buck-and-dance show."[5] Butts's church, the
same one that Benzel attended (out of curiosity), has had to pass out fliers to
visitors explaining how to behave during the service. Abyssinian's congregants have also complained that tourists turn on their cameras during prayer
and "snap away whenever a shout arises from the church's 'amen' corner."[6]
Rob Kerby of Beliefnet news stated, "Having to turn away crowds of international visitors are a number of evangelical neighborhood churches famous for
their joyous choirs, sermons delivered in dramatic traditional cadence and
unabashed congregations with an exuberant style of worshiping Jesus."[7]
Whereas most of the commentaries in the news report enjoyment in the

unique experience of attending black churches in Harlem, the tourists nevertheless come as "gawkers" and the church becomes a site to be observed, but not necessarily understood. Tourists are not there to learn or understand, to visit a significant historical site, like when visiting the churches in Italy or England, but to see and hear—a curiosity.

Whitney Houston's "home-going" (funeral) was covered by both the national and international press and shown in its entirety—three and a half hours—on numerous television channels. It was akin to villagers looking out and seeing a "stranger in the village."[8] The stranger, villagers could tell, had some similarities that they could identify with (in this case, casket, pallbearers, prayers, singing, music, and eulogies), but there was strangeness about it all the same. The villagers (white Americans) also were not looking to learn about or understand what they were seeing—an African American cultural experience that is a part of many black churches.

To the "foreigner" (people who are unfamiliar with what they are seeing and hearing), this might have been interpreted as being in a space that was exotic, frightening, and different. The scene was further complicated because of the people who were present and in charge—people who aren't usually invited over for Sunday dinner. Some across the country voiced surprise at what they were hearing and seeing during the broadcast of Houston's funeral. When the service wasn't referred to as a funeral, but rather a "home-going" to God, many white Americans were hearing a different perspective, or at least different terminology about the service after a black person dies.

Commentary about the service in the social and news media included positive statements, such as observations that the music was beautiful and Kevin Costner's remarks were great.[9] However, the single story that white Americans were used to hearing and seeing about a church service was disrupted. Many of the negative statements pointed out the speakers' lack of knowledge about the black experience, and a lack of patience or a disregard by white Americans for learning about and understanding this important aspect of the black experience.

The clapping, shouting, and laughing in a sacred space were criticized as disrespectful, and reference to the service as a "home-going" was regarded as alien or inappropriate.[10] Critics of the home-going described it as an overblown spectacle that was out of the mainstream.[11] The fact that some of the TV anchors covering the home-going had very little knowledge of the service contributed to the criticism. Many of these negative statements made about the rituals at Whitney Houston's home-going would not have occurred if there had been widespread respect, appreciation, and acceptance of black people and their history and culture.

Kevin Costner spoke at the funeral and, according to some, he looked out of place—a white man speaking for seventeen minutes to a church filled with mostly black people while eulogizing a black woman. But as Costner spoke, increasingly radiating confidence with a posture and delivery that said "I am comfortable here, and I too have a Baptist church story to tell, one that Whitney and I used to talk about," it was not Costner who became comfortable in his own skin, but those who were watching who had never been inside of a black church, who through him and because of him began to feel more relaxed and engaged with the home-going celebration, not just as observers but as participant-observers.

The style of preaching seen in Whitney Houston's home-going celebration was, according to Carl's friends and colleagues at Madison, different, but not mysterious, exotic, or any other negative adjective. Through the full portrayal of the church service, people were able to recognize the many similarities to other religious church services, such as the closed casket, location of family members near the coffin, and the order of the service. This Sunday occurrence in black churches across America is a deeply rooted and cherished tradition. But when snippets of a sermon are shown on television (especially those of a black preacher) to the unfamiliar eye and a mind filled with prejudice, viewers' misinterpretations, fears, and anxiety can cloud their understandings.

The prevalence of this alien perception of the black church motivates this chapter. We hope to demystify the black church and build toward a greater understanding of black people, their religion, and their worshiping customs. In doing so, we hope to help readers make sense of the voices of the Trinitarians whose perspectives on the Wright controversy are given in chapter 5.

Prejudicial statements, Gordon Allport argued, are those that show "an antipathy based on faulty and inflexible generalization that is felt, expressed and directed toward a group or an individual of that group."[12] Many of those voicing criticism about Jeremiah Wright would dismiss the relevance of Allport's claim, arguing that their comments are merely observations of an event and a legitimate investigation into a political candidate's background. But this argument loses its currency when prejudicial and racist statements began appearing on the Internet, on the walls of Trinity Church's restrooms, and on the signs of those protesting outside of Trinity Church. Some parishioners experienced these statements firsthand:

> There were times when I would get the calls that I wanted to cuss back but I didn't. [They made] racial slurs. They would say things like "is Reverend Wright there?" And I'd say no. [And they would say] "that racist S.O.B. . . . We'll be there this Sunday to do so and so."

> One caller said, he [Barack Obama] was betrayed by a smooth-talking preacher whose recent behavior is a clear example of how low the black church has sunk in the days after the death of Rev. Dr. Martin Luther King Jr. It is heartbreaking.

# THE ORIGINS OF THE BLACK AND
# AFRICAN AMERICAN CHURCH

The title of this chapter, "The Black Church and the African American Church in Chicago," is intended to honor not just the contemporary African American church but also those blacks born in Africa who were brought here as slaves and founded the institution under the direst of circumstances. These individuals struggled against tremendous odds to start a religious institution in which they could worship God, dream of freedom and equality without interruptions, and have a place, even if it was in a swamp, where for a millisecond they could feel human, at peace in life. This "invisible institution" of the black church was a crucial element in the spiritual survival of slaves. It was the organizing principle around which the life that enslaved blacks had some control over was structured. It was their school, forum, political arena, social club, art gallery, music conservatory, and sanctuary. It was the lyceum, the gymnasium, and the sanctum sanctorum. The black church, founded under slavery, survived, flourished, and developed into the full-blown black church that we have today.

Religion was the sustaining force that gave blacks the strength to endure when endurance foretold no promise, and it gave blacks the fortitude to be courageous in the face of their own dehumanization.[13] Arguably, not since the bombing of the 16th Street Baptist Church in Birmingham, Alabama—which killed four African American girls on Sunday, September 15, 1963—has the black church received such attention and undergone such a racialized attack that brought forth major national media attention.

Knowing the pain and joy of the black church from its conception as an invisible institution during the days of enslavement to its place in present-day American society—and its role in the African American community writ large—should provide insight into why the unspoken voices at Trinity United Church of Christ need to be heard. This anecdote by Henry H. Mitchell, author of *Black Church Beginnings*, was echoed by many members of Trinity when they said Rev. Wright had preached to them "Know who you are and whose you are." Mitchell states:

> In 1973 in the introductory course in African American church history at Colgate Rochester Divinity School, I—the instructor—was accused thus: "you teach Black church history like it's your own family album." My answer was, "you're absolutely right, and that's how every one of you should view it. It's not abstract data required to pass a course. It's the spiritual history of our family. Until you see it this way, you won't even know who you are. Among other handicaps, you'll be the helpless victim of widespread misinformation about our family's faith, as having come from the slave masters."[14]

This "spiritual history" reaches back to the Revolutionary War period of the 1760s and 1770s. While some black churches, such as the African Methodist Episcopal (AME) Church, are predominantly African American, many black churches are members of predominantly white denominations, such as the United Church of Christ (which developed from the Congregational Church of New England).[15] The history of the Presbyterian Church provides another example and greater insight into the historical tensions and struggles faced by black churches within predominantly white denominations over issues of slavery and racial exclusion.

The beginning of the black church is the beginning of a rich and glorious chapter of American history. This history includes the origin of the invisible institution (sometimes called hush harbor) where religious meetings were held on plantations across the South. These religious meetings gave those who were enslaved inspiration and hope to plan for the day without shackles or having to be called "boy." In addition, the black church became the educational institution where newly emancipated African Americans received schooling during the years following the Civil War. The black church also built colleges and universities that helped African Americans assume their place in society, rising to different levels of accomplishment and enjoying a diversity of careers. Perhaps most significantly, the black church served as the "drum major" to mobilize communities to peacefully march during the turbulent civil rights era, challenging both black and white Americans to model the biblical values of equality and justice upon which this nation was founded.

At the beginning of the twentieth century, W. E. B. Du Bois asserted, "The Negro church . . . is the social center of Negro life in the United States, and the most characteristic expression of African character."[16] Although today many African Americans may question this thesis, the African American church remains a dominant force in the lives and experiences of black people and its influence is present in other racial and ethnic communities. At some church services during the year members of the congregation tell stories of racial oppression passed on to them by their parents and grandparents, stories that remind today's congregations that at one time in this country "the church was the only place African Americans felt free." In *Born to Rebel*, Benjamin Elijah Mays, former president of Morehouse College, explains the importance of his church to him as a young man in rural South Carolina:

> Old Mount Zion was an important institution in my community. Negroes had nowhere to go but to church. They went there to worship, to hear the choir sing, to listen to the preacher, and to hear and see the people shout. The young people went to Mount Zion to socialize, or simply to stand around and talk. It was a place of worship and a social center as well. There was no other place to go.[17]

Throughout the growth and development of the black church, different religious affiliations have influenced it. An excellent account of the growth of Protestant religion among African Americans from the birth of the black church through the nineteenth century in the United States comes from Laurie Maffly-Kipp.[18] She contends that black religious tradition was born out of several experiences: from white Baptist and Methodist missionaries sent to convert Africans to the earliest pioneers of the independent black denominations, black missionaries in Africa, and the eloquent rhetoric of W. E. B. Du Bois.[19] In the South during the 1770s, increasing numbers of enslaved people converted to evangelical religions such as the Methodist and Baptist faiths. Many white clergy within these denominations actively promoted the idea that all Christians are equal in the sight of God, a message that provided hope and encouragement to those enslaved.[20] White clergy encouraged worshiping in ways that drew upon African worship patterns. There was enthusiastic singing, clapping, dancing, and even spirit-possession.[21]

Maffly-Kipp also describes how some whites used the institution of the church to control African Americans:

> Many white owners and clergy preached a message of strict obedience, and insisted on slave attendance at white-controlled churches, since they were fearful that if slaves were allowed to worship independently they would ultimately plot rebellion against their owners. It is clear that many blacks saw these white churches, in which ministers promoted obedience to one's master as the highest religious ideal, as a mockery of the "true" Christian message of equality and liberation as they knew it.[22]

To keep their enslaved blacks subservient, white slave owners told blacks that God created them to be servants, and if they faithfully and obediently fulfilled this duty, they would be rewarded in heaven.[23] However, in slave quarters blacks organized their own churches in reaction to the lies they were being told and the oppressive church services the whites offered. Signals, passwords, and messages that whites could not discern were used to call fellow believers to church services. During their own services, enslaved black drew on beliefs from evangelical Christianity and sang songs using a mixture of African rhythms. They spoke and dreamed of freedom and calculated ways to escape to freedom.[24] Maffly-Kipp writes:

> It was here that the spirituals, with their double meanings of religious salvation and freedom from slavery, developed and flourished; and here, too, that black preachers, those who believed that God had called them to speak his Word, polished their "chanted sermons," or rhythmic, intoned style of extemporaneous preaching. Part church, part psychological refuge, and part organizing point for occasional acts of outright rebellion . . . these meetings provided one of the few ways for enslaved African Americans to express and enact their hopes for a better future.[25]

Invisible institutions were central to the lives of enslaved blacks; they were where they dealt with loneliness as best they could and dreamed of freedom. These institutions provided mental support and physical caring for enslaved persons, who were constantly faced with the disruption of their family and other kinship networks. Invisible institutions were organized and conducted by individuals who stepped forward or who were selected by the group.[26] To keep the meetings "invisible" to slave masters, they were sometimes held in swamps and fields (brush harbors) or inside slave quarters. There is not one model or a single story about these "hush harbors." Whereas the typical hush harbor had a pastor, in some cases it also had the slave owner's approval. In these circumstances, the message in the sermon was tamer than the message heard at the secret meetings.[27] The following song sung by black enslaved expresses the needs that the invisible institutions fulfilled:

> Oh, that I had a bosom friend,
> To tell my secrets to,
> One always to depend upon
> In everything I do!
>
> How I do wander, up and down!
> I seem a stranger, quite undone;
> None to lend an ear to my complaint,
> No one to cheer me, though I faint.[28]

It was during their secret religious meetings, when the enslaved had moments of spiritual freedom, that they developed different ways and means to "speak truth to power" and to remember that "power concedes nothing without a struggle." These meetings helped to establish a tradition, a tradition in which the black church became a space where black men and women gathered to discuss and develop plans to resist and push back against racial oppression, to encourage resiliency and agency, and to offer thanks for burdens that were lifted or achievements that were hard won.

At the risk of severe punishment the enslaved crept to the secret meetings. Punishment by the slave masters if caught could include whippings, loss of limbs, or worse. Peter Randolph shares a firsthand account of the dehumanization of enslaved blacks for worshiping God.

> Sometimes the slaves meet in an old log-cabin. . . . If discovered, they escape, if possible, but those who are caught often get whipped. . . . In some places, if the slaves are caught praying to God, they are whipped more than if they had committed a great crime. The slave-holder will allow the slave to dance, but do not want them to pray to God. . . . he is forbidden to do so under the threat of having his throat cut, or brains blown out.[29]

The primary qualification for a preacher in the hush harbors was some knowledge of reading. Many times this qualification was not to be found, and so a man (usually) was willing to develop the skills to preach. A former enslaved person explained, "Our preachers were usually plantation folks like the rest of us. Some man who had some education and had learned about the bible."[30] The ministry of the preacher was extremely important to the enslaved because their need for guidance and comfort was immense. Mitchell states, "The awesome importance of this spiritual and emotional support can be seen by the fact that the time to engage in worship was taken from the already too brief free time away from field work. Work time already ran from sun-up to sundown. Time for worship was taken from the brief period left for the personal needs for sanitation, sleep, food and child rearing."[31]

Mitchell also points out that the development of many great churches was conceived and executed by a generation of leaders among whom almost all had been legally and forcibly denied being taught to read.[32] The result of this repressive act was that incorporation papers for numerous churches were signed with X's. Additionally, Mitchell argues that charismatic preachers of the gospel and lay leaders in prayer were not deterred because of (Western) illiteracy, nor were they believers and supporters of anti-intellectualism. Quite the contrary: in response to being denied the opportunity to learn to read, black preachers developed superior memorization capabilities, much like their griot forefathers (storytellers in Africa), which allowed them to hear biblical stories a few times and then accurately recall them.[33] This artistic skill enabled the early black preachers to make the Bible come alive with their dramatic articulation of biblical stories.[34] According to Paul Oliver in his book *Savannah Syncopators*, "Though [the griot] has to know many traditional songs without error, he must also have the ability to extemporize on current events, chance incidents and the passing scene. His wit can be devastating and his knowledge of local history formidable."[35]

Mostly absent from the discussion of the "black preacher" is the presence and voice of the black woman preacher. There was a regular shortage of outstanding preacher talent and black churches were always on the lookout for the exemplary church leaders, but consideration of women for the role of senior pastor was marginalized and/or nonexistent. "The word church still [to this day] subtly implies male pastoral leadership in the minds of too many people."[36] This was exceedingly troubling to black women because the staunch, early pushes of the African American churches for social justice nonetheless ignored the idea of equality for women. Although we now have black woman preachers, this concern is still not completely alleviated.[37]

By 1810 the slave trade to the United States had come to an end, but the enslaved population continued to increase as female and male enslaved blacks "jumped the broom" (a marriage ritual used by enslaved blacks, who were often prevented from legally marrying), giving rise to a native-born population. With fewer native Africans living who had experienced Africa personally, the various cultures and language groups of enslaved Africans blended together, making way for the preservation and transmission of religious practices that were increasingly African American rather than purely African.[38]

These practices, the blending of African and African American, gave rise to religious traditions central to black churches today. The African belief systems, the traditional religious doctrines, are still present and are merged with traditions of the orthodox Christian faith. Mitchell records the points of correspondence: "The parallels are amazing, as with the omnipotence, justice, omniscience, and providence of God."[39]

After the Emancipation Proclamation was signed by Abraham Lincoln on January 1, 1863, blacks in the South immediately faced several complex and challenging problems: finding and reuniting with family, securing jobs, and discovering what it would mean to live in the United States as citizens and not as property. A narrative by former slave Isaac Lane takes us inside of the challenges blacks faced and the role of religion in guiding them through that tough time:

> After [Robert E.] Lee had surrendered and the Confederacy had gone to pieces and Jefferson Davis had become a refugee, our owners called us together and told us we were free and had to take care of ourselves. There I was with a large, dependent family to support. I had no money, no education, no mother nor father to whom to look for help in any form. Our former owners prophesied that half of us would starve, but not so. It must be admitted, however, that we had a hard time, and it seemed at times that the prophecy would come true; but the harder the time, the harder we worked and the more we endured. For six months we lived on nothing but bread, milk, and water. We had a time to keep alive; but by praying all the time, with faith in god, and believing that he would provide for his own, we saved enough to get the next year not only bread, milk, and water, but meat also.[40]

Part of what it meant to be citizens and not property included exercising religious freedom. So, along with the task of human survival and giving aid and support to that survival, there was the effort to organize religious communities and determine the nature and structure of black religion—that is, establishing the black church. Since religious unanimity was not a goal, numerous denominations developed, many of which have survived to the present day. Drake and Cayton comment on the diversity of denominations that flourished within the black church community:

> If you wander about a bit in the Black Metropolis [Chicago] you will note that one of the most striking feature s of the area is the prevalence of churches, numbering some 500. . . . Nowhere else in the Midwest Metropolis could one find, within a stone's throw of one another, a Hebrew Baptist Church, a Baptist

Believers' Holiness Church, a Universal union Independent, A Church of Love and Faith, Spiritual, a Holy Mt Zion Methodist Episcopal Independent, and a United Pentecostal Holiness Church. Or a cluster such as St. John's Christian Spiritual, Park Mission African Methodist Episcopal, Philadelphia Baptist, Little Rock Baptist, and Aryan Full Gospel Mission Spiritualist.[41]

## THE AFRICAN AMERICAN CHURCH IN THE NORTH

Northern blacks escaped the lash and the whip, but still had to deal with a harsh racial divide in most northern institutions: segregation on public transportation, in schools, and in churches was the rule.[42] Underlying this rule was an ideology of white superiority that was held not only by the everyday white person but also by some abolitionists. Sernett stated, "Even those whites who held up the abolitionist flag, often at the risk of social ostracism in their own families and community, rarely conceived of a reconstruction of the North along lines of racial and social equality."[43]

Richard Allen and Absalom Jones, along with other blacks, withdrew from St. George's Methodist Episcopal Church in Philadelphia because they were forbidden to pray at the altar with white members. In 1793, Allen and Jones founded the Free African Society. Jones went on to organize the African Protestant Episcopal Church of St. Thomas, and Allen organized the African Methodist Episcopal (AME) Church. These churches served as a sanctuary from theological indignity and racial exclusion.

Similarly, other blacks left white churches. Jeremiah Asher stopped attending church because he was required to sit in the "Negro Pew." The Negro Pews, wrote Asher, "were about six feet square, with sides so high it was impossible to see the minister or the rest of the congregation. The pews were design to accommodate about fifteen or twenty black people."[44] Because of the oppressive conditions, blacks in New York City, Boston, and other northern cities began to leave white churches. In more southern states such as Maryland, Virginia, Georgia, and Kentucky, African Americans begin to establish independent Baptist churches.[45]

C. Eric Lincoln's observation about this period, especially the social action by Allen, provides an explanation as to why the eleven o'clock hour on Sunday became segregated:

> Ever since Richard Allen and his black fellow worshippers had been forcibly ejected from Philadelphia's St. George Methodist Church as they knelt in prayer in a segregated gallery, the resulting establishment of a separate church had symbolized even at its beginning the black American's commitment to dignity and self-determination.[46]

This commitment to dignity and self-determination throughout the life of the black church has been led by the black preacher. This is so in part because, within the black church, preachers have had (and mostly continue to have) the greatest freedom of any member of the African American community to plan for and promote racial equality and social justice: "The preacher tells us of days long ago and of a people whose sufferings were like ours. He preaches of the Hebrew children and the fiery furnace, of Daniel, of Moses, of Solomon and of Christ. What we have not dared feel in the presence of the Lords of the Land, we now feel in church."[47]

Preachers can say what they please about current political and social affairs, including race relations, and many do. There is little chance that leaders higher up in the church hierarchy will discipline ministers because they primarily answer to their congregations. In addition, there are rarely whites in the audience that might cause economic or social reprisals for comments made against white privilege. It is because of these conditions— the need to eliminate racism and the absence of white ears and eyes—that African American preachers were and are expected to be "real Race people."[48] James Poindexter, pastor of the Second Baptist Church of Columbus, Ohio, in the 1870s—a time when the ideology of Jane and Jim Crow was in full bloom—told fellow preachers at a pastor's union meeting about how it is the black preacher's duty to be involved in the political discourse and the behavior of the government:

> Nor can the preacher more than any other citizen plead his religious work or the sacredness of that work as an exemption from duty. Going to the bible to learn the relation of the pulpit to politics, and accepting the prophets, Christ, and the apostles, and the pulpit of their time, and their precepts and examples as the guide of the pulpit today, I think that their conclusion will be that wherever there is a sin to be rebuked, no matter by who committed, and ill to be averted or good to be achieved by our country or mankind, there is a place for the pulpit to make itself felt and heard. The truth is that all the help the preachers and other good and worthy citizens can give is needed by taking hold of politics in order to keep the government out of bad hands and secure the ends for which governments are formed.[49]

The fact that black women were placed on the margins of discussion and action regarding pastoral leadership did not mean that they quietly and submissively accepted it. Knupfer cites Lucy Smith as an example of a woman preacher who during the first two decades of the twentieth century became one of the most popular evangelical preachers of Chicago. Similarly, Knupfer identified Pastor Mary Evans and her protégée, Dorothy L. Sutton, as holding a pastorship and ministering a congregation at the Cosmopolitan Community Church in Chicago of up to nine hundred congregants. Following in Evan's footsteps, Sutton became the minister of Cosmopolitan Community Church and established programs for children such as Sunday school, a choir drama guild, and a Boy Scout troop that had a special appeal to the many young professionals in her congregation.[50] Beside the efforts of individual women, women's collective work could be seen throughout black churches' activities. In addition, Knupfer points out that black women in Chicago promoted social activism in numerous other areas including working at public housing projects; promoting the institution of perhaps Chicago's first multicultural curriculum in the schools; developing women's clubs that focused on assisting orphaned children, poor mothers, and the unemployed; working with the YMCA; and promoting the expressive arts and encouraging social protest.[51]

In the last thirty years, African American women theologians have written extensively about the double burden that they experience as both blacks and females. Many—such as Delores S. Williams, Katie Geneva Cannon, Emilie M. Townes, and Kelly Brown Douglas—identify themselves as "womanists," borrowing Alice Walker's term, which is defined as "a black feminist or feminist of color." For Williams, womanist theology brings black women's experience into the discourse of all Christian theology, from which it has previously been excluded. Womanist theology attempts to help black women see, affirm, and have confidence in the importance of their experience and faith for determining the character of the Christian religion in the African American community. It critiques black male oppression of black females while it also critiques white racism that oppresses all African Americans, female and male.[52]

Closing the racial gulf within the church has a history of stubborn progress. The inability to eliminate racial segregation at the eleven o'clock hour on Sundays dates back to enslavement and was kept alive after emancipation by Jim Crow laws. From the Reconstruction era onward, black and white Christian churches have for the most part gone their separate ways. When blacks left or were ejected from white churches early on, it created the conditions for black and white churches to develop with different style and substance. While African Americans shared a common belief with European American evangelicals, a belief that the biblical account of God's past dealings with the world offered clues to the meaning of life in America, there was a fundamental difference. White Protestants often likened America to the Promised Land—the New Israel—a "city set on a hill." Black worshipers, however, were more likely to see America as Egypt—the land of their captivity. They longed for their own emancipation, just as God had delivered the Israelites from their captors in the book of Exodus.[53]

Missed opportunities to close the racial gulf within the larger church community also came about because whites feared equating the enslaved blacks with groups in the Bible. This created a good deal of controversy since religion permeated most aspects of life during that time for both the clergy and owners of the enslaved. Most religious denominations voiced an opinion about slavery. Quakers were known to be the most vocal against it, and over time other denominations—Methodists, Baptists, and Presbyterians—voiced opposition. Some feared that blacks would relate groups and conditions of human equality discussed in the Bible to their own situation and seek to free themselves.[54]

Slave owners had debated the slavery and religion connection. Some held the view that if they converted the enslaved, it would cause problems, but they contended that slaves who were Christians might cause fewer problems than those who were not converted. Other owners of enslaved blacks believed that if they converted their slaves, they would learn to praise God and that would eventually lead to the enslaved praising them. Enslaved blacks, however, did not look at religion in this manner; their interpretation of the Bible related to their life and condition. They believed that the Exodus of the Israelites from Egypt meant that they should escape their shackles and head to freedom.[55] "Daniel being delivered from the lion's den prompted the thought that God freed men from their difficult situations, and the Resurrection symbolized a man being brought from death to life."[56]

After emancipation, the white church had many missed opportunities to forge a place within their halls for black worshipers. One such misstep was their refusal to overtly deal with the status of black people. Blacks wanted to be seen and treated as more than black people without shackles and someone to "fetch" coffee, plow the field, and care for little white babies. They were no longer property. They wanted the respect that being a man or woman afforded.[57] However, after the Civil War, efforts to make blacks seen and accepted as fully human, not the ignoble "three-fifths" of a person that the Supreme Court had argued, did not move forward without struggle. Most progress came through efforts initiated by African Americans rather than the white churches. For example, whites had a difficult time assenting to blacks in positions of respect, such as a pastor. Religious denominations gave little encouragement to the acceptance of black men as ordained preachers. For the average white man and woman, such an idea was not taken into account when the enslaved were freed.[58] This lack of support was perpetuated and reinforced by the refusals or delays in granting licenses to black men to preach.[59]

Resistance, delay, and neglect were strategies that were used in both the North and South to stall the advancement of African Americans in the clergy and other professions and to forestall opportunities for the races to come together. The fact that such tactics were employed by members of the church speaks volumes about the depth to which racism had invaded the country's ideological and philosophical core.

At the beginning of the twentieth century the racial gulf in church and state was still firmly in place, notwithstanding the Civil War and emancipation. In 1906, Reverdy C. Ransom that argued major efforts were needed to close this racial gulf:

> On this question of race, the history of our past is well known. The Race Problem in this country is still with us, and constitutes perhaps the most serious problem facing us today. In Church and state, from the beginning, we have tried to settle the problem by compromise, but all compromises have ended in failure. It is only when we have faced it courageously and sought to settle it right that we have triumphed, as in the case of Lincoln's immortal "Proclamation of Emancipation." American Christianity will un-christ itself if it refuses to strive on, until this Race Problem is not only settled, but settled right; and until this is done, however much men may temporize and seek compromise, and cry "peace! peace! peace!" there will be no peace until this is done.[60]

Almost fifty years later, during the civil rights struggle, Martin Luther King Jr. spoke directly about this racial gulf in American's churches: "It is appalling that the most segregated hour of Christian America is eleven o'clock on Sunday morning, and Sunday school is still the most segregated school of the week."[61] Since King's statement decades ago, very little has changed about who sits in church pews. Consequently, many American churches look much like they did in 1953.

Trinitarians who were present during the founding of Trinity in 1961 spoke about the Unity Church of Christ's dream of the church having black and white co-pastors and an interracial congregation. A statement by one Trinitarian puts into perspective the struggle to desegregate the eleven o'clock hour: "Many in the congregation were willing to go along with the co-pastor. But some were not because of racism toward blacks from that community, especially when black people would cross Halsted. But then, the decision was taken out of our hands as the whites began to flee their neighborhood. They didn't really want to have service with us, to sit by us; and that was OK. [Looking back] we really didn't need them." The idea of a post-racial society in America at the eleven o'clock hour on Sunday remains a tall hurdle to overcome.

An exception to the patterns of division among black and white churches is observed in David Van Biema's *Time* article "Can Megachurches Bridge the Racial Divide?"[62] Van Biema supports Martin Luther King Jr.'s thesis that despite the growing desegregation of most U.S. institutions, churches remain an exception. He noted that, based upon a 2007 survey, fewer than 8 percent of American churches have a significant racial mix. Van Biema believes that one reason for the racial gulf is that "people attend the church they are used to; many minorities have scant desire to attend a white church, seeing their faith as an important vessel of cultural identity. And for those who desire a transracial faith life the opportunity is discouraging."[63] Van

Biema continues, observing that in an age of mixed-race malls, mixed-race pop music charts, and a mixed-race president, the church divide seems increasingly peculiar: "It is troubling, even scandalous, that our most intimate public gatherings—and those most safely beyond the law's reach—remain color-coded."[64]

That said, Van Biema argues that there are various reports that the racial divide is beginning to fade in some churches, especially evangelical Christian congregations. Referencing Michael Emerson, a specialist on race and faith at Rice University, Van Biema states that the "proportion of American churches with 20 percent or more minority participation has languished at about 7.5 percent for the past nine years. But among evangelical churches with attendance of 1,000 people or more, the proportion has more than quadrupled, from 6 percent in 1998 to 25 percent in 2007. Call it the desegregation of the megachurches—and consider it a possible pivotal moment in the nation's faith."[65] Yet a growing concern is that while the racial divide in the church is fading, it is focused on the men to the exclusion of both white and black women, who continue to be treated and viewed as subordinate to men within the church and who face a lack of gender inclusion and continued gender inequity.[66]

Offering still another perspective, Emerson and Smith, in a 2000 publication, argued that although evangelicals have good intentions they may be participating in the preservation of America's racial chasm. White evangelicals, Emerson and Smith claim, do not believe that structural discrimination exists against blacks and they deny the existence of any ongoing racial problem in the United States.[67] They believe that the liberal media, African American culture, unethical black leaders, and the inability of African Americans to "get over" the past is the cause of any perception of a black problem. Emerson and Smith disagree and argue that evangelicals' attitudes are the natural outgrowth of their theological worldview rooted in individualism, free will, personal relationships, anti-structuralism, and premillennial eschatology—the belief that world conditions will only worsen until Christ returns—so there is no need to bother with social issues.[68] Such ideas are held firmly in place, Emerson and Smith say, because evangelical churches are segregated churches and are located in segregated neighborhoods, and this makes it difficult for white evangelicals to see the pervasive and systematic injustice that perpetuates inequality, going on every day in the real world of black America.[69]

Mitchell argues that "the story of the Black church is a tale of variety and struggle in the midst of constant racism and oppression." In the context of race and oppression is the knowledge that "prior to 1800 no (black) church, North or South, evolved without some form of white denominational recognition, trusteeship of land title, and/or certification to the government by respected whites that the Blacks involved would cause the slave system no trouble."[70] Additionally, Maffly-Kipp states that the story of the black church is one "of constant change, and of the coincidence of cultural cohesion among enslaved Africans and the introduction of Protestant evangelicalism to their communities."[71]

"Go North" was the call heard by future members of Chicago's African American churches. In a letter written by an African American minister in the early twentieth century, one man describes the conditions that motivated the Great Migration: the blatant racism of the South with the all-consuming need to feed family:

> Doubtless you have learned of the great exodus of our people to the north and west from this and other southern states. I wish to say that we are forced to go when one thinks of a grown man's wages is only fifty to seventy five cents per day for all grades of work. He is compelled to go where there is better wages and sociable conditions. Believe me when I say that many places here in this state the only thing that the black man gets is a peck of meal and from three to four lbs. of bacon per week, and he is treated as a slave. As leaders we are powerless for we dare not resent such or show even the slightest disapproval. Only a few days ago more than 1,000 people left here for the north and the west. They cannot stay here. The white man is saying that you must not go but they are not doing anything by way of assisting the black man to stay. As a minister of the Methodist Episcopal Church I am on the verge of starvation simply because of the above conditions.[72]

The Great Migration transformed Chicago politically, socially, and culturally. Between the years of 1900 and 1910, the African American population grew rapidly. From 1916 to 1920, more than fifty thousand blacks, mainly from the South, migrated to Chicago. Up until World War I, about nine-tenths of the African American population lived in the South, most in very rural areas. "The War created an unprecedented demand on the part of northern industries for workers, especially large numbers of unskilled workers. The War cut off the immigration of workers from Europe and many European immigrant workers returned home in order to fight for their home lands."[73] Drake and Cayton explain, "As country after country was drawn into the First World War, foreign-born men streamed home [to Europe] from Pittsburgh and Cleveland, Detroit and Toledo, from mills and mines, to shoulder arms. Immigration virtually ceased; Chicago, too, lost thousands of workmen.[74]

As word went out about employment opportunities in the meat-packing plants and steel mills, African Americans headed north. The *Chicago Defender*, a weekly African American newspaper, was one of the major voices calling on African Americans to come north. Train porters helped distribute copies of the *Defender* throughout southern states. The newspaper highlighted employment opportunities and offered to help new migrants get settled. Nikki Giovanni has written about the role of the Pullman porters in the Great Migration: "This is for the Pullman Porters who organized when people said they couldn't. And carried the Pittsburgh Courier and the Chicago Defender to the Black Americans in the South so they would know they were not alone."[75]

Robert S. Abbot, a Georgian who came north in the 1890s, started the *Chicago Defender* and is credited with being a major force in the migration movement. The *Chicago Defender* was barred in many southern communities because whites did not want to lose their black labor force. Abbot wrote to African Americans:

> Turn a deaf ear to everyone. . . . You see they are not lifting their laws to help you. Are they? Have they stopped their Jim Crow cars? Can you buy a Pullman sleeper where you wish? Will they give you a square deal in court yet? Once upon a time we permitted other people to think for us—today we are thinking and acting for ourselves with the result that our "friends" are getting alarmed at our progress. We'd like to oblige these unselfish souls and remain slaves in the South, but to their section of the country we have said, as the song goes, "I hear you call me," and have boarded the train singing, "Good-by, Dixie Land."[76]

Because of this concise, truthful, and compelling message, many African Americans living in the South vigorously pursued the opportunity to get away from racial cruelty and poverty, and headed north to seek a better life.

## THE CHURCHES OF CHICAGO IN THE EARLY TWENTIETH CENTURY

From its humble beginnings, the history of the African American church in Chicago was one of racial and social activism: hiding escaping slaves; protesting against political, economic, and educational discrimination or racial bias; and supporting the less fortunate.[77] The African American church in Chicago was a space where people's own reality, life circumstances, challenges, and cultural context were not only reflected but also respected, supported, and nourished. It filled a void, gave voice to people's reality, and provided much-needed spiritual strength. Even on the Sundays when race was not mentioned in the sermon or discussed in Sunday school, the message from the pulpit was to "do good" as a people and as individuals because the entire African American community must be engaged in "uplift" to bring about social and racial equality. To understand the soul of African Americans of all ilks and stripes is to know that there is very little separation between the black church and black community; both are concerned with the effects of racism and the racial divide.

The oldest and perhaps most stable African American institution in Chicago was and still is the church. For decades the African American church has been a place of influence, serving as an agent for positive change in both moral and civic respects. It was arguably the only institution that African Americans owned and controlled. This has been the case since the 1840s, when significant numbers of black people begin arriving in Chicago. Within two decades, fugitive slaves from the South and free blacks from the East formed the core of a small Negro settlement of approximately one thousand people.[78] This small community of people organized an African Methodist Episcopal (AME) church—the nation's first African American denomination—in part because blacks were denied the opportunity to worship as they pleased during slavery and in part because of their great love of religion.[79]

Quinn Chapel AME, founded in 1847, fourteen years after Chicago was incorporated, became the first African American church in Chicago. It still stands at 2401 S. Wabash. Between 1900 and 1910, Chicago's African American population grew rapidly. By the end of the century there were a dozen African American churches, and between 1900 and 1915 that number doubled. The majority of the churches were affiliated with the two largest African American denominations—African Methodist Episcopal and Baptist—and were controlled and supported exclusively by blacks from the beginning. New churches continued to open as the community grew. Most Baptist churches in the African American community were offshoots of Olivet, the oldest and largest African American Baptist church in the city, whereas the new AME churches were offshoots of Quinn Chapel.[80]

The church was the one institution in Chicago where African Americans as a group could go and feel relief from the nuanced and overt racism that elsewhere shaped their life experience. African Americans did not experience this freedom while spending their money in department stores in the Loop, riding public transportation, job hunting, or seeking health or city services. The African American church in Chicago was a meaningful place where African Americans could "make a joyful noise onto the Lord" in keeping with the black collective memory—a joyful noise necessary for survival in a hostile world. In addition, the African American church was a place in Chicago where African Americans could match their theological needs to a liturgical mode consistent with their lives, thereby demonstrating the human agency to create their own churches to worship as they please.[81] Worshiping as they pleased included preaching that sought to provide both oral and aural satisfaction, delivered with a sincerity that led to a complete surrender to the Spirit of the Lord.[82]

In 1943 Langston Hughes set pen to paper and captured the African American within his or her church. He offered reasons for the leaping and shouting—to "feel better"—and explained the mental anguish and dismay that racism heaped upon African American citizens, even as they were serving as soldiers, doing their part to bring freedom to others in foreign lands.

> Dancing and shouting have a lot in common. Both are a kind of relief, an outlet for pent-up emotions, a savior from the psychiatrist. Rhythm is healing. Music is healing. Dancing and shouting are healing. Father Devine knows this, so does Rev. Cobb. Exhorters and gospel singers know it instinctively. Shouters know it in their souls. Folks who work hard all week, all year, all their lives and get nowhere, go to church on Sunday and shout—and they feel better. Colored, and poor, and maybe born in Mississippi, "Jesus Knows Just How Much I Can Bear," so you holler out loud sometimes and leap high in the air in your soul like Pear Primus does when she dances "Jim Crow Train" which is pretty hard thing to bear, especially when you got relatives fighting in North Africa or New Guinea, and you at home riding in a Jim Crow car.
>     "Lord, I wish this train wasn't Jim Crow!" the song cried on the record. . . . Paul Robeson had just got through singing "Water Boy," "Joe Hill," and a Russian song which he dedicated to the Negro flyers who took off recently from the soil of Africa to bomb Italy, having ridden on the Jim Crow trains of Alabama themselves not so many weeks before. [83]

Quinn Chapel and several other Baptist and Methodist churches became major players in Chicago's abolitionist movement. The authors remember hearing stories as children about how Quinn Chapel was a place where runaway slaves could find food and shelter as they journeyed to freedom. These churches served as stations on the Underground Railroad to freedom. [84] In 1850, the U.S. Congress passed the Fugitive Slave Law, which stated that any white person with a sworn witness could claim a black person as his escaped slave and legally secure the individual through a petition before a federal commissioner. Quinn Chapel responded to this law by passing the following resolution: "We who have tasted freedom are ready to exclaim, in the language of Patrick Henry: 'Give us liberty, or give us death.'" Quinn Chapel then took immediate action to put in place a look-out system for slave hunters. [85]

In reaction to this legislation, Marsha Freedom Edmond stated that with the passage of the fugitive slave law, "many of the poor colored people were so frightened at what it portended that they fled to Canada." [86] When Lemuel C. Freer, an attorney, asked whether any Negroes were ever sold in Chicago, he was told, "Yes, a free Negro was one day arrested [in 1842] and put up to auction to be sold to the highest bidder. [But] it would have been hazardous for any man to buy him to keep in slavery or to sell him again. . . . Mr. Ogden bought the Negro for 25 cents and set him at liberty." [87]

## THE AFRICAN AMERICAN CHURCH TODAY

Today, Chicago's African American churches continue working together for racial and social equality as they have done throughout their existence. Francis argues, "Sure there was a difference in worship style, but when it came to the Black church's role in the Black community, it didn't matter whether you were Baptist, AME [African Methodist Episcopal], CME [Colored Methodist Episcopal], Pentecostal, Episcopalian or Catholic."[88] African American churches are a core institution for organization and dissemination of information, and a vehicle for action in African American communities.

The authors recall attending a Mother's Day service at Liberty Baptist Church on Chicago's South Side, where Dr. Martin L. King Jr. was speaking during the civil rights movement of the 1960s. The message from the pulpit was about how the congregants could and should engage in the civil rights struggle. King's message was a message that has been spoken and heard throughout the history of the black church. Many of the Trinity UCC parishioners that we interviewed recalled hearing similar messages in other churches. During the early days of the civil rights movement, when some African Americans questioned the extent to which they could be openly active without white retaliation, it was the African American church that gave both encouragement and direction to members' involvement.

As African Americans continued to arrive in Chicago, the number of church denominations increased and so did the size of their congregations. Olivet Baptist grew to a membership of ten thousand parishioners, becoming the United States' largest African American church. AME churches also continued to attract new members.[89] With the increase in black population came increased diversity within the African American church family. Pentecostal and Spiritualist storefront churches became part of the religious community.[90] According to a 2002 estimate, the African American church nationwide has evolved to more than four hundred denominations, with about forty-five thousand predominantly African American congregations.[91] Particularly in the 1990s, this growing membership included college-educated, middle-class African Americans.[92]

During the 1980s, African American churches increasingly recognized the need to expand their range of community programs. Churches begin to offer multiple Sunday morning services to accommodate the lifestyles of a new generation. Additionally, churches increased the outreach programs that already had a rich service history within the African American church tradition, such as providing holiday meals, organizing clothing drives, and developing programs for senior citizens and needy families.[93]

Today Chicago's African American churches are experiencing an adjustment period as membership in older churches—the ones that sustained the community for decades—dwindle in number. According to CBS reporter Jim Williams, churches are making use of technologies such as multiple cameras, live feeds of the services on the Internet, and smartphone applications to increase the number of young churchgoers: "Facebook and Twitter are as much a part of growing churches as tent revivals were years ago."[94] The younger parishioners Williams interviewed for his report said that church services are "stiff, boring and not fun." Another change in the black church is movement away from "Sunday best" clothing to a more casual look, including wearing jeans.[95]

Still another significant change in African American churches is the attention given to HIV/AIDS. As the rate of HIV infection and AIDS has risen among African Americans, compassion has replaced condemnation.[96] Dahleen Glanton, a *Chicago Tribune* reporter, noted that on a recent Sunday morning, "the Rev. Stephen Thurston stood on the pulpit before a packed New Covenant Missionary Baptist Church of Chicago while a health care worker swabbed his upper and lower gums. After his sermon, the health care worker announced the results: Thurston had tested negative for HIV."[97] According to Glanton, "increasing numbers of black churches are slowly becoming outspoken advocates for HIV testing, increased government funding, and education. For some, it has meant changing their views about religion and opening their doors to gays and lesbians, whom they once shunned."[98]

For some African American churches, decades of residential segregation kept their attendance relatively constant. However, the opportunity to move to neighborhoods with better schools and lower crime rates that arose as a result of the elimination of segregated housing policies caused many middle- and upper-income African Americans to move to the suburbs, and this affected the membership of churches in the urban area. In some ways, black migration from the city to the suburbs mirrors the black migration of earlier periods.[99] Some suburban African Americans have joined megachurches. Jaynes and Williams observe, "American religious institutions including Black churches are thus facing difficult times expanding the growth of their memberships. Increased social stratification within the black community, suburbanization of the middle class, and loss of worshippers as well as many talented ministers . . . make this trend especially difficult for Black churches."[100] Trussell explains that megachurches are having a significant negative impact on urban churches' membership rosters.[101] Blacks moving out to the suburbs have found new church homes and do not feel the need to make the drive back to their former church homes in urban areas. The megachurches also have sought to reach out and appeal to a diverse group of people, thereby racially integrating the congregation and encouraging people of different racial and ethnic groups to be comfortable with one another.

Philanthropy and volunteerism are enduring qualities of the African American church since its days as a hush harbor. In keeping with this histori-

cal tradition, African American churches in Chicago today are major philan-
thropic institutions. Besides serving as faith-based houses of worship, they
organize, encourage, and promote efforts to meet basic human needs. They
provide food for the hungry; access to shelter and housing; psychological,
financial, and educational counseling; and connections to other community
organizations. A study of African American churches states, "During times
of illness, the informal financial and spiritual support and caregiving assistance offered by African American churches is second only to the support
provided by the actual family."[102] This statement can certainly be made
about Chicago's African American congregations.

African American churches, whether housed in a storefront, an apartment,
or a jaw-dropping architectural structure, serve as the one place in the community where black people's dreams are kept alive and refueled from week
to week. Members of the black community with social and political ambi-
tions often seek out the resources of the African American church. Such was
the case with Barack Obama and Trinity United Church of Christ.

Many of the criticisms of and reactions to the events during the 2008
presidential campaign might be attributed to a lack of knowledge among the
general public of African American history and the history of the black
church. According to the Pew Charitable Trust's recent survey about
Americans' knowledge of religious communities, "basic information on the
religious beliefs and practices of many groups is lacking and there is little
solid data on the demographic characteristics of many of America's newer
faiths. The increasing diversity of the American religious landscape, the
remarkable dynamism of its faith communities and the pervasive presence of
religion in the American public square all serve to underscore the pressing
need for up-to-date, reliable information on these and other questions."[103]

If Jane and Joe Public had understood African American history and
culture, the claims that Trinity Church was racist and its members were being
duped or fooled might have fallen on deaf ears.[104] The widespread ignorance
of the culture and importance of the black church is accompanied by an
ignorance of the negative aspects of white American history, leaving many
Americans in the dark about their own past and that of their neighbors. As a
nation of diverse people, with an educational system that does not include
each other's histories and a media that has a history of racial bias and a lack
of inclusiveness, we resort to interpreting what we hear and see about
American history and culture through a narrow perspective. A narrow perspective runs counter to the diversity that we say we so dearly prize in the
United States. As historian Howard Zinn reminds us, "There were themes of
profound importance . . . missing in the orthodox histories that dominated
American culture. The consequence of those omissions has been not simply
to give a distorted view of the past, but more important, they mislead us all
about the present."[105]

## Chapter Four

# Trinity United Church of Christ

*And the preacher's voice is sweet to us, caressing and lashing, conveying to us
a heightening of consciousness that the Lords of the Land would rather keep
from us, filling us with a sense of hope that is treasonable to the rule of Queen
Cotton.*

—Richard Wright

The black church, even in the twenty-first century, remains the taproot of the
black community and the life source and resource for black people. To tell
the history of Trinity United Church of Christ, the church that received a
concentrated attack from the media and others during the 2008 U.S. presidential campaign, we weave together its history with congregants' stories and
experiences and material from books and documents. Trinitarians' collective
and individual memories provide a narrative about the church's past and
recent history, including who the congregants are, who the preacher was, and
what led them to Trinity. They spoke about their participation in the church
and the church's motto: "Unashamedly Black and Unapologetically Christian." From the Trintarians' narratives, it is clear that the raison d'être for the
black church today is as significant as it was during the days of the hush
harbors and the early days of Quinn Chapel and Olivet Baptist Church.

Both authors of this book attend United Church of Christ (UCC)
churches. Shelby attends Trinity Church on Chicago's South Side at 95th
Street, and Carl attends the First Congregational Church of Madison, Wisconsin, located just north of the Camp Randall football stadium. The United
Church of Christ was founded in 1957 through the union of two Protestant
denominations: the Evangelical and Reformed Church and the Congregational Christian Church. Each of the denominations came from the union of two
earlier denominations that can be traced back to 1620 and 1629. Congregational churches were established when the Pilgrims of Plymouth Plantation

(1620) and the Puritans of Massachusetts Bay Colony (1629) acknowledged their essential unity in the Cambridge Platform of 1648. Congregants from the union came to what is now the United States of America seeking religious independence from persecution by British political authorities. Their beliefs centered on local church autonomy, covenantal church life, personal piety, and the priesthood of all believers. Eleven signers of the Declaration of Independence were members of churches in the UCC tradition. Ten percent of present-day UCC congregations were formed prior to 1776.

Over the decades, UCC congregations have held firmly to these beliefs and advocated for social justice through words and actions. In 1630 the denomination put into place democratic decision-making. The Congregational Church (prior to becoming part of UCC) was the first denomination to ordain an African American pastor in 1785 and in 1853 was the first denomination to ordain a woman. Other notable UCC firsts came in 1972 with the ordaining of an openly gay man and in 2005 with the decision to support same-gender marriage.

Congregationalists, as UCC members are known, helped inspire the Boston Tea Party in 1773. In 1777 congregants from the Old Zion Reformed Church in Allentown, Pennsylvania, hid the Liberty Bell from British forces occupying the town. Hundreds of distinguished colleges and universities such as Harvard, Yale, Dartmouth, Howard, Fisk, Wellesley, Smith, and Oberlin are in debt to UCC for their beginning. Eighty percent of UCC members are located in the Northeast and Midwest. There are more than 700 UCC churches in Pennsylvania and approximately 188 UCC churches in Iowa, where Obama won the Iowa Caucus and became a legitimate candidate for the presidency.


## THE EARLY DAYS OF TRINITY UNITED CHURCH OF CHRIST


Shelby is a charter member of Trinity UCC. He was one of the founding parishioners present at Eddie and Rose Butcher's home, where the initial meetings to establish Trinity were held. After holding several start-up meetings in members' homes, on December 3, 1961, founding members moved to Rudyard Kipling Elementary School. After one meeting at Kipling, the congregation moved to John Shed Elementary School. According to Shelby and the documents on Trinity's early history, twelve working- and middle-class families, many of whom were descendents of the black migration, joined together to start a UCC congregation.

Reverend Kenneth Smith, the assistant pastor at Park Manor Church at 70th Martin Luther King Drive, was assigned by the Chicago Congregational Christian Association to help establish Trinity. Rev. Smith told the congregation at Park Manor Church about the formation of a new church and invited those who were planning to move further south to join him in setting up the church. Both authors heard the invitation but only Shelby responded. He was planning to purchase a home on the far southside (at the time). Carl's thoughts, however, were on graduate school outside of the city.

Shelby, a GI Bill recipient and graduate of Tennessee State University (TSU), and his wife Doris (also a graduate of TSU) were characteristic of the group of young people who were in search of a new residence on the South Side of Chicago. Shelby and Doris purchased land and built a home located three blocks from where Trinity would later be constructed and four blocks away from Halsted Street, because, as he recalled, "Property for building a home was available in the area."

Early Trinity parishioners worked hard canvassing for new members. One Trinitarian took us back to that time: "Deacon Sunny Chapman came by circulating a UCC petition for people interested in joining and building a church. I said I'm on board. I have two children . . . and I'd like to become a part of a new church." Another charter member told of the canvassing and initial meetings that lead to the establishment of Trinity: "When Rev. Smith came out here [to] canvass the community, [my wife] went to one of the first meetings. They held meetings in peoples' homes in order to find interested people. That's how we got here. It was Congregationalist, and it was in line with what we were doing as a new couple."

Two values that were constants among the founders and that became and have remained core values of the church were respect and love. Respect and love for each other were steadfast among the founders as they worked together to start a church family and to find a site to build a church. A founding member spoke of that time: "When Rev. Kenneth B. Smith was our pastor and founder, we were like one happy family. The congregation was so small. We started out with about 125 members. We treated each other with such great respect, and there was good Christian love within our group. We had a leader that was so caring and prayerful. So we banded together like one big family." Another founder explained how the respect and love they had for one another helped them to remain resilient throughout the struggle to find a permanent church home: "When Trinity was getting started we had our first business meeting at the Kipling School in 1961. We lost our contract there [because] someone underbid us and got the all-purpose room. We left Kipling School and went to Shedd School at 99th and Forest. We held our Sunday service there. We had only one day, Sunday, to take care of church business. Service was usually one hour. Whenever there was a need for a business meeting, we would meet from house to house."

The love that the charter members saw and felt was also experienced by others joining Trinity years later and has continued to serve as a primary reason for joining the church:

I fell in love with the church's mission: its desire to be a black church in a black community, doing good things for black people and making sure that we were aware of who we are as a people and building up our self-esteem. You know, just being a force in the black community, a force that engages people and makes sure that our people are as healthy mentally and spiritually as they can be.

I went to Trinity with my sister in 1981 and I cried like a baby. I felt all of the love in the congregation. I cannot remember the scripture, I remember crying and I remember Pastor Wright preaching about love and I remember the congregation showing a lot of love.

In 1966, Trinity congregants moved into their first church building, which remained the church home for the next twenty-eight years until they moved into their current location. The original building had a seating capacity of two hundred. Its location at 523 W. 95th Street was significant because at that time Halsted Street—only four blocks away—marked "the color line" where the Black Belt stopped. Because of the possibility of physical harm, encountering prejudicial attitudes, and threats of violence, African Americans usually did not journey past Halsted and real-estate agents resisted showing or selling property to blacks on the west side of Halsted. This redlining further exacerbated existing patterns of residential segregation and kept racial unrest in place. "The bulk of blacks were between State and Halsted. There was a push [west] and it became a bitter push to get pass Halsted to Ashland [the next major street]. I mean, war in the schools and everything. There was a Catholic priest, Father Lawler, who led the movement to keep the blacks east of Ashland. There's been a struggle to move west."

At the time of Trinity's founding, the civil rights movement of the 1960s was already well under way. Six years and two days had passed since December 1, 1955, when Rosa Parks refused to give up her seat to a white man on the Montgomery, Alabama, bus. Young African American veterans were taking advantage of the GI Bill to complete college and vocational school and were returning or migrating to Chicago. They, along with middle-aged African Americans who had accumulated the down payment for a home and secured a job that allowed them to earn enough money to make monthly mortgage payments, began to search for new living spaces, homes with a bit of "elbow room," to borrow Davy Crockett's words. The black community in Chicago, especially the Bronzeville area, was overcrowded and much of it was in need of revitalization. Additionally, black Chicagoans inspired by the civil rights movement and black participation in military service during World War II demanded to live where they wished: "We were living on 75th Street and we bought a home on 98th Street. We wanted to move. We wanted a change."

When the UCC Association assigned Rev. Smith to establish a church, the hope and vision was to establish a church of middle-class blacks that would merge with a white UCC congregation and have white and black co-pastors. Although this was a progressive idea, the vision was consistent with a line from Dr. King's "I Have a Dream" speech: "I have a dream that one day on the red hills of Georgia the sons of former slaves and the sons of former slave owners will be able to sit down together at a table of brotherhood."

Rev. Smith and the parishioners moved forward with the association's plan. They supported the idea of a black-white congregation with black and white co-pastors. In addition, Trinity congregants believed that the idea was consistent with the fundamental doctrine of the United Church of Christ— "That they may all be one"[1]—and the congregation's belief in equity and equality. But these plans were stymied for several reasons: First, the association's plan called for a middle-class African American congregation. At the time, Trinity's congregation was becoming increasingly working class and the church was attracting parishioners who came from the working poor. Second, the association believed that African Americans in the congregation would gladly assimilate with white UCC members without hesitation, that they would welcome and take pride in having fellowship with white congregants, since this was the time of a heightened push for racial integration in Chicago. But the association did not take into account the white flight that occurred as black families moved into the area. Third, some of the black parishioners were fearful that there would be retaliations for crossing the color line. Harassment and violence in both the North and South in pursuit of civil rights were well known and understood by the Trinity membership. In reflecting on the failure of the association's plan, the overall perspective among congregants was that an opportunity to foster better race relations between blacks and whites was lost. A Trinitarian explains, "We [blacks and whites] did not work at working it out. There was no real discussion about living together in the community. Sometimes, some of us wonder what things would be like now, if we had worked at it."

That said, throughout the black community, many people were questioning the effectiveness of assimilation efforts. This was especially so regarding the education of black students. African American parents of schoolchildren argued, "Why does a black child need to sit next to a white child in order to receive a quality education?" "Why can't a black child sit next to another black child and receive a quality education and be taught from a curriculum that addresses African Americans' history, culture, and contributions to America?"

During this time, the statement "Black Is Beautiful" was echoed throughout the African American community and the Black Power movement gained momentum as an alternative to the civil rights movement. In Julia Speller's

*Walkin' the Talk: Keeping the Faith in Africentric Congregations*, an illuminating study of Trinity Church, she wrote, "The failure of the Civil Rights Movement to usher in an era of genuine integration and harmony between the races turned into a search for an alternative experience of purpose and belonging for many African Americans."[2] Speller goes on to argue that corresponding with the search for an alternative experience, Trinity parishioners began to debate with one another about the direction of the church. Some argued that the church and its members should adopt the ideology and strategies of the Black Power movement. Other parishioners argued for staying the course of the civil rights movement and trusting that Americans would soon come to honor one's achievements regardless of race. Speller states that Trinity members "held tenaciously to their Congregational tradition, finding Unity in their connection to American Protestantism and Purpose in the lifestyle of black 'middle-classness.'"[3]

In 1971 Trinity membership dropped from 250 down to 100, causing major concern and anxiety within the congregation. Church leaders and the membership could not explain the cause of the decline. Pastor Rev. Willie J. Jamerson resigned and Trinity was faced with the decision to either close its doors or move in a different direction. Closing the doors of Trinity Church was quickly dismissed in favor of bringing on Rev. Reuben A. Sheares as an interim pastor.

Rev. Sheares's tenure was short (1971–1972) but significant. He directed the church to reexamine its sense of purpose and reasons for the decrease in membership. He led discussions about important issues facing Trinity, such as the debate over an integrationist or Afrocentric philosophy. Soon the congregation came to believe that they had a handle on the problem of their decline. Vallmer E. Jordan, interviewed by Speller, described the problem of the church as reasoned by the church leadership: "For years we had prided ourselves on being a middle-class congregation within a mainline denomination, but suddenly the *values* within the black community shifted. Aspirations for integration and assimilation were being replaced by those of black pride and separation."[4]

According to Shelby, Trinity was face with a major dilemma about how to stay within the principles and guidelines of the United Church of Christ and still make the church and its activities and enterprises culturally responsive to the African American community. After serious deliberation, the church leadership decided to embrace an Afrocentric focus within the context of the principles of the United Church of Christ. The focus was on remaining with the United Church of Christ's statement "Who We Are, and What We Believe": "Through the years, members of other groups such as Native Americans, African Americans, Asian Americans, Volga Germans, Americans, Hungarians, and Hispanic Americans have joined with the four earlier groups. Thus the United Church of Christ celebrates and continues a variety of traditions in its common life."

Trinity celebrated the paradigm shift by informing the wider Chicago community of the transition and encouraged any and all citizens to join the church. Rev. Sheares adopted the motto "Unashamedly Black and Unapologetically Christian." Most church members were supportive of the motto and did not believe it meant Trinity was anti-white. Reverend Sheares stated that the purpose for the motto was "to acknowledge [blacks'] rich African American heritage and CHRIST as center of their life." Professor Martin E. Marty, a scholar of religious history, also rebuked the anti-white thesis: "For Trinity, being 'unashamedly black' does not mean being 'anti-white.' . . . Think of the concept of 'unashamedly': tucked into it is the word 'shame.'" Underlying this idea, according to Marty, is a diagnosis "of 'shame,' 'being shamed,' and 'being ashamed' as debilitating legacies of slavery and segregation in society and church." Marty also explained that the Afrocentrism contained in the statement "should not be any more offensive than synagogues should be 'Judeocentric' or that Chicago's Irish parishes be 'Celticcentric.'"[5] In addition, Speller argued that the motto "has remained as a reminder of not only who [Trinitarians] are but Whose they are, continuing to emphasize both meaning and belonging." One Trinitarian offered her understanding of the motto: "It means that you are to worship God and serve him in the way that he intends you to be. You don't have to be European, you don't have to be Caucasian, you can shout, clap, and praise God the way you want to." This explanation permeated much of what we heard from the Trinitarians about their understanding of the motto and the meaning they attributed to it. Another congregant elaborated, "It teaches us not to be ashamed of who we are. Not to apologize [for] who we are. . . . whatever happened to us in the past is nothing to be ashamed of or nothing to apologize for." The motto's origin was discussed by another congregant: "It was the second pastor of the church who came up with it. He said his reason for it was because of the civil rights movement, for all of the pain that came out of that movement. That was a profound statement."

Since the 1970s, Trinity's motto of "Unashamedly Black and Unapologetically Christian" and the black liberation theology thesis have served as the foundation for the Afrocentric curriculum, teaching, and experiences that undergird much of what takes place in the church: sermons, music, ministries, and personal interactions:

> What we were learning at the church about our history and culture, basic information, they were not teaching us in the schools. I wanted my children to know who they are and whose they are.

My mom says, "Hey, you should listen to this [Rev. Wright's sermons on tape]. They are really good." He gives a black historical perspective which she believes the younger generation is missing, I agree.

This was an interesting and exciting time in history, the early 70s. There was this idea of being black and proud, knowing your heritage. Singing songs from out of our cultural tradition was far more empowering than singing old fuddy duddy songs from the Pilgrim hymn book.

The motto and black liberation theology continue to be instrumental in attracting members of the African American community to Trinity:

Trinity Church is where you come when you wish to attend a church where people say what's on their mind. If it's wrong, we apologize, but if we are right we have nothing to apologize for. We [believe] in being unashamedly black and unapologetically Christian.

## TRINITY'S BLACK VALUE SYSTEM

In 1981 the Manford Byrd Recognition Committee of Trinity Church, chaired by Val Jordan, developed and put forward what they called the Black Value System.[6] Dr. Byrd was recognized because, despite his hard work and credentials, systemic racism in Chicago denied his appointment as Chicago public school superintendent for several years. The Black Value System included twelve precepts and covenantal statements. In our interview with Byrd, he noted that the twelve precepts are based upon the way he lives his life and has provided service to the entire Chicago community. In the introduction of the Black Value System, Jordan stated:

Dr. Manford Byrd, our brother in Christ, withstood the ravage of being denied his earned ascension to the number one position in the Chicago School System. His dedication to the pursuit of excellence, despite systematic denials, has inspired the congregation of Trinity United Church of Christ. We have prayerfully called upon the wisdom of all past generations of suffering Blacks for guidance in fashioning an instrument of Black self-determination, the Black Value System.

In Jordan's comment about the shaming of Dr. Byrd, there is a reminder of Marty's statement "of 'shame,' 'being shamed,' and 'being ashamed' as debilitating legacies of slavery." Trinity instituted an annual Black Value System Educational Scholarship in Dr. Byrd's name in 1981 as a way to recognize the man or woman who best exemplifies the Black Value System. The Recognition Committee honored Dr. Manford Byrd with the first award.

The Black Value System consists of a set of black ethics that must be taught and exemplified in homes, churches, nurseries, and schools, wherever blacks are gathered. They consist of the following concepts:

1. *Commitment to God*: "The God of our weary years" will give us the strength to give up prayerful passivism and become Black Christian Activists, soldiers for Black freedom and the dignity of all humankind. Matthew 22:37—"Thou shalt love the Lord thy God with all thy heart, and with all thy soul, and with all thy mind."

2. *Commitment to the Black Community*: The highest level of achievement for any Black person must be a contribution of strength and continuity of the Black Community. John 4:20—"If a man say, I love God, and hateth his brother [or his sister], he is a liar; for he that loveth not his brother or sister whom he hath seen, how can he love God whom he hath not seen."

3. *Commitment to the Black Family*: The Black family circle must generate strength, stability and love, despite the uncertainty of externals, because these characteristics are required if the developing person is to withstand warping by our racist competitive society. Those Blacks who are blessed with membership in a strong family unit must reach out and expand that blessing to the less fortunate. Deuteronomy 6:6–8—"And these words, which I command thee this day, shall be in thine heart: And thou shalt teach them diligently unto thy children, and shalt talk of them when thou sittest in thine house, and when thou walkest by the way, and when thou liest down, and when thou risest up. And thou shalt bind them for a sign upon thine hand, and they shall be as frontlets between thine eyes."

4. *Dedication to the Pursuit of Education*: We must forswear anti-intellectualism. Continued survival demands that each Black person be developed to the utmost of his/her mental potential despite the inadequacies of the formal education process. "Real education" fosters understanding of ourselves as well as every aspect of our environment. Also, it develops within us the ability to fashion concepts and tools for better utilization of our resources, and more effective solutions to our problems. Since the majority of Blacks have been denied such learning, Black Education must include elements that produce high school graduates with marketable skills, a trade or qualifications for apprenticeships, or proper preparation for college. Basic education for all Blacks should include Mathematics, Science, Logic, General Semantics, Participative Politics, Economics and Finance, and the Care and Nurture of Black Minds. Matthew 22:37—"Thou shalt love the Lord thy God with all thy heart, and with all thy soul and with all thy mind."

5. *Dedication to the Pursuit of Excellence*: To the extent that we individually reach for, even strain for excellence, we increase, geometrically, the value and resourcefulness of the Black Community. We must recognize the relativity of one's best; this year's best can be bettered next year. Such is the language of growth and development. We must seek to excel in every endeavor. Ecclesiastes 9:10—"Whatsoever thy hand findeth to do, do [it] with thy might; for [there is] no work, nor device, nor knowledge, nor wisdom, in the grave, whither thou goest."

6. *Adherence to the Black Work Ethic*: "It is becoming harder to find qualified people to work in Chicago." Whether this is true or not, it represents one of the many reasons given by businesses and industries for deserting the Chicago area. We must realize that a location with good facilities, adequate transportation, and a reputation for producing skilled workers will attract industry. We are in competition with other cities, states, and nations for jobs. High productivity must be a goal of the Black workforce. II Thessalonians 3:7–12—"For yourselves know how ye ought to follow us: for we behaved ourselves not disorderly among you; neither did we eat any man's bread for nought; but wrought with labor and travail night and day, that we might not be chargeable to any of you: Not because we have not power, but to make ourselves an example unto you to follow us. For even when we were with you, this we commanded you, that if any would not work, neither should he eat. For we hear that there are some which walk among you disorderly, working not at all, but are busybodies. Now them that are such we command and exhort by our Lord Jesus Christ, that with quietness they work, and eat their own bread."

7. *Commitment to Self-Discipline and Self-Respect*: To accomplish anything worthwhile requires self-discipline. We must be a community of self-disciplined persons if we are to actualize and utilize our own human resources, instead of perpetually submitting to exploitation by others. Self-discipline, coupled with a respect for self, will enable each of us to be an instrument of Black Progress and a model for Black Youth. I Peter 1:4–7—"To an inheritance incorruptible, and undefiled, and that fadeth not away, reserved in heaven for you, Who are kept by the power of God through faith unto salvation ready to be revealed in the last time. Wherein ye greatly rejoice, though now for a season, if need be, ye are in heaviness through manifold temptations: That the trial of your faith, being much more precious than of gold that perishes, though it be tried with fire, might be found unto praise and honor and glory at the appearing of Jesus Christ."

8. *Disavowal of the Pursuit of "Middleclassness"*: Classic methodology on control of captives teaches that captors must be able to identify the "talented tenth" of those subjugated, especially those who show prom-

ise of providing the kind of leadership that might threaten the captor's control. Proverbs 3:13–14—"Happy are those who find wisdom and those who gain understanding, for her income is better than silver and her revenue better than gold." Those so identified are separated from the rest of the people by killing them off directly and/or fostering a social system that encourages them to kill off one another; placing them in concentration camps and/or structuring an economic environment that induces captive youth to fill the jails and prisons; and seducing them into a socioeconomic class system which, while training them to earn more dollars, hypnotizes them into believing they are better than others and teaches them to think in terms of "we" and "they" instead of "us." So, while it is permissible to chase "middle-classness" with all our might, we must avoid the third separation method—the psychological entrapment of Black "middleclassness." If we avoid this snare, we will also diminish our "voluntary" contributions to methods A and B. And more importantly, Black people no longer will be deprived of their birthright: the leadership, resourcefulness, and example of their own talented persons.

9. *Pledge to Make the Fruits of All Developing and Acquired Skills Available to the Black Community.*
10. *Pledge to Allocate Regularly a Portion of Personal Resources for Strengthening and Supporting Black Institutions.*
11. *Pledge Allegiance to All Black Leadership Who Espouse and Embrace the Black Value System.*
12. *Personal Commitment to Embracement of the Black Value System*: To measure the worth and validity of all activity in terms of positive contributions to the general welfare of the Black Community and the Advancement of Black People toward freedom.

During the 2008 presidential campaign, many asked, "What is black liberation theology? How did it come about and where does it come from?" The questions seemed to hang in the air, with limited or superficial attempts to objectively answer.

Black liberation theology's origins can be traced to Professor James Cone's scholarship in the 1950s and gained prominence with a July 31, 1966, full-page advertisement in the *New York Times* placed by fifty-one African Americans professors who demanded a more aggressive approach to eliminating racism. The ad voiced demands consistent with the Black Power movement and located its source of inspiration in the Bible.

Barbara Hagerty's article on black liberation theology helps provide an in-depth explanation for the theology through her interviews with scholars.[7] In her article, Anthony Pinn, who teaches philosophy and religion at Rice University in Houston, states, "God is so intimately connected to the community that suffers, that God becomes a part of that community and God's presence in the world is best depicted through God's involvement in the struggle for justice."[8] Dwight Hopkins, a professor at the University of Chicago Divinity School, also states, "Black liberation theology often portrays Jesus as a brown-skinned revolutionary." Hopkins argues "that in the book of Matthew, Jesus says the path to heaven is to feed the hungry, clothe the naked, visit the sick and the prisoners. And the central text for black liberation theology can be found in Chapter 4 of Luke's gospel, where Jesus outlined the purpose of his ministry."[9] Hopkins continues by addressing "freedom and liberation," two ideas central in the life of African Americans: "Jesus says my mission is to eradicate poverty and to bring about freedom and liberation for the oppressed."[10] Another point that Hagerty makes is that black liberation preaching is often loud and passionate; the preacher is seen as angry and the message is inflammatory.[11] Linda Thomas, who teaches at the Lutheran School of Theology in Chicago, suggests that this interpretation can be attributed to the fact that many white people are not familiar with African American churches.[12]

## THE WRIGHT PASTORSHIP

In 1971, Trinity turned its attention toward hiring a new pastor. Preachers interested in the position received the church's mission statement to review and were asked to address it or give their interpretation of it during the interview process. Five applicants interviewed for the position, including Rev. Jeremiah Wright Jr., whose interview took place on December 31, 1971. Wright, Shelby recalled, was very positive about the mission statement and stated that he was the person for the job. Wright believed he could move the church forward in keeping with the black freedom and liberation thesis. One Trinitarian recalls:

> Reverend Wright came to Trinity on a Sunday afternoon and spoke. He seemed to have something about him that a lot of us liked; his style of preaching. Not everyone in the congregation cared for Reverend Wright, but enough did to vote him in. Let's say if there were 100 members present that Sunday afternoon 75 members stood for him; maybe 25 did not stand. There were members that did not like Pastor Wright's style, but he delivered a message that was warm and so spiritual that a lot of us related to it.
>
> The church has grown under Pastor Wright from 87 initial members to at least 8,000. It's not that [it is] a large congregation that makes you know that you are great; it was his teaching and preaching. Reverend Wright's preaching holds me. He is a great teacher and a great preacher.

Jeremiah Wright Jr. was born and raised in a racially mixed section of Philadelphia called Germantown. His parents are Jeremiah Wright Sr. (1909–2001), a Baptist minister who served as pastor of Grace Baptist Church in Germantown, Philadelphia, from 1938 to 1980, and Mary Elizabeth Henderson Wright, a school teacher who was the first black person to teach an academic subject at Roosevelt Junior High. Wright's mother was also the first black person to teach at Germantown High and Girls High, where she became the school's first black vice principal.[13]

Wright graduated from Central High School of Philadelphia in 1959. The school was considered one of the best schools in the area. The school population was approximately 90 percent white. His high school yearbook describes Jeremiah as a respected member of the class. A statement in the yearbook reads, "Always ready with a kind word, Jerry is one of the most congenial members of the class of 1959. His record at Central was a model for lower [younger] class members to emulate." After graduation, Wright attended Virginia Union University in Richmond from 1959 to 1961. He left school to enlist in the United States Marines, where he served for two years. Next, Wright joined the United States Navy and entered the Corpsman School at the Great Lakes Naval Training Center. Here he received training as a cardiopulmonary technician at the National Naval Medical Center in Bethesda, Maryland.[14]

A high point during Wright's service to his country occurred when he was assigned to be a part of the medical team charged with President Lyndon B. Johnson's care after his 1966 surgery. The surgery was to correct a protrusion in the area where his gall bladder had been removed the previous year and also to remove a throat polyp. Before leaving the navy in 1967, the White House physician, Vice Admiral Burkley, personally wrote Wright a letter of thanks on behalf of the president. Following his service in the navy, Wright attended Howard University in Washington, DC. He earned a bachelor's degree in 1968 and a master's degree in English in 1969. In 1969, Wright earned a second master's degree, this time from the University of Chicago Divinity School. In 1990, Wright received a Doctor of Ministry degree from the United Theological Seminary in Dayton, Ohio, where he studied under Samuel DeWitt Proctor, mentor to Martin Luther King Jr.[15]

The Trinitarians were impressed with Wright's educational accomplishments, his background, and his ideas for moving the church forward. He was offered and accepted the position of senior pastor at Trinity UCC. Wright took on the stewardship of Trinity at the time when African Americans were robustly promoting cultural and historical awareness.[16] References to early proponents of black consciousness and present-day black activists were a part of ongoing discussions in the African American community. Churches, social clubs, political groups, and other organizations throughout the black community increasingly engaged in discussions of black pride and affirming black consciousness.

Wright was not only cognizant of the Black Power movement but also aware of the opportunities and problems that came with it. Parishioners at Trinity were wrestling with "whether they wanted to be a white Congregationalist church in black face or a black church in the black community."[17] Speller contended that Trinity was dealing with its own "double consciousness"[18] brought on by the Eurocentric religious traditions of Congregationalism. Also, some parishioners were continually questioning their earlier support of the civil rights movement. Some members were concerned about the fairness of the American system of justice and argued that more attention should be given to black empowerment.[19] Speller claimed that it was at this point that Trinitarians decided to begin the process of shedding the shame associated with blackness and lay claim to a new purpose, a purpose that called them to a Christianity of liberation and empowerment.[20]

From the time he stepped into the role as senior pastor, Wright reached out to attract the youth of the community. His personality was described as charismatic, warm, and welcoming; his style of dress included dashikis; and his ability to know and the ability to call all his parishioners by their names, even as the church membership grew into the thousands, was unique. In addition, his ability to speak several African languages and his passion for getting people involved in serving in Trinity's ministries came through in our interviews with parishioners. One member exemplifies the comments about Rev. Wright's connection and devotion to the congregation as she spoke about how he encouraged her and her husband to get involved with the youth ministry: "In 1972, when Pastor Wright came he was trying to find young people to help attract the youth. My husband and I were probably one of the few young couples. He said, 'I need someone to help me with the youth.' So he wrote my husband a letter and my husband said, 'Well, I don't know, I don't think we're going to do it.' But finally, he decided to go ahead and assist Pastor Wright. So we become co-sponsors of the Youth Fellowship."

Later during the interview process we caught up with the husband of the above interviewee, who added his words to the story: "After Reverend Wright came [to Trinity] he kept asking my wife and I to work with the youth of the church. I wasn't a member of the church, but he continued asking anyway. I said I don't want to work with young teenagers. I had just gotten out of my teens. I was 20 years old. He just kept asking me to come; so finally I did. I started working with them and I joined the church. I worked with teenagers for about five years; then I went from [working] with the Youth Fellowship to becoming a Scout Leader. Next, I became a Scout Master. I was the Scout Master of Troop 705. The [Scouts] were all members of the church. I was also in the Trinity Choral Ensemble, which was [instrumental] in the expansion of the church. I then went from the Trinity Choral Ensemble to Sanctuary Choir and to the men's choir."

A hallmark of the African American church—music—was critical to Trinity's development. Du Bois argued in 1903 that preaching, music, and the Holy Spirit are the three core ingredients to every black church.[21] One of the first changes under Wright's leadership regarded the music, particularly the youth choir. Shelby's daughter Sharon, who was sixteen when Wright became pastor, recalled how Trinity's worship style and musical selection shifted with his arrival away from traditional UCC hymns toward gospel music and visual props:

> One of the things that came about when Reverend Wright became senior pastor was the development of the Trinity Choral Ensemble. At first we were the Youth Fellowship Choir, but then Reverend Wright started introducing gospel music to the church. This was unheard of because our church services mainly consisted of hymns. However Reverend Wright brought a new sound to our church; he called it "new gospel." And with that the Youth Fellowship Choir was formed and started to singing gospel music and contemporary music that contained themes that dealt with the world's concerns: "Keep Your Head to the Sky," "The World is a Ghetto." We did 200 years of music and received help in preparing the song from Thomas Dorothy and Mama Ermaquin; the Spirit Campbell sisters also helped us.

Speller explains that this moment marked a psychological and spiritual shift as the youth choir was "usher[ing] in a new day at Trinity Church, and through their singing and musical selections they ignited a flame that burned off the dross of black shame to reveal the refined gem of self-love."[22] In addition, with call-and-response becoming a prominent part of the eleven o'clock service and the tradition of singing songs from the Pilgrim Hymnal falling out of favor, some parishioners begin to feel that this "new" Trinity was no longer their church.

Speller states that some parishioners left the church because of what Wright described as "fear of change—change in the style of worship but, more importantly, change in the kind of members that would desire to join our church."[23] In a Sankofa moment Rev. Wright stated that in keeping with the motto "Unashamedly Black and Unapologetically Christian," the congregation was developing a new consciousness; Trinitarians were changing from "Negroes to being Black!" Wright contributed a chapter to the compilation volume *Living Stones in the Household of God*, published in 2004, in which he described his feelings about the change in membership that began to take place following his arrival at Trinity: "Having a witness among the poor and having a ministry to the poor is one thing, but making the poor folks members of your congregation is something else altogether. . . . Failure to have the black poor at the table with you as equals means you are doing missionary work," while having "poor black folks" who "sit down at the table as equals" means you are "serious about talking or doing . . . black theology."[24]

Although Speller spoke about those who left Trinity in her book, in our interview, she also told us about the effect of Rev. Wright and Trinity on the African American community: "Trinity church had a great effect, especially on the young kids. We started with the youth fellowship and we got the choir started, from word of mouth a lot of young people start coming . . . they wanted to find out what was happening. Many of their friends, parents, girlfriends were coming to the church. . . . They came to see and all of a sudden they were joining the church, the choir."[25]

Sharon spoke passionately about how the young people at Trinity, with Rev. Wright's support and encouragement, argued for a greater role in the church. They also learned how to look out for someone other than oneself. Sharon recalled:

> Reverend Wright gave us [the youth] a lot of responsibilities in the church that a lot of older people thought we shouldn't receive, including the opportunity to represent the church at local and state religious meetings. I remember when I was chosen to be on the Ecumenical Society and later The Renewal Council. We were responsible for representing not just our church but the United Church of Christ for the Chicago South Side. This taught me a lot about dealing with people, about understanding different cultures and different people. Also I had the opportunity to see ideas or projects that we put in motion come to fruition. For example, the Community Renewal Council as well as United Church of Christ deemed it important to set up certain venues for [Latinos arriving in Chicago in the mid-1970s]. We provided immigration help and we assisted people who were junkies or addicts; we helped prostitutes to get off the street; provided help to homeless people without demanding that they come to the church. Reverend Wright always says, "Always in the heart of the community, ever seeking the community's heart." I can think of so many issues that the United Church of Christ and Rev. Wright have stood for that many people my age have no idea about: the Wilmington Ten, Bishop Tutu, Free Mandela—these were active parts of our service, not just a news story.

Rapidly, Rev. Wright was winning the hearts and minds of his congregants. Soon the word about the dynamic, well-dressed, young, handsome minister spread throughout Chicago and especially within the black community. Trinitarians reminisce:

> When Reverend Wright came to Trinity nobody knew what Trinity was or even where Trinity was. At first, if you told people you were from Trinity Church, they'd ask "Where is that?" You'd tell them the address, and they would say, "Oh, that little church sitting on the corner." After a few years when you would tell somebody you are from Trinity and the first thing they would say was, "Oh, that's where Reverend Wright is, isn't it?"

Before Reverend Wright came to the church, on Sunday mornings you could come into the sanctuary and choose any seat. . . . After Reverend got here and word got around about him—young, light skinned; they called him a radical minister—everybody start coming to see what he was all about. If you didn't get there early, you were going to sit in the aisle, or stand up in the back. Word of mouth just started spreading.

The general consensus among Trinitarians was that Rev. Wright not only preached well but his intellectual assets were also "off the charts, and his personality and charisma were exceptional." Another parishioners notes, "He's a brilliant man, even though they [whites] did not want to hear what he was saying. He was always speaking the truth. He didn't say anything that was a lie."

The new pastor wrote personal letters of condolence, empathy, care, and well-being to his flock when he could not reach them by phone. Wright's heart and office door remained open to the members and others in the broader Chicago community who were struggling, with no strings attached. As the member of another church noted, "I belong to a smaller church, but my minister does not write the letters that Reverend Wright writes. My minister did not call me when I had a death in the family. He [Wright] called when my father passed. He writes letters and he knows his members. There are tons of people in the church but he can pick you out and say, 'I saw you and you were wearing . . . this color dress.' I mean to me that's absolutely amazing."

Wright's pastoral connection to members is evident from one who decided to leave Trinity: "I left for one reason . . . I was kind of hiding. I wasn't really working in the church; I'd sing in the women's chorus. I love to sing so that wasn't a big deal. I really felt like I wasn't being involved and at that time I was visiting a smaller church. I got involved there. I wrote Reverend Wright a letter because I wanted him to know that I wasn't leaving because of anything he did or because of anything that was going on inside the church. I didn't have any problem with Trinity at all. I just needed to work more. I needed to be more active."

As Trinity's membership grew into the hundreds and then thousands and streams of young people came to worship, the single Sunday service grew into three services: 7:30 am, 11:00 am, and 6:00 pm. A congregant states, "Trinity moved away from a one-hour service when Reverend Wright informed the congregation that there would no longer be a scheduled time for the conclusion of the service. Services would no longer last from 11 to 12 noon, so people could return home to watch the Chicago Bears." Instead of the Chicago Bears, Cubs, or White Sox on Sunday, Trinitarians could look forward to a lecture on black history and culture and a seminar on national and international affairs. Congregants enjoyed Wright's preaching-lecture on black history and culture, and it became another reason people joined Trinity.

Perhaps the most significant change that Wright brought to Trinity was a change in philosophy, a perspective on the regard that black people should have for one another and for other people. Wright discussed the very early days of Trinity in the 1970s and argued that the church had to change its identity and the way it perceived its purpose. Wright asserted that Trinitarians had to stop looking at the neighbors around the church as "those people" and contending that the church had a mission to "those people." Instead, he argued that the church's goal should be to make those people "our people." He stated, "The members of Trinity Church of Christ began to realize that they had no 'mission to' the people in the [housing] projects and the people who did not make as much money as they did. What the congregation of Trinity needed was a ministry with all of God's people across cultural, educational and socioeconomic lines."[26]

Trinity's change in philosophy led Trinitarians to "move away from the concept of church as a place to enhance and validate their social position to one [where they] accept the church as a place for spiritual formation."[27] This was a change from a purpose and pursuit of a celebration of "middleclassness" to a purpose and pursuit where devotion to God and the poor took on a much greater prominence.[28] Thus Trinity, under Wright's leadership, embarked on a journey "from assimilation and fear to liberation and courage" with a spirit of freedom and a disposition to be black as a matter of cultural identity, and to be Christian as a matter of purpose and belonging to God.[29]

The core values of love and respect informed the seventy-two ministries that members could join in order to connect with one another and do outreach to the African American community and the wider Chicago community. The ministries were organized to help the poor, homeless, and destitute. The ministries put into practice the idea that "I am my brother's [and sister's] keeper" and that everyday African American men, women, youth, and children must be held in the highest esteem. These ministries served as the social network of the church, the technology that connected the parishioners and helped them fashion a collective identity. They prompted people to get to know one another, to have face time and learn and teach the significance of serving, a long historical tradition in the black community. Each member chose one or more ministries that best fit their lifestyle, identity, and personality as well as their desire to serve, give back, and learn about the plight of others. As you walk through the doors of Trinity Church on a weekday, but especially on a Sunday, you will still see members of the ministries in action, very visible but quiet and efficiently making certain that each and every person who enters, for as long as he or she remains, is made to feel welcome.

In African American communities, information, both good and bad, spreads quickly and pretty much intact. The word about Rev. Wright, his love of all people, dynamic sermons, the shift to gospel music, its seventy-two ministries, and democratic participation by the church's membership, including the youth, in the church's business affairs spread rapidly throughout Chicago's black community. The old, the young, the poor, the working class, the middle class, and black professionals all came and joined Trinity. In some ways Trinity became a site in the black community much like African American neighborhoods before civil rights, when all brothers and sisters—teachers, doctors, salespersons, professionals, those out of work—lived together and richly benefited from the togetherness. Most of the newcomers to Trinity stayed and made it their church home.

Du Bois noted in 1903 that, along with music, preaching was a core factor of the African American church. Wright's preaching, his informative message, and bombastic style were powerful attractions pulling the black community to Trinity. One Trinitarian spoke passionately about how Rev. Wright's message helped him to fill the religious void in his life:

> One Sunday I had attended my traditional Lutheran church, the one I grew up in, the one where I was an altar boy, an usher, and where I was confirmed. [But] I just didn't get the essence of what church was about on that Sunday. I wasn't fulfilled. I was left with a void. So I decided to make the trip over to Trinity. When I got there I heard this phenomenal gentleman, Dr, Jeremiah Wright. I was moved beyond belief. Phenomenal! He touched me. He touched the fiber of my being. Immediately the traditional Lutheran Church had no real substance for me anymore. I began to go back and back and back, but I was very reluctant to join. I would tell my mother and other people about this gentleman and what his sermons were based upon, how he stimulated me. They began to follow me, to attend church and they joined, vigorously and happily.

Another congregant spoke about how much she appreciated Reverend Wright's sermons:

> That weekend my godsister invited me to come to Trinity. I can remember it, as if it was yesterday. 1993, a sermon called "Grasshopper Mentality." That sermon changed my life because it was about the small mindedness of some people and how we have to put God first, family second, and everything else after. It was, like okay, I need to line up the priorities in my life.

Other congregants said that Reverend Wright made the scriptures far more accessible:

> The introduction to his version of the scriptures—and when I say his version, I'm not saying he distorted the scriptures in any manner—but he presented them in the way you can understand. A lot better than the King James' version. At that time in my life I was truly in need of renewing my understanding of the Bible.

Rev's sermons were something you could use in everyday life. All of his sermons tend to deal with how we can do better today; you know, not down the road, but today; so you could continue going down the road. His sermons were educational.

Several Trinitarians spoke about how Wright's sermons were educational about local, national, and international affairs:

He would educate you on everything . . . on the election for the president. He would tell you the history about people and things that you didn't read yourself. Reverend Wright read and would bring it to the congregation. He informed you about what was happening in the country. . . . If you checked his facts, [you would find him correct]. He had facts about Walmart, about the salary, about the union. He is really well read, well educated. He shared it with his congregation. You didn't leave Reverend Wright's church not knowing what was going on in the world.

Congregants asserted that Rev. Wright and Trinity's philosophy about education was not one of degree counting to decorate a wall with diplomas and certificates or of accumulating wealth and becoming middle class or more; it was about how to use one's education as a service or tool to help others, those who are forced to take shelter under a bridge or live on the street in a cardboard box: "Trinity stresses so much about education in order to [help] yourself; and as equally as important to help others. We have afterschool programs to help the students and we provide scholarship funds. Trinity wants young black children to go to school. . . . My parents were educators, and the whole family stressed school and church; anything else they would allow the kids to debate, but you had to go to school and to church."

As we look across the interviews, the take-away is that Wright's message helped congregants, especially members who were not previously members of a Baptist church or a church that openly embraced the black culture, to better understand the scriptures. Instead of connecting scripture to European Christian religion and interpreting the Bible in that context, Wright interpreted scripture within an African Amrican historical and cultural context. And for those who joined and were previously members of a Baptist church or another religious domination that more readily took into account the black experience, Wright's message demanded more of them. It required that they embrace and include at the table of political, social, and economic life black brothers and sisters not only from middle, wealthy, and professional classes but also the poor, the beggar, the jailed, and the prostitute. Any who sit in the pews at Trinity, regardless of the path that they have walked to get there, heard from Wright a request that comes out of black history and culture: to use education as a tool to help yourself and flourish as a Christian and as a tool to facilitate an engagement in which people who are othered have the opportunity to demonstrate their agency as they seek a flourishing life.

Some Trinitarians discussed Wright's preaching style, and the majority liked it and was very pleased and comfortable with it. It was not the calm, collected delivery and message that is often found in most UCC churches. But most blacks are familiar with "black preaching" due to growing up in African American communities. One Trinitarian stated that he liked it because although the preaching style and delivery was robust, it was not the old-fashioned fire, brimstone, and damnation: "I think the greatest thing about Rev. Wright's preaching was that he did not deliver the fire and brimstone like many of the old-time black preachers, like you are going to hell."

The preaching style found in many black churches arguably dates back to the Second Great Awakening, a Christian revival movement at the beginning of the nineteenth century. Geoff Alexander contends that African American preaching usually consists of "inflection and timing so musical that many have compared it in style to improvised jazz."[30] It is delivered by a preacher who is often "orator, singer, theologian, spiritual leader, law-giver, scholar and administrator";[31] as such, he or she represents "the most significant thread weaving through the long history of the black church in the United States."[32] Much of the preacher's "sermon is improvised around a matrix both sacred and profane, and the style is cohesive enough that one can enter virtually any black Baptist, Methodist, or Pentecostal church from coast-to-coast and hear a sermon of similar form. This is assured in part by the congregation, which answers the preacher verbally at every opportunity, creating a call-and-response pattern, which often builds to a frightening intensity."[33] Although threatening to some ears, such a preaching style is a rich thread in the cloth of American spiritual life.

In February 2008, in the midst of controversy, Rev. Jeremiah Wright adhered to a preestablished retirement date. He retired after thirty-six years as the senior pastor of Trinity Church, turning over the daily responsibilities of the church to Reverend Otis Moss III, who began his duties as interim senior pastor in June 2008. Nearly a year later, on May 31, 2009, Moss was officially installed as senior pastor. Moss is a native of Cleveland, Ohio, an honors graduate of Morehouse College, and a graduate of Yale Divinity School. During an interview for the *Chicago Defender* a few days prior to his installation, Effie Rolfe asked Moss about the effect of Wright controversy on his calling: "In light of the controversy with the Rev. Jeremiah Wright and former member, then presidential candidate Barack Obama, did you ever question God about your assignment as pastor?" Reverend Moss responded, "Absolutely! Wow, my first day in the pulpit was the day the media controversy started and my question was, 'OK God, now you called me and now I am in the middle of a storm' . . . looking back in hindsight I realized God had placed us here in Chicago for such a time as this."[34]

We later asked Rev. Moss a similar question about the transition period. He responded, "[It was] incredibly difficult and at times brutal but also a blessing in many ways to come into a position like this. The church having to depend upon you making the transition . . . [as they] mourn someone who had been there for x number of years. . . . I think it was the uniqueness and the blessing of the moment. [It is when something] is challenging, difficult and stressful that God utilized it to create something unique and different."

Members of the congregation also recognized the difficulty of the transition, and while they appreciated Moss's efforts to make the transition as smooth as possible and many agreed that he was doing a fantastic job, a few others were smarting from Wright's retirement and the media's attack on the church. One Trinitarian stated, "They [church members] are still pining away over Pastor Wright and are not ready to give their full loyalty; [it's] difficult, very difficult." Another congregant observed, "There is pain from the separation and there is pain from the [media] attacks. With all of this is going on [Reverend] Moss doesn't know who to trust in order to get people to support him." Still another Trinitarian noted the chaos and framed it as how attacks from the outside are placing their new pastor in a challenging position: "I think there were a lot of unfair accusations being made against the church as well as against Reverend Wright. Reverend Moss being the new pastor had to deal with it. He inherited something he never expected. As a young pastor, having to be in the national spotlight under those circumstances had to be extremely challenging for him."

"So God was with Moses, so God will be with you," Otis Moss Jr., pastor emeritus of Olivet Institutional Baptist Church in Cleveland and the young Rev. Moss's father, told him during his installation service. Rev. Moss's father foretold what the majority of the congregants said they saw and liked in their new senior pastor: "Reverend Moss has a strong abiding faith in God; and although he was challenged by the media chaos he believed that with his trust in God he and the church would be okay. Now, he is well accepted by all of us [Trinitarians] and you only hear positive statements about him. And everyone is pulling for him to be successful."

Although Moss is a part of a new generation of ministers committed to preaching prophetically that love and justice are the inseparable companions that form the foundation of the Gospel of Jesus Christ, his preaching style continues in the tradition of Rev. Wright and other black preachers. One congregant complimented Moss's ministry in this way: "I think Reverend Moss has been a wonderful pastor. I think he's been that breath of fresh air that the church has needed. . . . His whole style is different. He's not as fiery; passionate, but not as fiery." In addition, Moss's sermons are informed by the works of the black artists of the Chicago Renaissance discussed in chapter 3.

Moss identifies the works of Zora Neale Hurston, August Wilson, Howard Thurman, and jazz and hip-hop artists as increasing the richness of his ministry and personal self.

The primary mentors for his spiritual formation are the work and legacy of Dr, Martin Luther King Jr. and his father, Dr. Otis Moss Jr.[35] One Trinitarian stated, "Pastor Moss is keeping the focus on culture, Christ, and community. His vision for the church is bridging the generation gap. I see other churches beginning to do that as well because [we are in] the hip hop era. . . . I'm old school, but Pastor Moss has educated me to use what the Lord gives you to save souls." Another Trinitarian described Moss's efforts to reach the youth: "I love him; he has brought forth so many things which have to do with dealing with the younger generation. You have do that with churches with an aging population. If you do not attract and make attractive the church for younger generation, you do not grow."

On Sunday, as you drive across 95th Street between State and Halsted, following the thirty-mile-an-hour speed limit is impossible. Cars of all years and makes are heading toward Trinity. Drivers are searching for a parking space and they know that if it is anywhere between forty-five minutes and an hour before Sunday services, especially the 7:30 and the 11:00 services, they probably will not find a parking space. The University of Wisconsin–Madison group who visited Trinity (a visit we will come back to a bit later in the book) had to park five blocks away from the church. Thankfully, on that occasion it was a pleasant November day in Chicago, a bit windy, but not unusually so for the Windy City. Over the years the heavy traffic that surrounds Trinity, as well as hundreds of people hustling to get to church, has served as an invitation for others to come and join. One congregant was so enthralled by what she saw that she decided to leave her husband at their present church home and come to Trinity by herself: "I used to take a friend home west of Trinity and I would come across 95th Street and see all the cars out in the parkway. I would say something is happening here; so for about five years I attended Trinity before I joined. My husband was at Park Manor [a UCC church]; he didn't want to come. I left him there and I came to Trinity." In case you are wondering, the husband did "wise up" and eventually followed his wife to Trinity.

The voices of the everyday people at Trinity point out that they come from far and wide throughout Chicago and its suburbs to Trinity seeking spiritual love, a church home for themselves and their family members, to learn a cultural history that has not been taught to them, and to hear and get to know a pastor who is learned and caring. They spoke eloquently about Rev. Wright's, and now Rev. Moss's, caring disposition, the individual attention they gave them, as well as their energy and charisma. They appreciated that the content of the sermons connects biblical scripture to everyday life—

their lives—and African American history and that the church advocates liberation theology.

On Carl's first visit to Trinity with Shelby, he noticed the warmth and cordiality of the greeting, and how each and every person who enters is immediately made to feel welcome and special. Outside of the sanctuary, members of different ministries directed and served children, latecomers, visitors arriving on buses, and people searching for parking spaces in a friendly, courteous, and professional manner. There is no shortage of members for the various tasks and in some cases two members will service a party.

On that first Sunday visit, Carl joined Shelby at the charter/founder member luncheon. The Hospitality Ministry, wearing white gloves and displaying a lot of love and respect, ushered a group of about twenty charter members into a dining room where they were served and fussed over in a manner that fitted and suited their station. Members of the ministries say they love what they do, helping and serving, and note that they are often members of more than one ministry. A member of the Hospitality Ministry explained, "I'm currently with the Hospitality Ministry. Hospitality has various functions, including repast that we do at the church for members that have passed; extending fellowship to visitors, preparing food, serving food, and making people comfortable in any way that we possibly can. [Also] I'm a member of the Grandparent Ministry and I was a member of the Readers Ministry because I love people. My husband is a deacon. He was a chairperson for the Deacon Board for about six or eight years. He teaches many classes. He really knows the Bible inside and out."

At the outset of our writing, we argued that we were on a challenging and ambitious journey to contribute to America's story, to fill a void that was not only going unnoticed but also being dismissed, or at best being dealt with on others' terms. We specifically noted that the history—points of view, dispositions, stories—of everyday African American people was not heard within the mainstream narrative.

The next chapter presents the narrative of the everyday parishioners' experience of the Wright controversy, the Obama campaign, and their aftermath. These stories constitute a counter-story to the "single story" presented by much of the media that used video snippets to frame Rev. Wright as a crazed individual who differed greatly from the pastor that Trinitarians know. Their narratives make it clear that media efforts to portray Trinitarians as anti-American go against the concepts of "We the People" and "Liberty and Justice for All." As Rev. William Sloane Coffin, Yale University chaplain, said, "There are three kinds of patriots, two bad, one good. The bad ones are the uncritical lovers and the loveless critics. Good patriots carry on a lover's quarrel with their country, a reflection of God's lover's quarrel with all the world."

To bring you the Trinitarians' story, we conducted interviews that sometimes resulted in visiting homes, having coffee, and holding conversations after Sunday church services; talking about all of Chicago's sport teams, national and global politics, black and white people in general, Barack Obama, and any and everything else. What we learned was that the Trinitarians are fair and open minded but, like all people, they have their personal biases about their Chicago sport teams (many do love "Lovie," the Bears' coach, and Derek Rose and the Chicago Bulls); are vexed about the small amount of African American power and lack of representation in city politics and the treatment of black people in general; and are frustrated by the gang violence and the murder of black youth and with blacks who are not doing their best or who are "pulling the race down." Trinitarians have more than just a pedestrian understanding of national politics and are pleased to be moving up on the learning curve regarding international and global politics. They love "Barack" but would like to have five minutes with him to discuss some of his policies and other political actions.

The Trinitarians' voices would embrace the words of Katherine Lee Bates in "America, The Beautiful" (1893), especially the last verse. Here they can envision the "patriot dream"—images of black soldiers who fought for America's freedom and Americans' liberty since the Revolutionary War, with special attention to the African American Tuskegee Airmen, who were the first African American military aviators in the U.S. armed forces during World War II. Similarly, they would find hope in the phrase "crown thy good with brotherhood" because they are serious and forthright about welcoming, accepting, and being appreciative of other racial and ethnic groups, and all who are "othered."

*America, The Beautiful*

> Oh, beautiful for patriot dream
> That sees beyond the years;
> Whose alabaster cities gleam
> Undimmed by human tears.
> America, America,
> God shed His grace on thee
> And crown thy good with brotherhood [sisterhood]
> From sea to shining sea.

Additionally, Trinitarians are like most Americans, people who have risen up personally and collectively from being "a wretch," as stated in "Amazing Grace." And they are especially grateful to God for being with them as they journeyed from enslavement to the present day, from blindness to a time where they can now "see":

*Amazing Grace*

Amazing grace! (how sweet the sound)
That sav'd a wretch like me!
I once was lost, but now am found,
Was blind, but now I see.

*Chapter Five*

# The Unheard Voices of Trinity Church

*Four hostile newspapers are more to be feared than a thousand bayonets.*
—Napoleon Bonaparte

In March 2008, a firestorm descended upon Trinity United Church of Christ much like the wind-driven blaze that destroyed the hillsides of northern Oakland California and southeastern Berkeley in 1991. A firestorm can be accidentally ignited or naturally caused. However, instead of being a natural phenomenon, in this case it was a conflagration, a white-hot blaze brought on by the media, particularly throngs of reporters and hate-mongering protesters who produced uncontrollable chaos, threatening the sacredness of the church and the life, health, and property of its congregants. The chaos that it created left congregants and black churches across the United States facing tremendous racial turbulence. Narrowly selected portions of Reverend Jeremiah Wright's sermons had been picked up by the press and played over and over in the media in what might be called a stack effect. In a fire, a stack effect occurs where there is a temperature and pressure difference between the outside air and the air inside the burning building. In this case, the differential between the images produced by outside media and the reality of the interior life of Trinity Church caused a stack effect that threatened the well-being of those inside.

## THE MEDIA

When Barack Obama became a candidate for the Democratic Party nomination, the media arrived at Trinity to learn more of Obama's church life. Reporters were greeted cordially and individual congregants consented to be interviewed. Trinitarians for the most part welcomed the attention. They were accustomed to visitors and people of all races coming to the church, and they knew that the world wanted to know about the Obama family and their church. They were very proud to be able to say to friends, "Our church member has moved from U.S. senator to presidential candidate—wow!" As one congregant said, "I recall everybody was quite elated that one of Trinity's members, Barack Obama, was going to run for president. There was excitement."

Trinitarians said they understood that any person seeking the presidency undergoes intense scrutiny and that this would be more so with Obama because the black man has not yet received unconditional acceptance by all members of society: "We knew that with an African American running for the presidency, and especially since there was the possibility that he could win, the scrutiny would be intense." Some argued, in fact, that they understood and appreciated that the media's job was to tell the full life story about anyone whose chances of becoming president and commander-in-chief were good and that the media wanted to know about family and friends close to candidates: "We understand that in the research into Senator Obama's background, some members of the media decided to pursue his membership at Trinity Church and relationship with Trinity's senior pastor Reverend Wright; that's fair." In sum, Trinitarians believed that Obama deserved a close examination and that it was appropriate to look at his house of worship. They knew that most whites had very little knowledge and understanding of the black church and hoped that this "examination" would help to remedy that shortcoming. In addition, they were supported by their knowledge of the church growth and development in Christ over more than forty years, and that as a people they were "Unashamedly Black and Unapologetically Christian" and had no reason to fear anyone.

The congregation's early feeling of confidence, however, began to dissipate after short snippets of Rev. Wright's sermons were picked up by the media and broadcast widely. These were small portions of sermons that seemed inflammatory and, to an outsider, potentially anti-American. Pundits and members of the public alike, lacking an understanding of the black church in general and of Trinity specifically, interpreted these snippets in the worst way possible, accusing Wright and the congregants of racism and hatred of America. It was a nightmare for the congregants of this close community. Opponents stalked them, picketed outside the church, and left angry, hateful phone messages. The media relentlessly pursued parishioners with inflammatory questions and cameras and microphones in their faces. The media and protesters thus became a fiery blaze of great size and intensity that generated and was fed by strong inrushing winds of horrific rhetoric and images from all sides.

One parishioner recalled, "I was very angry. I thought it was unfair to Obama, the way the media portrayed Reverend Wright as this radical person . . . totally out of control. It's like you and I talking and someone who is listening to us takes bits and pieces of our conversation and makes it into something different. It was unfair not only to Obama and Reverend Wright but the church as well." Trinitarians said they soon learned that the reporters could not be trusted. They were on a mission, searching for information that would support a single, narrow, biased story of the church. That said, some congregants wanted to give reporters a chance to do an interview in which they would get a fuller and truer picture of Trinity. They reasoned and hoped that meeting with reporters would help both Trinity and the media.

One Trinitarian recalls an interview she granted to a reporter after being assured that the interview would be fair and honest:

> The first part of the interview was okay, but she [the reporter] continued to try to push me to make some commentary about Pastor Wright's relationship with Louis Farrakhan. She kept asking why he would want to have anything to do with Louis Farrakhan, something to that effect. I said, first of all you need to step back and look at Pastor Wright and Louis Farrakhan. You need to look at the black community more broadly in terms of how [and] what we have to do as a community to survive. We have to help each other. I was trying, you know, to give the larger picture. [But] she kept trying to push me to make some definitive statement, I guess, condemning Pastor Wright's relationship with Louis Farrakhan. I chose not to do that. She flipped around and she asked me a few more questions and we ended the interview. . . . I trusted that she would do a good job that she would be honest and forthright, but she was looking for some statement; that was her agenda. I recognized that and since then I have not taken any interviews with anybody about anything about Trinity. I've been very angry about that [interview] and felt very violated.

E. A. Sovik, in *Notes on Sacred Space*, tells us that "to the faithful of any congregation, their own church buildings are commonly thought of as 'sacred.' Even the most commonplace church building can become venerable in someone's mind, so holy that . . . even changes made in it are seen as sacrilege."[1] During the 2008 presidential campaign the "change" that took place at Trinity was not the change Sovik speaks of, for he is speaking of an architectural change. At Trinity, the change was even more extreme—it was a movement from peacefully and serenely worshiping God and giving warm love and care to fellow congregants and visitors, to tension, uncertainty, and feeling disrespected during Sunday worship hours.

Trinity's leaders quickly realized that they were in a firestorm that showed no sign of dying out, a storm for which their years in divinity school and church training had not prepared them. They knew that it was time to take stock of the situation and seek professional help. Additionally, they knew that calm, dignified leadership would allay—as much as possible—fear and uncertainty among the congregation. Trinity's leadership contended that, in order to deal with the media's aggressive efforts to get something—any-thing—with a foul or negative spin on their former pastor, Rev. Wright, presidential candidate Barack Obama, and Trinity Church, they needed to harness and to put into action all of the personal and professional resources at their disposal. The media's interest was in telling a fabricated single story that Wright was an "un-American, anti-white" minister, that Trinity was racist and, by affiliation, so was Barack Obama.

Recalling this turbulent time, Trinity's current senior pastor, Rev. Moss, stated, "I started here [when] the media barrage began on Trinity. My first day was the day or D-day in many ways. One of the things that we were not prepared for was the media, specifically Fox News, conservative outlets . . . that they were going to put such emphasis on the church [and] Pastor Wright. Since nothing like that had happened historically, there was no reference point." Reverend Moss noted that "all of a sudden the emails start, the calls [and] then the death threats. . . . It just kept growing from there. It would not stop. . . . Every Sunday there were throngs of people who were showing up specifically with devices like this [referencing our voice-recorder ] who were attempting to find the next unique sound bite." Continuing with his story, Reverend Moss described the media's incessant quest to find additional sound bites: "Our Akiba [bookstore] . . . helped the ministry out. . . . People were purchasing CDs and DVDs 100–150 at a time, looking for something. They didn't care what it was. They were just trying to find something."

As the search continued for additional segments of videos of Wright that could be used to exploit a racial division between blacks and whites, the church leadership decided that additional help was needed. They were not prepared to deal with the persistent and relentless media bombardment and other attempts to provoke reactions from the congregants. Moreover, the church leadership became aware that the media's investigation of Trinity allowed others who despised Trinity's motto of "Unashamedly Black and Unapologetically Christian" to use the "cover" of the media to attack the ideology of the black church and their use of black liberation theology. Rev. Moss observed that it was not only on Sundays that the church was violated, and it was not only the media that was disruptive. Picketers outside the church diligently attempted to interrupt church life. Trinity was in the bull's-eye of racial hatemongers. The ongoing media attention brought additional derogation to both the church and its surrounding neighborhood. Signs claiming that Trinity was a "racist church" and had a "racist pastor" were held up outside the church. Many Trinitarians dismissed the parade of signs as not deserving the kind of overt response that would bring attention to the church. But the shouted expletives were much harder to tolerate. For some, it was a return to the days of barking dogs and angry shouting militants as one walked the protest line with head held high. "What is really different, now?"

they seemed to be thinking. "They picketed our church. I saw them carrying the signs marching around the church. . . . I met a group outside carrying signs that said the pastor is racist. One shouted at me, 'Why do you go to church here? He preaches hatred.'"

Addressing the protesters outside of the church Rev. Moss stated, "We had protests. We had some group from Kansas that came up [to Trinity]. They protested out in front of the church and utilized some horrific racially charged language and other types of language. [They used] cameras to [try to] promote confrontation. . . . If a confrontation had happened, no matter how it played out, it would be framed as 'this is an African American man or woman who is attacking this white man,' [or] whomever it may be; this was the whole point." Rev. Moss continued describing how the church responded to this baiting: "What we did [in response was] send the choir out. . . . They surrounded everybody and started singing to the point they could be heard over the [picketers'] bullhorns. [The picketers] came back a few months later. It was really frustrating. It's the same group that protested a Marine who was killed in Afghanistan. . . . It was really horrific."

Some congregants spoke in angry tones about the picketers and the shouting and screaming outside of the church. Some voiced a "turn the other cheek" perspective. Some of the older Trinitarians argued that the church should be "smart," and that the church's thinking should be rooted in Mahatma Gandhi and Martin Luther King Jr.'s interpretation of Matthew 5:39–41. These older Trinitarian understood that both Gandhi and King had used Jesus' Sermon on the Mount as a foundation for their civil rights movement and as justification for political action. It was not a passive acceptance of injustice and oppression but a positive action that was an assertive but nonviolent form of protest. In addition, congregants reasoned that to respond negatively to any gesture or provocation made by the media would allow them to characterize Trinitarians as the "ugly person" and and to say, "Well, I told you so!"

The congregants' calm response is attributable to many things, including thoughts of King or Gandhi as well as church leaders who asked the congregants to be smart and civil. But as we listened closely to the interviewees, what registered above all else was their firm belief in Jesus Christ. One Trinitarian confirmed our observation:

> There is one good bright star to this whole thing; you didn't ask this, but I will tell this story. We were in prayer service one Wednesday and these three [two white women and a white man] came in to prayer service; they were journalists from some paper. They were taking notes, a lot of writing. One of the deacons came in [hoping] to pray with them. I said, "Pray with them? We ought to put them out! But okay we'll pray." I was with the two women and he was with the man; one was Jewish and the other was Catholic. One said, "You know we don't believe in the same things that you believe in." I said, "That's

okay, that's fine, but we [all] still serve God. You serve your God, we serve
our God. Our God has Jesus." . . . The other girl said, "Well, I was raised
Catholic and I haven't been to mass in years." I said, "It doesn't matter; God
will still hear you. Prayer is nothing more than talking to God; whatever fills
your heart just let it go." Well, the one who said she was Jewish started
praying and went on and on and on. It was a long prayer; then she said, "I feel
so revived." And the one who was Catholic said a prayer. Her father was dying
of cancer. After she prayed, I said, "Is it okay if I put your father's name on
our prayer list?" She said, "Would you do that?" I said, "Yeah, sure." I mean,
why not? Why wouldn't I? After prayer service they both hugged and they told
the minister, "We came here to do a story, but we got a blessing."

Moments like this, unfortunately, were few and far between. No one else
recounted a moment when reporters took the time to engage them as real
people in the sanctity of their church. All the Trinitarians we interviewed
exemplified the quality of behavior just described. They would welcome all
to the church, although they knew that they would not receive the same
treatment if the situation were reversed. That said, they also knew that while
remaining calm, they were not going to allow the media to disrespect them or
their church.

## PEACEFUL RESISTANCE

The violence of the firestorm resulted in plans to push back on the media. A
press conference was announced to lay out procedures for dealing with the
media and others who wanted information from the church. Guidelines for
dealing with both the media and church membership were laid out: "On the
day of the press conference we introduced our media protocol and guidelines.
We ask them [the media] not to call our sick and shut-ins." Congregants were
asked not to talk to the media but to refer them to designated spokespersons:
"We are very intentional about who will speak for Trinity. We [make] sure
that whoever speaks will integrate biblical paradigms, biblical scriptures,
[and] will intermix classical liberation theology and biblical scholarship into
the message." Church members were given guidelines that included procedures about what to do if the media requested an interview. A Trinitarian
spoke about following the church's guideline. "I was doing what we are
asked to do and that is to refer anyone to the person who was in charge of
publicity or public relations. That is what I did; I was not going to fall prey to
the media. I also notice that [since they had difficulty securing interviews
from Trinitarians] they had tried to interview people who lived across the
street [from the church] or lived in the neighborhood. It was pathetic." Every
now and then a congregant would take the bait and respond to a reporter's
question: "I am on my way to church one Sunday and they [the media] are

out and my wife asks me not to say anything but I do. He [reporter] asked me what I think about Reverend Wright. I take it to them! 'I view Reverend Wright as a freedom fighter, spiritual leader, and I will stand by him no matter what happens.'"

The relentless, assertive, and at times aggressive actions of the media in their efforts to get the story they wanted, or, as Rev. Moss argued, "to fill in the holes for a story already written," convinced Trinitarians that they needed to stop the way in which the sanctuary was being disrespected, individual congregants were being harassed, and the overall church was being made a victim of threats and epithets. In other words, Trinitarians decided to take action and develop a plan of resistance, to push back against racism and those who were intent on telling a "single story" about Trinity Church.

Trinitarians spoke about how the plan of resistance was designed to prevent the media from destroying the church and disrupting the flow of love among members and the pastor that many Trinitarians contended was the heart and soul of Trinity. Trinity's plan called for the church to exercise greater agency in getting out the message it wanted to congregants and the public, and making church services available to people in their homes who were afraid to attend church because of media violence: "Trinity has its own website, its own streaming abilities, and its own network. That was a saving grace from our perspective. We are able to take the church service into the home of our congregants who did not wish to walk by the screaming reporters and protesters." Congregants who were professionals in journalism, communication, and public relations met to strategize about how Trinity would push back to change the racialized story that was defaming the reputation of the church and narrowly framing Rev. Wright. "We have members of our church who are noted journalists, who are marketing people trained just as I am in public relations and public communications. We took ownership of the story."

Trinity's plans included inspecting packages and bags brought into the church, requesting that the media have recording devices examined by the director of communication, and searching for explosive devices between each of the three church services on Sunday. The ministry responsible for greeting and welcoming visitors increased their vigilance; church security officers were told to be watchful both inside and outside of the church. Trinitarians likened what they were experiencing at church to security checks that the public has to undergo at airports: cars in the parking lot were observed, large bags were inspected, and the hospitality ministry was assigned to be watchful over the coming and going of people.

Pushing back, standing up against oppression and the powerful, is in the DNA of African Americans. From the time of enslavement to the present moment, blacks as a people and as individuals have pushed back against institutions, people, and ideas that seek to oppress and undermine them. This action has taken place in all of the spaces where they have been present in every imaginable way over the years: guiding escaping slaves north to freedom; black soldiers launching the "Double V" (victory at home, victory abroad) campaign of World War II, in which they linked their fight for justice and democracy in Europe to the fight for African American equality at home; Frederick Douglass in 1852 delivering his speech "What, to the Slave, Is the Fourth of July?"; black artists introducing into the art world an ethnic consciousness and the creation of a new black identity; citizens boycotting racially segregated buses, conducting sit-ins at "white only" lunch counters, and writing protest poems, plays, novels and articles; legitimizing black dance and shattering the boundaries that tried to hold and control black dancers and choreographers; leading civil rights marches; writing protest letters from prisons; marching on Washington; and photographing the faces of blacks living in poverty and despair for "We the People" to see and contemplate. Trinitarians, like those who have come before them, stood tall in their resistance to the media's attacks.

The Trinitarians' horrific stories about the media were told as if the media firestorm had taken place within the past twenty-four hours. Trinitarians asserted that members of the media shouted at them and chased after them as they made their way to church and also as they left church. The media's goal (Trinitarians all believed) was to get a negative comment from a congregant about Rev. Wright that could be used on the six o'clock news in order to turn the voting public against Obama. "You could not leave Trinity without being besieged by the media. CNN, MSNBC, ABC, and CBS . . . they were all out there, the cameras were rolling, someone would stick a microphone in your face as they asked you questions." Some congregants said that black reporters were hounding them as well. They seem to have held out some hope that black reporters would have an understanding of what was happening in a black church and would have relayed that information to their employers in order to bring about new coverage that was fair and balanced. But that was not the case; black reporters, for the most part, performed as white reporters did: "Black reporters would run up to you, and I would tell them just like I told the white reporters, 'All media must report to the main desk [in Trinity] and someone will talk to you.' and I would walk on."

Trinity soon had to install further controls on the media's behavior. TV cameras and recording devices caused interruptions in the service and disrupted the atmosphere of reverence and piety that Trinitarians loved and had come to expect. Congregants claimed that the media had only minimal regard for the black church as a sacred place. They reminded us that the black church was and must remain a space to escape the racial tensions in the larger society and receive community support. It is not a space in which the white media can bulldoze and try to manipulate people in order to obtain the story it desires. In black churches, "unlike the workplace, where many blacks entered as disempowered producers dependent on wages for survival and beholden, ostensibly at least, to their superiors," people should feel safe and supported.[2]

Every Trinitarian we interviewed saw the media presence at Trinity as intrusive. They spoke not only with anger but also with disappointment regarding the media's actions in interfering with Trinity's hours of worship, including the hours before and after church service. "I saw this as being intrusive. Before church, during church, and after church, [those are] very private moments of reflection. When I leave church, it is a time when I'm collecting my thoughts, my ideas, formulating what I'm to do for the rest of my week spiritually. I don't need anyone to intrude and ask me about Trinity, what I feel about Trinity, or what I feel about Obama. That's private and it's intrusive." Another congregant reports, "I saw Fox News come in one Sunday with a camera crew and I was standing at the door with one of our pastors. She handled the gentleman very well. She told him that he could not bring the camera into church but he could come in and worship. As he went off, he was rude to her; he told her, 'Why would I want to worship here?'" This contempt for the black church was what shocked and dismayed many Trinitarians throughout the ordeal.

Sitting in the church with the choir singing softly and clapping rhythmically, along with the calm prayerful words of the preacher flowing out across the congregation, was still not enough to relieve the anxiety that congregants felt during the media firestorm. They explained that the expressions of care and love did not quiet their emotions. Feelings of tensions circulated throughout the sanctuary: "There was tension about who was in the building or whether someone was coming in with a camera. It was really very difficult. [In addition] I had several phone calls to my office as well as at home. Major news media outlets called trying to do interviews with me. Trying to find out what I knew. I refused each and every one because I kept seeing how they were treating other people on the media. I did not trust that anyone would actually do a fair job."

The media onslaught continued and reached a point where it became not only a distraction and disruptive but also a violation of the sacredness of the sanctuary and the surrounding space where the church is located. "At first, I tried to ignore the media, pay no attention, to 'stay in service'; but that was impossible to do. They had no regard for the church and the people in attendance." "It became a distraction with the news media out there every Sunday at all the services. The media attempted to isolate people going to church and ask them [questions]." Congregants were not only caught up in their own feelings of frustration and violation but also concerned for their fellow congregants. People tried to shield one another from the media attacks, attempting to preserve the sense of community and safety that had previously permeated the church: "The news media did not leave elderly people be, they approached anyone they hoped they could get a story from. One Sunday, I took the arm of one of our older members and walked along with her and told the media to leave us alone."

When congregants heard about and saw the media and others disregard the church's guidelines and smuggle cameras and recording devices into the sanctuary, this further added to their feeling of vulnerability and anxiety. A member of the sanctuary choir stated, "You can see [from the choir position, above the church pews] photographers crawling around on the floor of the sanctuary [trying] to get into position to take pictures [without permission] and this went on for weeks." Another congregant claimed, "They would get inside the sanctuary and we would figure that they were coming for service. Strangers are welcome at our services. But they were sneaking in all kinds of devices, bumping and squirming [to take pictures]. Some would take pictures and try to sell them. They were paying black and white people off the street to come in and try to get information for them."

For some congregants, when a person who they first believed was a typical Sunday visitor took out a recording device, ignored the congregants sitting around them, and pushed about in their seat in order to get a good picture, the line of respect for them as individuals and the church as a sacred space had been crossed. And although Trinity remained steadfast about keeping the church's doors open throughout the media attack, the fear and anxiety stemming from the ordeal caused some Trinitarians to avoid church services on Sunday.

As everyday people attending church, entering a sacred space where they normally come for mental and spiritual comfort, Trinitarians believed that not only were they being disrespected by the media but they were also being treated as second-class citizens in their own church house. It was as if someone had taken them back in time to a period when whites could do as they pleased and blacks had to accept it even though they hated it. David Abramtsov writes about behavior in the church in a way that supports the Trinitarians' experience:

> The House of God ought to be given the greatest of respect: "Reverence My sanctuary" (Lev. 26:2). Our Savior charged, "Make not the house of My Father a house of trade" (John 2:16). Even on the church grounds one must always remember that God's House is close by . . . the ground around a church is consecrated. . . . The Church Fathers admonish that, "Those, who heedlessly turn sacred places into that which is ordinary and behave without discretion around them, and act the same in them, we decree to put them away from them" (VI. Ecumenical. Council #97). We must conduct ourselves honorably in church auditoriums or halls which are located in the basement of some churches. Here too we must avoid . . . noisy transactions so as not to commit blasphemy and sacrilege on church property. As to the character of affairs which may be conducted in such halls it is best to consult the Pastor. [3]

Because of the disregard for the sacredness of the sanctuary and the church grounds in general, Trinity posted notices outside of the sanctuary that said, "No recording devices or cameras allowed into the sanctuary unless first cleared by the director of media." The notices remain in place to this day, a bitter reminder of their ordeal.

There were a few times during our interviews with congregants when recalling an incident caused an expression of fear to come over the interviewee's face or when the congregant's nonverbal expressions communicated, "Do we really need to talk about this?" Although this message was communicated nonverbally, the verbal response always was "Let's get started." Everyone we interviewed seemed to sense the importance of their contribution to this American story. One interviewee, who had answered phones during the time of the media firestorm, cautiously and hesitantly began. As she became more comfortable, she told of the calls she answered and the disrespectful treatment she received from some callers. She said some the callers issued threats and used a vile vocabulary: "We started getting phone calls that were threatening and the language was foul. I will not repeat it." A follow-up question about the nature of the threats led to her saying, "I was actually afraid for the church because you don't know. You couldn't trust people, you didn't know if somebody was going to come in [to the church and] try and do bodily harm to someone."

The most upsetting time for the Trinitarians was when some reporters started contacting congregants who were shut-in or hospitalized. In one case, a minister responsible for attending to the sick and shut-in stated that an attempt was made to contact a Trinitarian's father who laid dying in a hospice. In order to be sure of what was stated, we asked, "Did you say a call was placed to the HOSPITAL room?" "No, HOSPICE room!" was the reply. The minister continued, "We had to take the Sick and Shut-In List out of the church bulletin. Before we had a Christian fellowship policy; that when a person was sick and shut-in we listed their home address and their phone number. You could mail a card to the hospice or hospital. But we had to stop printing the information in the bulletin because members of the media were calling hospital rooms, the hospice, and congregants' houses. They were even going to their hopsitals or homes because the addresses were listed." The minister added, "Let me step back to the person that calls me about her father. She was literally in tears because members of the media kept calling his hospice room and they [the family] had to make arrangement so he [would be unable to] accept any calls."

This action on the part of the media raised questions about where they would draw the line, how far would they go to get their story. All-out contempt for Trinity Church was what the congregants felt they were up against, and they didn't know when it would stop.

Presently, the Sunday program no longer includes the name of the sick and shut-in. Now, the congregant's name and a brief statement about their condition is announced during service on Sunday. The Trinitarians we interviewed argued that the policy change limits the number of people who are informed about their fellow parishioners and cuts back on the number of visits, cards, and letters that a congregant will receive to cheer them and offer support.

In speaking about the media's lack of respect for members of the church—contacting the sick and dying, hounding congregants as they came to and from church, and allegedly writing threats with profane language and placing the same in the church's restrooms—Trinitarians spoke with pride about how they pushed back unafraid and undeterred. The day when blacks do not speak up or speak back against forms of tyranny and oppression, the congregants implied, has either come and gone or perhaps never existed. Trinitarians' resistance during the media firestorm was no exception.

When listening to the Trinitarians talk about the media firestorm, their prevailing emotions were disgust and anger. But unlike the media, theirs were not words of contempt. They were angry with the media for disparaging the black church but in their Christian manner they were not contemptuous. Congregants mainly spoke about the media's narrow framing of Rev. Wright and Trinity Church, and in doing so they offered full responses about the video snippets from Wright's sermons that set off the firestorm. They framed their responses in several ways, but to a person they were angry with the way the media handled and interpreted the snippets: "The way they produced it and [spoke about] it was only in a derogative manner. The snippets were not [presented in] reference to [problems and issues in] the world; in references to what was taking place in the U.S. and and its connection to the Bible." These were the issues, Trinitarians argued, that Rev. Wright was discussing in his sermon: social injustice in the United States and the world and locating these ills in a biblical context. They felt that, as a teacher and a preacher, Wright was a man who embodied honesty and a commitment to truth. They stated that he did not believe in one-sided stories; he pushed back against all kinds of oppression, and such was the case the day he delivered the sermon that created all the fuss. A Trinitarian who was present at the sermon offered her observation: "I was at that sermon. He was making a much larger point. The snippet made it sound like he was condemning the United States of America. No, he was condemning evil within our society that perpetuates oppression. He was always preaching liberation and he uses examples from the Bible to show how the same thing happens in the United States; and it happens over and over again."

This point was further illuminated on Melissa Harris-Perry's show on May 19, 2012, when she stated that her understanding of "God damn America" was that it was coming "out of a black liberation theology tradition that says inequality is sin, racism is sin; the sin isn't these personal things. The sin is sort of these big structural questions, so it isn't sort of the Americans who need to be rooting out their individual sin; it's the nation itself that needs to confront the sin of racism. But somehow it turns politically into just 'God damn America.'"

Dwight Hopkins from University of Chicago's Divinity School, on Melissa Harris-Perry's discussion of Rev. Wright on May 19, 2012, gave a theologian's perspective on Rev. Wright's statement "God damn America" within the context of the sermon and black liberation theology: "I think people are confusing two things. One, there is a political debate about the facticity or relevance of examples of what he thinks the U.S. government has done. But there is also a particular point where he literally points to the Bible. It's very clear that this tradition of the Bible is particularly a prophetic tradition and in fact it says in the Bible in the Old Testament that God damns the wayward Israel nation to bring it back to use the resources to serve as a model for the rest of the world. So when he points to the Bible, there's a theological point . . . and the whole point of Jesus, coming from the perspective of the Christian faith, is to free the poor, to free those who are oppressed, and that's the public announcement of Jesus Christ. And then the final point is when Jesus talks about how to get to heaven. . . . he specifically says that the only way Christians can get to heaven is to serve the poor, help those who are in prison, give water to those who are thirsty and visit the widow."[4]

Along these same lines, many Trinitarians stated that, for all of the love they have for the United States, they also believe that they have a right to criticize it. This tough and transparent love of country was conveyed in several comments like the one below:

> The United States has indeed been complicit in the oppression of many people and that's a fact. Anybody who denies this is looking at history through rose-colored glasses. He [Rev. Wright] reminded us of this. He does not do it to encourage us to be anti-American, but to make sure that we have a clear picture of what is going on in the world in order that we can make critical decisions about how to function in the world, how we vote and how we do ministry. He wants to make sure we see both sides of the coin. Historically, the story has always been one-sided. To say or to believe that our nation has never done anything wrong, that we didn't rape the land from the Indians, would be a lie. Pastor Wright always tells the real story, good, bad, or indifferent. He helped us to think critically. That sermon was just one example of what he did every single Sunday. What's so interesting [is that] he's not the only pastor that does it. There are many African American pastors who preach the same way about the same kind of issues across the nation all the time. There's a prophetic message being preached Sunday.

Congregants spoke about how the media misread the church services at Trinity. Their overall observation was that the media came to the church expecting to hear streams of disparaging comments about white people and the United States, and they asserted that those expectations had come from a biased framing of a people and a person: "A lot of them [the media and others] came there looking for Reverend Wright to be up there preaching. They thought that he would stand in the pulpit and preach negative thoughts to them. Everything would be negative. . . . But when they got here and saw that he is a preacher and teacher and his word is not about hate, that he was preaching love, they didn't know how to handle it."

"Why a 'single story,' an insulting story, about a black man who had contributed so much to his country as a marine, a medic assigned to serve President Johnson during his illness, and a fighter for social justice at home and abroad?" congregants asked. "People will start doing and saying anything to bring someone down or bring the church down." Although congregants understood, they were nevertheless disgusted that their pastor was being used as a tool by the media to attack Barack Obama: "I remember the Satanic attack vividly. I remember the media demonizing Pastor Wright who was preaching as he has always preached: truth to power . . . because the media could not find any skeletons in Obama's closet they chose to try to demonize the pastor. Even to this day, [Rev. Wright] and his family are still suffering from that. It angers me because the media is so powerful."

Some congregants claimed that there was much more to the media attack than the focus on Wright and Obama. Some of the charter members spoke about how the black church is a site where the white power structure has intruded before, and that although this is the twenty-first century, the attack on Trinity is as it was before, only today things are a bit more subtle: "People will do and say anything [to] bring the church down. In my opinion, that's what it was all about. It really wasn't about Reverend Wright; in my opinion it was about Trinity the church." Another parishioner argued, "There are a lot of people that want the media and other people in the world to think that there is something non-biblical, non-spiritual, and defaming to America going on here and that is not the case."

Trinitarians argued that the portrayal of Reverend Wright as an anti-American, racist pastor was a part of a scheme to attack the black church. On this point, Rev. Moss noted that the "African American community and specifically African American church is mysterious and exotic to those who are non-African American. It [then becomes] easy to create any type of perception that you want [of the black church] and make it believable. [This is so] because [if you are not African American] you are disconnected and you already see a group of people as exotic, mysterious and dangerous; all of those metaphors. It is then easy to attach the metaphors to Trinity specifically." Another Trinitarian also argued that the media firestorm had a larger purpose than Wright or Obama: "I think the media was trying to divide not only the Trinity community but the black community by starting the debacle.

They [the media] thought people would either choose Wright's or Obama's bandwagon. That would split the black community because black people wouldn't be able to support both of them."

Members of the church questioned the media's portrayal of Trinity on several points, but the major issue was the fairness of the media. To Trinitarians, "fairness" was a big deal. They talked about how fairness and democratic participation are expected and common virtues within the church. Fairness is central to their collective identity as African Americans. Their historical identity rests on the notion that African Americans as a people have a strong record of reaching out to other groups and welcoming them into their neighborhoods, churches, and homes. Trinitarians contended that the Fourth Estate left fairness at the office when they descended on Trinity: "I don't think [the media] was fair at all. I think they deliberately did a chop job in order to paint this ugly picture." Another Trinitarian added, "Newscasters came looking for a certain thing, but it didn't happen so they left with negative thoughts in their heads."

More than a few congregants pointed fingers at Fox News as the major culprit in the unfair attacks on Trinity, Wright, and Obama: "When I say the media stirred things up, I don't want to make it like everybody [every media outlet] was doing this. I [would] say the main culprit was Fox News. They were something terrible. Their whole job was to bring down this candidate for the presidency and it was also to bring down this pastor." While Fox News was identified by some as the major culprit, other congregants complained that other media outlets came to Trinity with closed minds as well. They came seeking only certain information that would enable them to frame Trinity and Rev. Wright in a preconceived, negative manner.

> They were low-down, opportunist, manipulative, and short-sighted. They only told one part of the story, and they presented the news as sensationally as they could.

> Always digging . . . to take an old sermon and just play a piece of it and not the whole thing was not fair. It was poor journalism; to keep the snippets playing over and over again made you feel like it was the 1980s when I was DJ. We would mix records, we'd take a sampling of James Brown. The part that says "aaaaaaaa give me some more, aaaaaaaaaa give me some." You would just keep mixing that. . . .When I saw those little snippets it was like [the media] was mixing it.

Many videotapes were purchased from Trinity's bookstore by the media in the search for additional footage from Wright's sermons to support the accusations of Wright and Trinity as racist and anti-American. But we could find no evidence that any new material was discovered or shown on television. Much of the material presented to the public had already been aired at an earlier date by the media, such as the sermon "U.S. of K.K.K.A.," which received attention in the media during mid-March 2008.

On this point Eli Saslow of the *Washington Post* wrote on March 18, 2008, "Internet and television news shows recalled Wright's praise of Nation of Islam leader Louis Farrakhan and played a greatest-hits compilation of Wright's most incendiary comments: that September 11, 2001, meant 'America's chickens are coming home to roost.' That former president Bill Clinton 'did the same thing to us that he did to Monica Lewinsky.' That 'racism is how this country was founded and how this country is still run.'" That said, Saslow stated, "To his supporters, the messages Wright wove through more than 4,000 sermons were now disseminated in a handful of grainy, two-minute video clips that tell only part of his story."[5]

Some of the congregants argued that, in addition to their overall unfairness, the media had "missed the point" in their reporting. The general sentiment was that they missed an opportunity to move toward the post-racial society that some like to talk about. They asked why, since Obama's pursuit for the presidency brought the media to Trinity, didn't some reporters take advantage of the opportunity to do at least a few stories that would foster better race relations between blacks and whites? They wondered, does "if it bleeds it leads" always have to be the only principle? And should stories that bleed be most of all that is written or reported? A few charter members spoke of the "old days," as they call them, when the *Chicago Daily News* and the *Chicago Tribune* did human interest stories or would offer a "people's point of view" on a story that was in the headlines. They said they knew that "it was about money and power," but nevertheless they asked "Why?" and argued that human interests and understanding between people of different races are the glue the country needs to move toward a post-racial society.

## OBAMA'S RESPONSE

The "glue" that would foster understanding and bring the country together, especially black and white people, was delivered by Barack Obama before a small audience of supporters, clergy, and elected officials during his March 18 speech at Philadelphia Constitution Center, which attracted more than 4 million live television viewers and was viewed 1.2 million times in the first twenty-four hours on YouTube.[6] The speech, titled "A More Perfect Union," is one that Trinitarians recalled with pride. It elevated Obama's statesmanship and was seen as comparable to, if not greater than, the speech John F. Kennedy gave on his Catholicism in Houston in 1960 when he was pursuing the Democratic presidential nomination. "I thought it was great and well received nationally." The speech generated comments on a range of issues:

Obama's defense of Rev. Wright, race and racism in the United States, the speech as a political tool, and the speech as a tool to foster unity between the races. Most Trinitarians listened to the speech primarily to see how Obama would handle the Wright controversy. The major concern voiced was this: "How is he going to treat Jeremiah?"

Obama was discovering some truths about the archetypal American news community, that race is what bleeds and leads, especially at this time when a black man was closing in on the presidential nomination. Race, in all of its blatant and nuanced manifestations, was the line pursued and reported. Race was not explicit, but rather the underlying driving force behind the nuanced, racialized terms of this "post-racial" election used in news reports and the questions asked the candidate. In addition, explicit conversations about race were characterized as anti-American and divisive and were used to try to undermine or bring down the Obama campaign. Trinitarians knew that the media had pushed Obama into a corner and they were pounding him unmercifully. He had been unable to quiet the controversy over Trinity's motto ("Unashamedly Black and Unapologetic Christian") and his twenty years as a member of a church where the preacher said "God Damn America," although he had granted interviews to both conservative and liberal commentators in addition to publishing an article in the Huffington Post. His pursuit of the presidential nomination was being dogged by race and racism. Many Trinitarians expressed their concerns at the time: "We knew he needed to do something big in order to get the media off of his back. Several of us thought that he would give a speech because he is good at it; but we did not know how good it would be until we heard it. Nevertheless, we still worried and wondered if it will be enough to stop the media assault on him."

Millions in the country heard "A More Perfect Union" because of the nature of its content—race and Rev. Wright—and because of its significance to the presidential campaign. Trinitarians were no different; they were glued to their television sets too. Most Trinitarians were not disappointed with the speech. Many spoke gleefully about how one of their own members, who many thought was on his way to the White House, had delivered a brilliant speech. They proudly claimed that the speech moved the nation forward in race relations and took a big step toward neutralizing right-wing propaganda designed to exploit race as a divisive tool to marginalize discussions on socioeconomic and class issues in the United States. But more important for some congregants, Obama had also stuck up for his pastor and discussed race not in the way it is often presented in the media as a spectacle (e.g., the O. J. Simpson trial and Hurricane Katrina) but as a part of our national character that we have yet to perfect and as a dynamic structure shaped by power and privilege that demands perceptive exploration and action. "I can no more disown him," said Obama, "than I can disown the black community. I could no more disown him than I can disown my white grandmother . . . who once confessed her fear of black men who pass her by on the street, and who on more than one occasion has uttered racial or ethnic stereotypes that made me cringe."[7] This particular statement caused many Trinitarians to assert that he defended Wright rather than rejecting him: "I thought it was an extraordinary speech and I thought he stood up for his pastor; not only did he stand up for Pastor, he didn't give into the [pressure of the media]." "He tried in my estimation to save his relationship with Reverend Wright in front of the media and the nation." "A More Perfect Union" was made "more perfect" to the congregants because as they listened to it they could tell that not only did Obama write much of the speech but also much of the "heart and soul of the speech came from the twenty years he [Obama] spent at Trinity."

Some congregants contended that because Obama was mixed raced he understood both black and white problems and issues. They asserted that he had acquired that knowledge and understanding living with his white mother and white grandparents; being treated as a black man in the United States and a minority in other places; and spending twenty years as a member of Trinity Church and having married a black woman and fathering two black children. These experiences along with his undergraduate, graduate, and law school training equipped him with the knowledge, skills, and disposition to present a case for a post-racial America and to deliver that idea in a speech to the American people. Some congregants who acknowledged that Obama's life experiences prepared him to write and deliver the speech nonetheless engaged in friendly debate over which aspects of his life experience most enabled him to perform as he did: "I don't know, I think it's an accumulation of his life experiences, Trinity, Harvard, his white mother, his black father and grandparents, where he lived as a child, Michelle, living in Chicago, *and* let's not forget the man's special." Another said, "His clarity of understanding of both black and white America is much more Trinity and Chicago than Harvard and Boston."

"A More Perfect Union" was delivered at a key moment of the 2008 presidential campaign, and just as some Trinitarians had surmised, Obama returned to his unique strength, oratory eloquence, to save his chance to win the Democratic presidential nomination of 2008. The power of oratory has been expressed in numerous adages, such as "A blow with a word strikes deeper than a blow with a sword." Obama and his campaign staff put into practice what many scholars, religious leaders, emperors, and the Bible itself have argued for centuries regarding the power of the well-spoken and delivered phrase: words can influence men and women. And for Obama, the truth that the pen is mightier was borne out by comments from both the young and old at Trinity. Congregants felt the speech addressed multiple issues of concern, including standing up for Rev. Wright and the church, and said it was "awesome," "on target and frank," "straightforward," and focused on bringing the nation together.

The speech was on target. It was frank. The question of the twenty-first century will be race [because] no one has really tackled it in an effective way.

I think the speech needed to be made. I believe it woke a lot of people up about his concern about race in America, It had to be said and there was no fear; there was no acquiescence, no compromise. This was a straightforward look at who we are and what we have in front of us.

I think Obama's speech was about unity, bringing people together of all races, all colors, all whatever. His thing is trying to bring us together. You know like King wanted us to do. He believes that in order for us to succeed in the world we're going to have to begin to work together, live together and treat each other like human beings.

Words are powerful, yet sometimes even the most well-thought-out phrases and crafted explanations do not satisfy everyone. Obama's speech annoyed some people, including the congregants he was trying to convince. Some Trinitarians believed that Obama's speech was grounded as much in his political ambition as his altruistic ambition couched in "hope and change" for all Americans.

I thought that he was talking like a politician. He was trying to reach the largest number of people without them getting angry with him. He said a lot of the things that I agreed with, like when he referred to Reverend Wright as being an uncle. But his main purpose was trying to get the greater number of people not to be upset with him.

He's campaigning for office. He's trying to defend his position. His main concern at the time was to get votes. He's a politician and he did what was necessary in order to be accepted. You go along to get along.

In addition to Obama's discussion of Rev. Wright, Trinitarians were also interested in his comments on a post-racial society: "There is not a black America and a white America. . . . There's the United States of America." While the comment was considered aspirational and some positive developments have taken place between blacks and whites in recent decades, they are not convinced that it has come to pass. To many congregants, that was the message in Rev. Wright's sermon—that America still has a long way to go in order for achieve social justice for all Americans. In addition, because some congregants have personal knowledge of the civil rights struggle of the 1960s and those without this firsthand knowledge have learned about it through life experiences, they are hopeful but not convinced that a post-racial society will come to be. Looming large in their minds are the few successes and continual failures to achieve real integration, equality for all people, and to acquire genuine civil rights in Chicago and America. So climbing aboard Obama's post-racial train does not bring with it the hope and optimism that it did when their grandparents in the South climbed aboard the train headed north to Chicago.

> He is saying to us that there is no place for racism as we knew it. I hope in my life time that it will become a day when racism does not plays a part [but] I believe it's always going be. It's just like crime. There's always going be crime.

> He was trying to get us to understand that this is a new day, that it's time to change the way we look at race and racism. I feel he is being sincere, more so than anybody we have heard. Every president mentions race. Some discuss it a bit and others a bit more. Bill Clinton always tried to make it as if race wasn't an issue. I don't know how that can be. Obama's speech is more authentic and sincere about [black people]. But he cannot change racists' views or opinions.

Many Trinitarians celebrated the fact that Obama's speech helped to quell the firestorm that had descended on Trinity along with the racist and anti-American language about Rev. Wright. But while the firestorm had died down (at least momentarily), giving Trinitarians a chance to take stock of the damages from the storm they had encountered, some spoke about the opportunities lost, such as the opportunity for the American people to gain an understanding of the black church and black people, to learn about black liberation theology and its significance to African Americans. Congregants contended that opportunities to have conversations with whites and other social and ethnic groups should have been encouraged as people observed the racial bifurcation. They argued that the reporting on Trinity should have opened up discussions that would consider larger social issues, like the school-to-prison pipeline, the failure of schools with large numbers of African American students, and the increasing lack of employment for black people. But although most of the topics they wanted discussed focused on black people, the overall sentiment was that they were prepared to listen and participate in discussions that would take other problems and issues into account in order to make life better for all.

## WRIGHT'S PRESS TOUR

On April 25, 2008, less than a month after Obama gave his "More Perfect Union" speech, which had lessened the media focus on Trinity, Jeremiah Wright began a three-day press tour that would make him the big newsmaker for the week of April 28 to May 4, 2008. The controversy that he created generated more news coverage than both Hillary Clinton and John McCain that week. During the week Hillary Clinton accounted for 41 percent of the campaign stories, McCain registered 14 percent, and Wright and Obama's relationship accounted for 42 percent.[8] Wright's press tour was designed to address a range of issues (the accusation that he was anti-American and unpatriotic, his sermons, the black church, Trinity Church, and his relationship with Obama) in order to rehabilitate Wright's public image.

The tour started on April 25 with *Bill Moyers Journal* on PBS. The interview on PBS was Wright's reentry into the media spotlight. In the hour-long interview with Moyers, Wright discussed the history of the African American church in a dignified, professorial, and genial manner and portrayed a much different character than the crazed caricature shown in the video clips on television and YouTube. He spoke of his two years as a marine and four years as a navy cardiopulmonary technician who cared for President Johnson after his gallbladder surgery. He spoke of the services at Trinity that he started to help the community since becoming senior pastor in 1972: women's groups, HIV ministries, and tutoring programs, among others. He was taking large steps toward demystifying the media image of him and putting in its place an image of a sophisticated, intelligent pastor. During the interview he explained that the "Not God bless America, God damn America" comment in his sermons was taken out of context. He said that he did not begrudge Obama for denouncing them, noting, "He's a politician, I'm a pastor, we speak to two different audiences. And he says what he has to say as a politician, I say what I have to say as a pastor. But they're two different worlds."[9]

The interview was followed by a speech at the NAACP annual meeting on April 27. Wright opened the speech calling attention to the NAACP's incomparable record as a champion in the fight against discrimination, racial prejudice, and unjust public policies. Within the context of the conference theme, "A Change Is Going to Come," he then spoke about the mis-education of black students and the need to change the ways they are taught, as well as the need to change conditions in society that divide people. He pointed out that the remarks in the videos of his sermons were taken out of context and viewed the wrong way by white viewers who were not familiar with the traditions of the black church. In closing, he stated he remains hopeful because "many are changing how they see others who are different." Wright's appearance at the NAACP generated only mild media attention; while he was not as erudite and soft spoken as he was when he did the Moyers interview, he was nevertheless professional and informative.[10]

On April 28 Wright delivered a lecture at the National Press Club in Washington, DC, that was followed by a question and answer period (Q&A). There was very little media coverage of the lecture itself, in which Wright spoke about the history of the black church and its centrality in lives of African American people. However, the Q&A session following the lecture was widely rebroadcast and caused CNN's Anderson Cooper to refer to

Wright as "Hurricane Jeremiah," who, for someone who supports Barack Obama, couldn't be doing any more damage to his candidate. Wright's performance at the Q&A reawakened the media focus on him and Obama. Trinitarians, like the rest of the public, saw the televised Q&A. Many of them were startled by Wright's behavior, and they were forced to consider questions about their beloved pastor that they had never before entertained.

During the Q&A Wright was a different person from the "professor" who delivered the lecture on the history of the black church. His demeanor was sarcastic, defiant, cocky, inflammatory, sometimes humorous, and at times vague with his snappy responses. He sidestepped questions about Louis Farrakhan and argued that "this is not an attack on Jeremiah Wright, this has nothing to do with Barack Obama, this is an attack on the black church."[11] He stated at least four times that he was speaking not for himself but for the black church that he believed had been viciously attacked by the media. Dana Milbank of the *Washington Post* offered his "Rough Sketch" on what took place:

> Speaking before an audience (and thirty television cameras) that included Marion Barry, Cornel West, Malik Zulu Shabazz of the New Black Panther Party, and Nation of Islam official Jamil Muhammad, Wright praised Louis Farrakhan, defended the view that Zionism is racism, accused the United States of terrorism, repeated his view that the government created the AIDS virus to cause the genocide of racial minorities, stood by other past remarks ("God damn America") and held himself out as a spokesman for the Black church in America.[12]

Most Trinitarians were glued to their televisions for each of Wright's performances. This rehabilitation tour in which he placed himself front and center in the 2008 presidential campaign made him the number one newsmaker in the week's political coverage. But he blew it, according to the majority of the Trinitarians interviewed. Trinitarians did not meld together the individual performances in the triathlon and offer up a single score, but instead compared and contrasted each performance, because they believed that the context, audience, and questions asked contributed to Wright's responses.

Congregants at the church at first had feelings of pride and admiration during the Moyers interview, which then turned to anxiety, frustration, and disbelief during the Q&A at the National Press Club. Many contrasted his performance at all three events, noting that at the Press Club Q&A he did not represent himself well:

> I thought the Bill Moyers interview was excellent, that he was right on point, and I think his composure was how it should have been. I believe he should have stopped after that interview. There was no need to go on. By the time he

got to the Press Club, he was frustrated and set up. He wanted to show them: "you will not make me conform to your world."

> If you go through that weekend, starting on Friday with the Bill Moyers interview, that was great. The Sunday night event in Detroit at the NAACP dinner was a mixed bag. He still was on top as far as I'm concerned. The Press Club thing was not so good for him; in terms of his image, it was disastrous.

Trinitarians supported the idea that Wright took the initiative to explain the controversy in his own words during the interview with Bill Moyers and that he used the speech at the NAACP event to let the mostly black audience know that he was not a "demon." He was not trying to upset Obama's run for the presidency. "At the first interview, he was explaining his situation. He's giving you the history as to what took place [at Trinity Church]; what initiated it. At the second interview [NAACP] he was trying to convince people 'I am not a demon. I did not preach to destroy world, [I am not anti-American].' [In the third interview] he got tired of trying to defend himself, tired of being called a N(word). At some point, you strike back."

Some congregants claimed that Wright's performance at the Press Club Q&A was because of his hurt and anger from being attacked by the media. His patience had run its course and he was fed up with hearing and seeing the negative statements about himself absent of context and with little or no discussion about the validity of his statements. Trinitarians argued that if he had stopped his lecture tour after the Bill Moyers interview, everything would have been better.

> Well, I'm going be honest. I think that the interview that Pastor Wright did with Moyers was very good and that should have been it. I think the Press Club was a bad choice; he should not have done it. I think at [the Press Club Q&A] things spiraled out of control. Rev got angry. He did the same thing that he does in the pulpit. But you can't do that on national TV. When he rants and raves in the pulpit, we understand. We get the message. We move on. You cannot do that in a broad context and that's when it spiraled out of control. I don't know what was going on, but I did recognize at that point he was taking it very personal. He was hurt, hurt, hurt, wounded, and I still think he's wounded personally. That's when it went awry.

> I think it wasn't necessarily that he meant to be mean. He had been hurt, he had been jumped on. All of the things had been insinuated about him. He had been brutalized.

> It wasn't anything towards Obama. He was expressing what he was feeling. I think the one [interview] with Bill Moyers was low key. He spoke truth to power. At the Press Club, it was like retaliation, but I don't really think it was retaliation; I think it was just that he had enough. He was fed up with all that had been said and what all had been done.

I recall the Q&A at the Press Club more than the Bill Moyers interview because I was really hurt. It was disappointing because it didn't sound like my Reverend Wright, my pastor. It sounded like he might have been exhausted . . . the movements, his facial expression, his hand expressions and the finger movement. I was disappointed. Not necessarily [with the] words, but it was the expressions on his face. I was disappointed.

"That's not the Rev. Wright I know." Being exhausted, exacerbated by the media's dogged attacks to paint him as a crazed anti-American, was too much, some argued, for a person who had earned an honorable discharge from the Marines and had cared for an ailing president: "It was a really rough week for him in terms of the preaching or speaking in different cities. He was very tired, burned out; by the time he got to the [Press Club] the weight on him was very heavy."

Why did he do it? Was it bad counsel? Some congregants argued it was because Wright received bad advice or did his own thing: "Let me answer it this way. Either Reverend Wright got bad counsel or he got good counsel and he ignored it, one of the two. He should not have done either one of the interviews. When all the flak hit the fan, he said he was going be quiet until June, after the last primary. THAT's what he should have done."

The media had been hostile, and Wright was walking into an iconic symbol of the institution, the National Press Club. When most people walk into the lion's den, they want friends with them who will have their backs. But when friends are the ones encouraging unsuitable behavior, the situation can get out of hand, which is what some Trinitarians argued was the case at the Q&A session. Such was the sentiment expressed by many congregants:

The moment I turned the television on I knew that it was not good. I blame the people who were around him, those who were cheering, applauding, and urging on the quick answers and the snaps (with the fingers). I think they told themselves that there was going be opposition [at the Press Club] so we're going to be ready to meet them head on.

I think there was a feeling about the Press Club, that it was really going to be antagonistic grounds. I believe some of the people thought that he was going to be attacked; that some people attending would be anti-Obama and anti-Wright. Therefore you had to have some Wright supporters. The Wright supporters became a cheering squad. That led to some of the responses, which some said were intemperate, and it made the young lady who was the moderator a sympathetic figure. A lot of stuff was heaped upon her simply because she asked him questions.

Although Trinitarians understood the reason the entourage accompanied Wright to the Press Club, they were dismayed and annoyed by the fraternity symbols (e.g., hand gestures) that Wright used during the Q&A.

> I saw on the front page of one of the newspaper papers—I can't remember which one—that had this picture of him, where he was doing something with his hands. My daughter says that he is speaking to the Omegas [a Greek fraternity]. He is a member and he was "throwing up the hoofs." It's something that they do when they are speaking to each other, but the way he was acting made him look like he was out of control.

> I call it my Saul Complex. When I saw Jeremiah at the Press Club, it was a person I had never seen before; maybe that part of him was always there but hidden. He made all of those Omega signs, all that stuff that he was doing; you think either this guy's totally lost it or he's bitter. [Because] Obama literally kicked [him] off of the bus. I think the Saul Complex set in because [Wright] thinks, here is a guy that I have nursed; I have been the surrogate father and he has put me down.

Some parishioners reasoned that Wright was taking the opportunity at the Press Club to separate himself from Obama. They argued that Wright did not want to give in to the demand for him to shut up or change and get in step with the Obama campaign. Some congregants argued that when you speak up as Wright did, you will be ganged up on by all involved, both friends and hatemongers, all of whom are more interested in the end result they want than in whether there is truth in your remarks. Therefore, your option is to fold or speak up.

> I'm clearer about the Press Club because I thought Reverend Wright was separating himself from the now President Barack Obama. I know Reverend Wright, [and he] always said what he felt. He never sugar coated; he always said I'm not changing because somebody from this church is running for president. I'm going to continue to bring the word the way I have been bringing it. That speaks volumes to me because we've seen so many times that when politicians have people around them that are outspoken, when media attention comes they try to cover it up. I think his strength and character as a man threatens some people. We live in a country where if you're not on my team, then you are a threat to my team. The Press Club was his way of separating himself from the candidate.

"A sad day" for the church and Rev. Wright is the way in which many Trinitarians described the Q&A at the Press Club. Some wondered if Wright's ego was running loose and if he was trying to damage Obama's presidential chances.

> Well, I think it was a very sad period in the church's history. I felt that
> Reverend Wright's behavior was uncharacteristic of a minister in the sense
> that he had built the church and he had not only given it a national presence but
> an international presence. I believe that he felt that he was bigger than the
> church and I also felt that perhaps subliminally he was trying to sabotage
> Barack Obama's chances of being president of the United States. Some of the
> things that he did were such that you had [to question] his motives. Why
> would he say things like this? Was his ego out of control?

However, some Trinitarians saw his ego as a source of strength and resistance for Trinity and himself in the face of an aggressive and persistent media. Rev. Wright, Trinitarians argued, is a very intelligent, gifted man, the master of several languages, a person who is a teacher and preacher, and someone who does not hold back on issues of social justice. That said, he has an ego (and not a small one). He does not lean back when he deals with racism in white power structures—the role of slavery in the development of the country, the orchestration of Jane and Jim Crow laws to keep blacks marginalized, and the neglect of federal, state, and local government officials in adhering to American's democratic principles of equality for black people. In addition, and more to the point, Wright was pushing back on the media that was depicting him as a crazed anti-American who not only hated white people but also had over the years encouraged his congregants to dislike white people. A Trinitarian asserted, "He has an ego and he wasn't going to let the white man get the best of him."

Some Trinitarians looked on the bright side. They were supportive of Wright and tried to explain his actions: "There were some things at the Press Club that might have been okay if he had not done all the moving around and throwing the signs. If he had phrased his comments in another way, it might have gone very well." Some argued that Wright should not have been silent: "I will answer it this way, a lot of us at Trinity love Pastor Wright like a mother loves her child. I feel that Pastor Wright is a prophet and you cannot silence a prophet." Some found no problem with Reverend Wright's performance during the Q&A: "Reverend Wright tells it like it is. He doesn't pull any punches with anybody. He's going to say what he's got to say to you whether you like it or not."

The range of these responses to the Q&A speaks to Trinitarians almost four years later still trying to understand why Wright went on the media tour, particularly at the time he did, and why his behavior changed between the Moyers interview and the Q&A at the National Press Club.

The press tour, especially the Q&A at the Press Club, swung the spotlight back on Trinity, but more specifically back on Wright. The media remained the culprit, but Wright had temporarily become the wrongdoer. The spotlight was on him. His supporters did not know what to think and his enemies were hoping he would continue to make a fool of himself. His actions at the Press

Club had given the media what they wanted: confirmation of the image—the single story—that the media had created: Obama's pastor as a crazed radical and Obama as guilty by association.

Trinitarians were not the only ones troubled by Wright's performance during the Q&A. The Obama team knew that they needed to address Wright's performance; otherwise, the controversy would become white-hot again and the momentum gained by the "More Perfect Union" speech would be lost. The presidential hopeful moved swiftly to get ahead of a possible full-blown resurgence of the controversy on race and anti-American senti-ment in comments he delivered in Hickory, North Carolina. In a sharp tone, he stated that the Rev. Wright of the Q&A is not the person he met twenty years ago and that his comments "were not only divisive but destructive . . . and end up giving comfort to those who prey on hate . . . and do not portray accurately the perspective of the black church." Additionally, Obama stated, "Some of the comments that Reverend Wright has made offend me and I understand why they offend the American people. . . . He does not speak for the campaign." Included in Obama's remarks was a pushback on particular comments: "When he states and then amplifies such ridiculous propositions as the U.S. government somehow being involved in AIDS, when he suggests that Minister Farrakhan somehow represents one of the greatest voices of the twentieth and twenty-first centuries, when he equates the United States' war-time efforts with terrorism, then there are no excuses. They offend me. They rightly offend all Americans. And they should be denounced, and that's what I'm doing very clearly and unequivocally here today."

These words caused Trinitarians to feel terribly distraught; they believed that they were observing the final "I can't take this anymore; I am out of here" break-up: "Barack was moving on and doing what he needed to do. It was like a child who had to choose between mother and father in a divorce. Members could feel the tension."

For a month the church proceeded to return to some degree of normalcy, with one eye on news reports about Obama: How was he doing in the polls? How were his speeches and interviews received? Did he say anything else about Trinity or Rev. Wright? What were the liberal and conservative media saying? Spontaneously, congregants would offer their reflections on the me-dia, especially television with particular attention to the cable channels. Their feelings about these networks were strong and unabashed. Congregants spoke about not watching Fox: "It is too painful, they lie. They make me want to throw the TV out of the window." "Fair and balanced; are they joking? They are the worst!" Some argued that CNN and MSNBC gave a fairer analysis of the situation and that their stories on Obama were less biased. They did not believe what some media pundits were arguing, "that Obama was receiving a free ride by a liberal press." Some even wondered, "What is fairness for a black man? What is the rubric used to make the judgment?" "I like CNN the best. They seem a bit fairer." "MSNBC in the evening seems to be pulling for Obama; [Chris] Matthews years ago predicted he would become president."

Despite the perceived greater level of fairness seen in these news outlets, some Trinitarians argued that there was a lack of representation of African American news anchors on all of the networks, which added to the myopic portrayal of Trinity Church and its congregants: "I like MSNBC too, but they need more than one black anchor. She's great, but why only one? And don't say they can't find anyone." Another Trinitarian, taking advantage of the direction of the discussion, added that they do have "guest commentators, but it's not enough; also our kids need role models. There is just a lot of obvious racism in the media."

While one eye was on the media, the church's other eye was searching for signs of Wright. They asked each other, "Who has seen him? How is he feeling? Is he coming to his office in church? What should we do to help?" Regardless of the congregants' feelings about his media appearances, they loved and admired Wright and wanted only the best for him. That said, the majority of their attention was on Obama and his pursuit of the presidency. Congregants were feeling good and thinking optimistically as the polls indicated that *their* presidential hopeful was doing very well: "I would call my girlfriend each night and we would watch the news together; sounds crazy, I know, but we were excited beyond belief." Discussions over the months about the possibility of Obama winning the presidency changed from wishful thinking and dreaming to "Is this really happening?" Among the older congregants, the musing was as follows: "We may not only see a black man in the White House in our lifetime but a black man who is our brethren; thank the Lord." "I can remember how excited we were and how proud we were. Then things took a negative turn."

"This is not a decision that I come to lightly, and frankly it's one that I made with some sadness. . . . Trinity was where I found Jesus Christ, where we were married, where our children were baptized. We have many friends among the 8,000 congregants. . . . It's clear that, now that I am a candidate for president, every time something is said in the church by anyone associated with Trinity, including guest pastors, the remarks will be imputed to me, even if they totally conflict with my long-held views, statements and principles." With these words, Barack Obama affirmed his resignation from Trinity Church on May 31, 2008.

The Obamas' departure from Trinity was motivated by controversial statements made by Reverend Michael Pfleger while delivering a guest sermon at Trinity Church on May 25, 2008. Chicago's activist Roman Catholic priest mocked Senator Hillary Clinton from the pulpit during his guest appearance and also stated that the former First Lady was a white elitist who felt entitled to the Democratic nomination. Footage of the sermon was circulated on the Internet, and the comments sparked mass public controversy.

Trinity Church made a statement on May 31 regarding Obama's resignation: "Trinity United Church of Christ was informed today that Senator Barack Obama and his family will no longer be members of our church. Though we are saddened by the news, we understand that it is a personal decision. We will continue to lift them in prayer and wish them the best as former members of our Trinity community."

Obama's resignation from Trinity Church set off a flurry of comments. Most Trinitarians had strong views about the reasons for Obama's resignation and they were not shy about expressing them. Nevertheless, looking across the range of comments, the parishioners mentioned three key motivations for the resignation: (1) smart politics, (2) media pressure, and (3) personal expediency on the part of Obama.

Many interviewees thought that the resignation was smart politics. The resignation was a wise political move because he had to leave the Trinity if he wanted to win the election.

> Barack did what he had to do in order to be president. If he had agreed with or had aligned himself with Pastor Wright he would have never gotten elected. They would have used that to tear him down. He made a very difficult decision, but it was necessary for him to do it.

> I knew he was going to have to resign if he wanted to be president. After Father Pfleger did his thing at the church, I think his advisors and everybody else were telling him that the best thing to do is to resign so he could put some distance between himself and Trinity. This was necessary if he wanted to win that election.

> I think it was more of a political thing. I don't think he left because of Father Pfleger.

> I wanted him to resign because I felt that if Obama resigns from Trinity Church [he] would have the opportunity to become president. I thought maybe if he didn't [resign] and Obama lost the election, Pastor Wright would be blamed. The media would turn it around and blame everything on Jeremiah.

The second common theme was that the media's power forced the resignation.

> Well, I was expecting it. I knew the media wasn't going to let him stay at Trinity. I figured he was just going to have to leave.

> I was sad because I really didn't feel he should have had to leave his church. What was even sadder, even to this day, I don't think they have chosen a

church home. I could be wrong, but the last thing I remember is that they hadn't chosen a church home in DC. Every other president has been free to go to church wherever they chose to go. So why should he have to be worried about where he's going to go to church on Sunday. He shouldn't have to go through that. If he picks a black church is that going to be wrong. If he picks a white church is that going to be wrong. He's caught in the middle. And that's not good.

"Got what I want, time to go": Some Trinitarians had sharp comments about Obama's resignation and argued that, now that Obama had gotten what he wanted and the things had gotten hot, he was ready to move on:

> Losing votes and not garnering votes [motivated his decision]. He got what he wanted. The church was leverage, the church was red meat, and the church was a core, a bedrock, something he could grow from. He knows he's got the black vote. I think in my heart he used the church. He got what he wanted from the church and it was time to move on. He was not going to [risk losing] any type of creditability with the white polis.

There was another feeling among some congregants—a feeling of being betrayed by Obama. They believed that Obama did not stand up for Trinity or Rev. Wright:

> When all this came [down] I felt he never really stood up for the church. He didn't say anything about our feelings or how we felt. I just felt betrayed; how could you do this to your pastor? According to his book *Dreams from My Father* he said he didn't know who he was. He was sitting in the church and he just cried. Pastor Wright helped him to find out who he was. [He brought] him to his senses.

> I was sort of hurt by it. I thought that he should have stayed. I don't think I would have left my church; why should I?

> I thought it was so sad. I felt bad about it.

Despite these comments, the overall consensus was that Obama wisely did what he had to do. While a few congregants were upset with the decision, they were not deeply bitter. Theirs was not a resentful anger, nor an "I want to get you back" anger. It was "We understand that he did what he had to do or thought he needed to do." Trinitarians had Obama's back; they supported him, and they saw the more fundamental issue: the elimination of Shadrach's legacy from black children and black people's thinking forever: "BARACK, you have 'got self.'"

## HEALING

Despite the challenges of the last few years, the congregants continually expressed a sense of love and community for one another in their church family, including their love of Trinity Church as a black church.

A few congregants asserted that the healing process was completed: "Yes Trinity has healed. We pressed on. We just kept doing what we were doing, we didn't back down, we didn't stop; and then Reverend Moss was able to carry the torch just like Reverend Wright did. That's the reason we have healed." "I think Trinity has healed. We just picked up ourselves and kept moving."

Although it has been more than three years, some Trinitarians still talk about healing as an ongoing process and cannot suggest a time when things will be completely normal again, or if that will ever be the case. The need to fight for survival brings with it a different perspective on how to view the world, and when that perspective is shaped by experiences from an encounter with one of the most powerful institutions in the country in a battle for the most powerful position in the world, the rewind button cannot be pushed to return to yesteryear's peace and calm.

> I think that we are trying to heal because it's like when someone walks up behind you and hits you. You are not ready [and] you wonder why it happened; you wonder why they had the nerve to come and hit you from behind. At 75 years old I understand how white people work pretty much. We have just gone through what always happened to us when we don't fit into what they think we're suppose to do, be, and say.

> I think we're healing. We are resilient people.

> I think Trinity is still in the healing process but it's not as nearly traumatic as it was.

Good medicine for healing was an event that came about when a crowd of over a quarter of a million people jammed Grant Park and the surrounding area in Chicago, and Obama addressed the nation for the first time as its president-elect at 11:00 pm Central Standard Time. Another healing moment was when nearly 37.8 million Americans sitting in their homes and offices listened as President Barack Obama recited the oath of office and gave his inaugural speech between the hours of 10:00 am and 5:00 pm Eastern Standard Time on January 20, 2009.[13] "We had an inauguration party at the church and wanted everyone to come. We had a big screen in the atrium [of the church]. We had food and our own little inauguration party. [The atmosphere] was real joyous: cheering, clapping, and crying, all of that at certain points. You couldn't see a dry eye and you could hear a needle drop. It was very, very nice. We had a good time that day."

## WAS HE OR WASN'T HE?

One constant question throughout the firestorm of the Wright controversy concerned Obama's attendance at Trinity Church: Was he there? When was he there? Was he in the church on the day Rev. Wright said "God Damn America"? Trinitarians on a whole were less in agreement on this question than any other. They were not hot and bothered about if and when Obama was at Trinity. They understood the purpose and significance of the question as well as its political implication. That said, they also saw it as further validation of the media's (and America's) lack of knowledge about the black church and particularly Trinity Church with Rev. Wright as senior pastor.

Reverend Wright was Reverend Wright each time he preached, and black liberation theology was the ideology that drove his sermons. If some were in disagreement with black liberation theology and Trinity's motto of "Unashamedly Black and Unapologetically Christian," they could always find something negative to support the framing of a single biased story about what church in America is supposed to be. In addition, Trinitarians were not particularly mindful of Obama's presence because each and every congregant was special, and the Lord was the really special person.

> I guess I saw them [Barack and Michelle] about three times together with the children.

> Yes, I would see him. I can tell you exactly where he sat. The only reason you knew he was there is because Reverend Wright would say we have Senator Obama in the house today. Other than that, you didn't know he was there. He was never ushered to the front of the church or anything; he would just come in like anybody else.

> I recall seeing President Obama coming into the church during his campaigning. He had an entourage of security around him. He was extremely well received. He is a black man running for president, a young attractive man, acceptable in all aspects, totally qualified. It was time that we put an African American into office.

> I never saw him in church. If I saw him, I didn't know him. Remember, we had three services. I don't know which service [they attended]. They probably went to the 7:00 am service. Being in the choir I would go to the 11:00 am service and the 6:00 pm service and sometimes the 7:00 am service. Some congregants say they never saw him in church. We laughed about it.

Being on the Praise Team and being able to see everyone [I can say that] when Barack says that he was not there for those particular sermons, I recall that they were not there on those days.

I never saw President Obama, Michelle, or the family in church. I've asked other people, and some people say the same thing; that either they didn't see them or they only saw them on occasion.

## THE TRINITY LEGACY

Obama's take-away as a congregant at Trinity Church is evident to those who watch him perform his presidential duties. As one interviewee said, "When President Obama did the eulogy at the funeral for the little girl that was shot in Arizona, when Gabriele Giffords was shot, the eulogy was so powerful to us because he did it just like the order of service for eulogy at Trinity. His remarks were in the order, from biblical to how it relates to the world, to the God in that little girl, and the God in the rest of us. The outline of his remarks comes out of the teaching he received at Trinity."

Wright's influence and friendship with Obama is also part of Trinity's legacy. At times, Trinitarians spoke about their relationship without hesitation; at other times they seemed not to want to go there, because it was a reminder of a bitter break-up. Most responses captured the following sentiment:

I think Reverend Wright was impressed with this young gentleman. He was impressed by his style, mannerisms, his eloquence and articulation; the type of sashay that he held, his type of panache. He loved him like a father loves a son. He was moved by his young presence and his ideals. He became a surrogate son and Jeremiah brought him into the fold. Obama needed a core base and our greatest core base has been the black church of America. Everything is funneled through the black church of America. If you ain't got nothing, you still have the black church and I believe Obama's destiny was preordained and worldly scripted. He was smart enough to realize, I need a core. I need a foundation. I need some place to grow from. So I think he understood the game and he played the game wonderfully well. He linked onto Jeremiah and I think everything took fruition at Trinity. He was embraced by the membership.

## THE TELLING OF AN AMERICAN STORY

Some pages ago, we stated that this book was written to fill a void in America's story. Blacks across the decades have argued to have their history and culture included, as it rightfully should be, as part of America's story. On the numerous occasions when an interview was completed but the coffee in the cups was still hot, conversations turned to other things of interest. One day after an interview session, this question emerged: "How would you like to see this Moment written about in the history books? If your son or daughter, or your granddaughter or grandson, came to you with two friends—one white and one Latino—and said, 'We are responsible for preparing a report on the 2008 presidential election and we wish to prepare our report on President Obama and Trinity Church. And, because you are a member of Trinity, may we interview you for our report?' What would you tell them?" Two "okays," two nodded heads, and one "hum, hum" communicated that all of the coffee lovers understood the question. The second part of the question was this: "Would you speak to your African American child about Trinity and Obama differently than you would to the white and Latino students?" The response was unanimous: "Say the same thing to ALL the kids: black, Latino, and white."

> I will tell my fourteen-year-old grandson and his two friends the same thing, the truth. I would tell them [that Obama] was a member, he, his wife and family for over 20 years. I will say I met them at the church on several occasions. He wasn't just there toward the elections or when he was a senator. He and his family came often. They enjoyed the services. He was the delight of Reverend Wright. I would tell them that Reverend Wright was concerned not only with the people at Trinity, but people in general, especially black people. He stressed education, not so much for education's sake but so you can you use education to help somebody else. I would want them [to know] how the media came in and took some of the sermons and took them out of context and tried to destroy [Trinity].

What the Trinitarians would tell the students varied only in choice of words and phrases they used to say that Trinity Church was disrespected by the media.

> I would like the history books to say the projected perception of Trinity was wrong. The media tried to portray Trinity as this racist church, that it didn't care about America or didn't like white folks. I would like for the history books to say that some people in power tried to influence the American people about a black church.

> My fifteen-year-old daughter and her friends would hear the same story. I would tell them that white society did not want to hear about the things that black people feel. They do not want to hear that we have a value system that helps propel us up from the bottom of the barrel. It teaches us how to get along in a white society and what we have to do as black people to propel ourselves. I would tell them that they were taking some of the speeches that Jeremiah made out of context, [saying he is] anti-white. But what Reverend Wright was

doing while he was the minister of Trinity was trying to be pro-black instead of how society sees us, as negative blacks.

As we noted above, congregants spoke directly and with great pride because this question, more than any other, had to do with their children and their children's children and their friends learning America's story:

I would like for it to be accurate. I wouldn't want anything to be watered down. I would want the truth to be told.

I would tell my daughter and her friends how proud we were the night that Obama was at Grant Park. How our church was really behind him in so many ways. My daughter understands what happened with the media, that it tried to tear him down and Trinity down. I would tell them it was a proud moment in our lives and we just can't let the media take that away from us.

I would explain the presence of the media first of all and how they made it more negative than positive. They wanted to make Reverend Wright the bad guy. No one from the media could actually understand that sermon. I would tell them it should have been a much more joyous time for Trinity and Obama, how the church could have celebrated more with his candidacy and his winning the presidential race. I think about the times [when] Obama probably had a need or wanted to come to church, to Trinity, where he had belonged for so many years and couldn't. I'm sure during the campaign he had a spiritual need.

I would tell them that the first African American President of the United States met up with a lot of controversy, people trying to say he was not a legal American citizen and saying that he was a terrorist. But that portraying him as anything other than a legitimate American would be wrong.

I'd have to explain to them that Trinity should not have been portrayed like it was on the television and in the press. I would tell them that Trinity is African centered and that there is a great deal of love and pride in the church.

## FINAL QUESTIONS

As the coffee lovers were taking their last few sips, we had an opportunity to hear their reflections on one additional comment made by the media during the controversy: "Trinity is a racist church." The media argument that Trinity is a "black anti-American church" was seen by the congregants as a narrow way of thinking about and purposefully publicly framing a black church. This narrow framing, the congregants argued, was based upon a single story of the black church in America. Such a single story, in the minds and hands of the media, made Trinity vulnerable to acts of racism and/or sloppy, biased reporting, as well as causing congregants to have to take time away from the mission and duty of the church in order to develop counter-acts of peaceful resistance. So now, given the opportunity to speak truth to power, here is what the Trinitarians said:

> I would say to them [white Americans] that Trinity is a church that is pro-black and being pro-black does not mean that you are anti-white or anti-anything; that would be my response. We are definitely pro-black but we are not racist, not even a little bit.

> Absolutely untrue and I will tell you why. At one time Trinity had a nun in the choir. I've always seen white people in the church. They are frequent visitors. Nobody was ever escorted out. There's a white gentlemen in the choir now. White people have always been welcomed and they come. Can you imagine white people coming if that was true? I can't. What would be the purpose?

## ARE WE READY TO LISTEN?

In this chapter, the unheard voices at Trinity Church spoke. Their comments help more fully address questions about the African American church (and in particular Trinity Church) and Rev. Wright than any outside reporting could. Many reading *The Moment* may come away with more questions. Now, more than ever, we do not need to hear a single story; we need a more comprehensive and fuller story about issues and events. As one media critic put it, "Access to instant news has become so indispensable to modern society that major media companies now wield unprecedented influence over public thought. The media amplify those events they wish to while exiling others to the shadows; they fashion political and popular heroes one day only to tear them down the next; they interpret the meaning of the most earth-shaking or insignificant incident before our morning coffee or commute back home."[14]

Now that we have heard the voices of the Trinitarians, how has this changed your perception of the Moment: the media, Barack Obama, Reverend Wright, the black church, and the Trinitarians themselves? Does this differ from what you saw and thought about in 2008? What will this mean for how we see this moment in history? If your view is different, we must admit that current educational standards are failing us when it comes to including the history, culture, and contributions of the various groups that make up this country. Our current curricula perpetuate a singular notion of what it means to be American; it "others" all citizens and residents of this country who are excluded from this single story.

Questions that apply to education apply equally to the media. Are all voices given equal privilege in our society, or are some marginalized? What are the motivating factors influencing the content that people receive? Who is telling the story, and whose point of view is the shaping the telling of the story?

That said, we can see, with the information available through social media and other venues, that agency is within all of us. We all have the responsibility to see to it that education and the media do a better job serving everyone, and we must continually question the information that we receive and seek a more complete story, and not a single story. Through social media and networks, each of us has the opportunity to get our message out and counter or complete the single stories that continue to be perpetuated. It is a challenge to enforce our agency as everyday people in this era when the shouts and cries of individuals and groups that are "othered" are drowned out by money, corporations, and so-called big people who only want their way at any cost. Everyday Americans must use their intellectual resources and insist through our daily behavior that we are not passive spectators of events taking place around us but are critical inquirers into what is happening. Sir Francis Bacon in the sixteenth century said, "Knowledge is power." It is up to us—everyday people—to investigate, share, engage each other, and communicate this power to one another in through the technology we use daily. Mystification of events, groups of people, and individuals should no longer be accepted with the research tools that many of us carry on our person or next to us twenty-four hours a day.

Another fundamental truth is the fact that a moral tenet has been pushed to the side—the tenet of respect for one another in recognition of our shared humanity. This recognition demands mutual compassion and caring for one another and a willingness to listen to what others have to say about their experiences and beliefs. This was lost during the firestorm and continues to be lost on many occasions to this day.

There are more unheard voices waiting to speak. Are we ready to listen?

# Epilogue

The deadline for the manuscript of *The Moment* was May 18, 2012. This date fell on a Friday, so on May 16 we were feeling pretty good about pressing the "send now" key and enjoying a sigh of relief. Earlier that week we read the *New York Times* article that spoke about an attempt to revise the Reverend Wright and Barack Obama overture that took center stage during much of the 2008 presidential campaign. We decided not to press the send button and sit tight. Three days later, on Saturday, the story still had legs. Television pundits and newspaper opinion writers were having a field day. An article by Kathleen Parker in the Saturday *Washington Post* (published the day before) asked, "Is Mentioning Rev. Wright Racist?" and another article, one by Michael D. Shear published on May 18, 2012, in the *New York Times* (online), was titled "Race and Religion Rear Their Head." In the article Shear wrote that "events Thursday [referring to a *New York Times* article that revealed that Republican strategists and financiers were planning to rekindle questions about Wright] suggest that it does not take much to divert the presidential campaign conversation back into the sensitive and politically dangerous questions of Mr. Obama's race, his religion, and the place of his birth." Shear also correctly noted that "the issues of race and religion never go completely away, at least in some extreme quarters of the American electorate." But watching the scant attention given to the story on the Sunday talk shows suggested that it had lost its momentum. Good! An idea born out of some hard-boiled politics but mostly out of a high level of racism was being rejected. Yet, as we watched the reasons given for the rejection (e.g., people now know the president, this is old news, some consultants trying to make money, Obama already distanced himself from Wright), the one that received very little attention was that it was a *single story* told during the 2008 presidential campaign about Reverend Wright, Barack Obama, and

Trinity Church. The rhetoric and the *story* remained the same now and continued to characterize Wright as Obama's radical, anti-American pastor. Although more than three years have passed, there seems to be little acknowledgment of threat to democracy that from come from telling a single story about a black church and a black pastor. There also seems to be a lack of interest in an honest examination of the scorched earth in order to assess the resiliency of the inhabitants and the sacred space where the media firestorm occurred. Such actions undermine America's call for "unity and diversity."

# Interview Questions

These are the questions we used to begin and guide the interviews. That said, the Trinitarians often took hold of the conversations and led us to new insights in what came to be very fruitful discussions.

Interviews generally began with the following introduction: "We want to take you back to the time when President Obama was campaigning for election, especially during the time of April 2008 to November 2008. We have questions for you based on your experiences as a member of Trinity Church and your thoughts about some of the events that took place from April 2008 to November 2008."

1. Tell us about your history with Trinity Church.

   a. How long have you been a member?
   b. What attracted you to Trinity Church?
   c. What has been your involvement with the church? What roles have you played?

2. Tell us about your relationship/interactions with the Obamas.

   a. Have your relationship/views changed?

3. What do you remember about President Obama's campaign for the presidency?

   a. Have your views about the campaign changed over time?
   b. If so, how?

4. What do you remember about Reverend Wright during the time of campaign?

    a. Have your views about the actions of Reverend Wright changed since the campaign?
    b. If so, how?

5. Specifically share with us your thoughts about the following video clips:

    a. "Confusing God and Government" speech
    b. Obama's "More Perfect Union" speech (race speech)
    c. Reverend Wright's National Press Club speech

6. What are your reflections on these events?

    a. As a member of Trinity Church?
    b. As an African American?
    c. As a citizen of the United States?

7. How would you like to see this event—this moment in time—portrayed in U.S. history books?

# Notes

## INTRODUCTION

1. Thomas Carlyle, "Lecture V [May 19, 1840]: The Hero as Man of Letters," *Johnson, Rousseau, Burns: Heroic in History* (Release date: February 15, 2007, EBook #20585), 149.

2. W. E. B. Du Bois, *The Soul of Black Folks*, quoted in Christopher R. Reed, *Black Chicago's First Century, Volume 1: 1833–1900* (Columbia: University of Missouri Press, 2005), 9.

3. Robin Kelley, "'We Are Not What We Seem': Rethinking Black Working-Class Opposition in Jim Crow South," *Journal of American History* 80, no. 1 (June 1993): 75–112.

4. P. N. Stern, "Why Study History?" American Historical Association, 1998, http://www.historians.org/pubs/free/WhyStudyHistory.htm, retrieved July 8, 2011.

5. Stern, "Why Study History?"

6. Kelley, "'We Are Not What We Seem.'"

7. Kelley, "'We Are Not What We Seem.'"

8. Howard Zinn, Declarations of Independence, http://zinnedproject.org/about/a-people%e2%80%99s-history-a-people%e2%80%99s-pedagogy, retrieved August 12, 2011.

9. Chimamanda Adichie, "The Danger of a Single Story" (TEDTalk), July 25, 2009, http://www.ted.com/talks/chimamanda_adichie_the_danger_of_a_single_story.html.

10. Barack Obama, *The Audacity of Hope* (New York: The River Press, 2006), 99–100.

## PROLOGUE

1. Richard Wright, *12 Million Black Voices* (New York: Viking, 1941), xix, xx.

2. Stephen Tuck, *We Ain't What We Ought To Be* (Cambridge, MA: Belknap Press, Harvard University, 2010).

3. Quoted in Philip S. Foner, *The Voice of Black America: Major Speeches by Negroes in the United States, 1797–1900* (New York: Capricorn Books, 1975), 46.

# 1. BACK TO THE MOMENT

1. Edward Said, *The End of the Peace Process: Oslo and After* (New York: First Vintage Books, 2001), 283.

2. Thomas Carlyle, "Lecture V, The Hero as Man of Letters: Johnson, Rousseau, Burn," in *On Heroes, Hero-Worship, and the Heroic in History: Six Lectures, Reported with Emendations and Additions* (London: J. M. Dent & Sons, 1908), http://www.gutenberg.org/files/20585/20585-h/20585-h.htm, retrieved July 21, 2012.

3. Oscar Wilde, "The Soul of Man under Socialism," *Fortnightly Review* 49 (February 1891, 290): 292–319, OCLC 2158602, retrieved July 7, 2011.

4. Rory Brown and Neil Thackray, "Journalism Ethics and Standards," *The Media Briefing*, http://www.themediabriefing.com/issues/journalism-ethics-and-standards, last updated 2012.

5. Christopher De Santis, ed., *Langston Hughes and the Chicago Defender* (Urbana: University of Illinois Press, 1995), 25.

6. St. Clair Drake and Horace R. Cayton, *Black Metropolis: A Study of Negro Life in a Northern City* (New York: Harcourt, Brace, 1945), 401–2.

7. Bill Kovach, "Can Democracy Survive 21st Century Journalism?" 2006, http://www.concernedjournalists.org/can-democracy-survive-21st-century-journalism, retrieved July 28, 2011.

8. Kovach, "Can Democracy Survive."

9. Bill Kovach, "CCJ's Comment to the FCC on the Future of the Media," May 4, 2010, http://rjionline.org/ccj/research/ccjs-comment-fcc-future-media, retrieved July 27, 2011.

10. Juan Gonzalez and Joseph Torres, *News for All the People* (New York: Verso, 2011), 2–3.

11. Walter Lippmann, quoted in Gonzalez and Torres, *News for All the People.*

12. Other hard-boiled events include May 19, 2008—Obama "lay off my wife"; May 29, 2008—"Is Obama Wright" wearing of flagpin controversy; June—Father Pfleger speaks at Trinity; July 2008—McCain accuses Obama of playing "race card"; and September 2008—"lipstick on a pig" comment.

13. Media sources used for readers' comments include the *Huffington Post*, the *New York Times*, the *Washington Post*, *ABC News*, *CNN*, *Fox News*, *Black Commentator*, National Public Radio, the Public Broadcasting Station, the Pew Research Center's Project for Excellence in Journalism, the *Wall Street Journal*, and MSNBC. Readers' comments are not directly attributed to the news sources they were posted on because we feel this would change the reading of these comments. In addition, the comments are representative of readers' posts across media outlets and they should be read as such.

14. Brian Ross, "Obama's Pastor: God Damn America, U.S. to Blame for 9/11," ABC, March 13, 2008, http://abcnews.go.com/Blotter/DemocraticDebate/story?id=4443788&page=1#.T4cqNo5xU.

15. Ross, "Obama's Pastor."

16. According to what we learned, ABC purchased the videotapes of Reverend Wright Jr.'s sermons from Trinity Church.

17. Jeremiah Wright, "Confusing God and Government," April 13, 2003, quoted in Roland Martin, "The Full Story behind Wright's 'God Damn America' Sermon," CNN.com, March 21, 2008, http://ac360.blogs.cnn.com/2008/03/21/the-full-story-behind-wright%E2%80%99s-%E2%80%9Cgod-damn-america%E2%80%9D-sermon.

18. "America's Chickens Are Coming Home to Roost!" September 16, 2001, http://www.fireandreamitchell.com/rev-wright/americas-chickens-are-coming-home-to-roost.

19. Anthony Smith, quoted in Gonzalez and Torres, *News for All the People*, 1.

20. James Baldwin, "Autobiographical Notes" (1952), in *Notes of a Native Son* (Boston: Beacon Press, 1955).

21. "PEJ Campaign Coverage Index: March 10–16, 2008: Democrats Media Narrative Roiled by Racial Tensions," Pew Research Center's Project for Excellence in Journalism, www.journalism.org/node/10210.

22. Mark Jurkowitz, "Democrats' Media Narrative Roiled by Racial Tensions," PEJ Campaign Coverage Index: March 10–16, 2008, Pew Research Center's Project for Excellence in Journalism, http://www.journalism.org/node/10210.

23. Jose Antonio Vargas, "Internet Congregation Rresponds in Many Voices," *Washington Post*, March 19, 2008.

24. Vargas, "Internet Congregation."

25. Mary Ann Akers, "Obama Disavows Pastor's Remarks," *Washington Post*, March 14, 2008, http://voices.washingtonpost.com/sleuth/2008/03/obama_reacts_to_controversial.html.

26. Ed O'Keefe, "Obama: Wright Wrong," ABC, March 14, 2008, http://abcnews.go.com/blogs/politics/2008/03/obama-wright-wr.

27. "Obama Condemns Pastor's Statements," *New York Times*, The Caucus blog, March 14, 2008, http://thecaucus.blogs.nytimes.com/2008/03/14/obama-condemns-pastors-statements/.

28. Barack Obama, "On My Faith and My Church," March 14, 2008, http://www.huffingtonpost.com/barack-obama/on-my-faith-and-my-church_b_91623.html, retrieved July 10, 2012.

29. Obama's CNN interview took place on March 15, 2008, and was conducted by Anderson Cooper on the program *Anderson Cooper 360*. This video is not currently available online.

30. Steve Brusk and Alex Mooney, "Church: Obama Ex-Pastor Is under Unfair Attack," CNN.com, March 17, 2008, http://articles.cnn.com/2008-03-16/politics/jeremiah.wright_1_sermons-wright-black-boy?_s=PM:POLITICS.

31. Brusk and Mooney, "Church: Obama Ex-Pastor."

32. Eli Saslow, "Congregation Defends Obama's Ex-Pastor," *Washington Post*, March 18, 2008.

33. Saslow, "Congregation Defends Obama's Ex-Pastor."

34. Saslow, "Congregation Defends Obama's Ex-Pastor."

35. Martin Luther King Jr., "'I Have a Dream," speech delivered in Washington, DC, August 28, 1963, http://changingminds.org/analysis/i_have_a_dream.htm, retrieved August 23, 2011.

36. Saslow, "Congregation Defends Obama's Ex-Pastor."

37. Gao Xingjian, "The Case for Literature," 2000 Nobel Prize Lecture.

38. J. Zeleny, "Obama Urges U.S. to Grapple with Race Issue," *New York Times*, March 19, 2008, http://www.nytimes.com/2008/03/19/us/politics/19obama.html.

39. Zeleny, "Obama Urges U.S."

40. Zeleny, "Obama Urges U.S."

41. Mark Jurkowitz, "The Pastor, the Candidate, and the Speech Lead the News," Pew Research Center's Project for Excellence in Journalism, Campaign Cover Index, March 7–23, 2008, http://www.journalism.org/node/10319.

42. Jurkowitz "The Pastor, the Candidate."

43. Zeleny, "Obama Urges U.S."

44. Zeleny, "Obama Urges U.S."

45. Zeleny, "Obama Urges U.S."

46. Patrick Healy, "Clinton on Obama's Speech: I Haven't Heard It," *New York Times*: The Caucus blog, March 18, 2008, http://thecaucus.blogs.nytimes.com/2008/03/18/clinton-on-obamas-speech-i-havent-heard-it/.

47. Fox News, March 19, 2008, Frank Luntz breaks down Obama's race speech, Sean Hannity.

48. Fox News, March 19, 2008.

49. Fox News, March 19, 2008.

50. Ariel Alexovich, "Blogtalk: Obama's Race Speech," *New York Times*, March 18, 2008.

51. Alexovich, "Blogtalk: Obama's Race Speech."

52. Jurkowitz, "The Pastor, the Candidate."

53. Jurkowitz, "The Pastor, the Candidate."

54. Gao Xingjian, "The Case for Literature."

55. Gao Xingjian, "The Case for Literature."

56. Alexander Mooney, "Obama: Wright Flap Has 'Shaken Me Up,'" CNN.com, March 19, 2008, http://articles.cnn.com/2008-03-19/politics/obama.interview_1_obama-florida-and-michigan-race-and-politics?_s=PM:POLITICS.

57. Kate Phillips, "Wright Defends the Church and Blasts the Media," *New York Times*: The Caucus blog, April 28, 2008, http://thecaucus.blogs.nytimes.com/2008/04/28/rev-wright-defends-church-blasts-media.

58. Quotes from the transcript are presented here rather than people's comments in the media because, unlike Obama's speech, this interview received less media attention and did not have the same amount of commentary in the social media and news networks.

59. Phillips, "Wright Defends."

60. Phillips, "Wright Defends."

61. *CNN Politics*, "Obama Quits Church, Citing Controversies," May 31, 2008, http://articles.cnn.com/2008-05-31/politics/obama.church_1_obama-controversial-sermons-father-pfleger?_s=PM:POLITICS.

62. Daily News Staff, "Obama Quits Church after Long Controversy," *NY Daily News*, May 31, 2008, http://articles.nydailynews.com/2008-05-31/news/29433794_1_chicago-s-trinity-united-church-barack-obama-longtime-pastor.

63. Clarissa Pinkola Estes, "Senator Obama's Press Conference About Resigning from Trinity," *The Moderate Voice*, May 31, 2008, http://themoderatevoice.com/20073/senator-obamas-statement-about-resigning-from-trinity.

64. Lynn Sweet, "Obama Says in No Hurry to Find New Church: 'This Was One I Didn't See Coming,'" *Chicago Sun-Times*, May 31, 2008, http://blogs.suntimes.com/sweet/2008/05/obama_says_in_no_hurry_to_find.html#more.

65. Sweet, "Obama Resigns from Trinity."

66. ABC News, "Obama Quits His Church," May 31, 2008, http://abcnews.go.com/blogs/politics/2008/05/obama-quits-his.

## 2. RACE, MIGRATION, AND POLITICS IN THE WINDY CITY

1. Christopher R. Reed, *Black Chicago's First Century, Vol. 1: 1833–1900* (Columbia: University of Missouri Press, 2005).

2. Douglas Burns, "Why Barack Obama Will Win the Iowa Caucuses," *Carroll Daily Times Herald*, January 2, 2008.

3. David Yepsen, "The Illinois Caucus," *ABC News/Politics; Des Moines Register*, December 1, 2007.

4. White abolitionists were active on the behalf of the black migrants, but African Americans still had to confront segregation in schools, hotel, transportation, and restaurants.

5. Mary J. Herrick, *The Chicago Schools* (Beverly Hills, CA: Sage, 1971).

6. Dianne M. Pinderhughes, *Race and Ethnicity in Chicago Politics* (Urbana: University of Illinois Press, 1987).

7. M. W. Homel, *Down from Equality: Black Children and the Public Schools, 1920–1941* (Chicago: University of Illinois Press, 1984).

8. A. Fairclough, *Black Teachers in the Segregated South: A Class of Their Own* (Cambridge, MA: The Belknap Press, Harvard University Press, 2007); D. Douglas, *Jim Crow Moves North: The Battle over Northern School Segregation, 1865–1954* (New York: Cambridge University Press, 2005).

9. A. M. Knupfer, *The Chicago Black Renaissance and Women's Activism* (Urbana: University of Illinois Press, 2006), 75.

10. "Jim Crow Laws: Illinois," http://www.jimcrowhistory.org/scripts/jimcrow/lawsoutside.cgi?state=Illinois, June 12, 2001.

11. C. A. Grant, "The Multicultural Evaluation of Some Second and Third Grade Textbook Readers: A Survey Analysis," *Journal of Negro Education* 50, no. 1 (Winter 1981): 63–74; R. Butterfield et al., "Multicultural Analysis of a Popular Basal Reading Series in the International Year of the Child, *Journal of Negro Education* 48 (Summer 1979): 382–89.

12. Grant, "Multicultural Evaluation"; Butterfield et al., "Multicultural Analysis."

13. James R. Grossman, *Land of Hope* (Chicago: University of Chicago Press, 1989).

14. Richard Wright, "Introduction," in St. Clair Drake and Horace R. Cayton, *Black Metropolis: A Study of Negro Life in a Northern City* (New York: Harcourt, Brace, 1945), vii.

15. Abraham Epstein, *The Negro Migrant in Pittsburgh* (New York: Arno Press, 1969), 13.

16. Wright, "Introduction," vii.

17. Richard Wright, *12 Million Black Voices* (New York: Thunder's Mouth Press, 1941).

18. Wright, *12 Million Black Voices*, 108

19. Wright, *12 Million Black Voices*, 108.

20. Gwendolyn Brooks, *Selected Poems* (New York: Harper & Row, 1944), 3. Reprinted by consent of Brooks Permissions.

21. Wright, *12 Million Black Voices*, 92.

22. Michael Homel, *Down from Equality: Black Chicagoans and the Public Schools, 1920–1941* (Champaign: University of Illinois Press, 1984), 30.

23. Mary Pattillo, *Black on the Block: The Politics of Race and Class in the City* (Chicago: University of Chicago Press, 2007).

24. Patillo, *Black on the Block.*

25. Dick Simpson, quoted in David Bernstein, "Daley vs. Daley," ChicagoMag.com, September 2008, http://www.chicagomag.com/Chicago-Magazine/September-2008/Daley-vs-Daley/index.php?cparticle=6&siarticle=5#artanc, retrieved December 21, 2011.

26. Robert Crawford, quoted in Bernstein, "Daley vs. Daley," 6.

27. Lois Wille, quoted in Bernstein, "Daley vs. Daley," 6.

28. Tristram Hunt, "Barack Obama Should Swap Chicago for Phoenix," *London Times*, June 20, 2008, http://ray-theporch.blogspot.com/2010/10/barack-obama-should-swap-chicago-for.html.

29. The "Black Belt" was a term used by sociologists and vice commissions to highlight delinquency, dependency, and crime. The change of the name to Bronzeville brought with it deep political and social significance for the residents. See Anne Meis Knupfer, *The Chicago Black Renaisssance and Women's Activism* (Urbana: University of Illinois Press, 2006).

30. "African Americans," *Encyclopedia of Chicago*, www.encyclopedia.chicagohistory.org/pages/2402.html, retrieved June 2, 2011.

31. Wright, "Introduction," xix.

32. Katie Geneva Cannon, *Katie's Canon: Womanism and the Soul of the Black Community* (New York: Continuum Publishing, 1995).

33. Jonathan Mark, "Eugenics," http://personal.uncc.edu/jmarks/eugenics/eugenics.html, retrieved March 11, 2012.

34. Wright, *12 Million Black Voices*, 103.

35. Cannon, *Katie's Canon*, 51.

36. Sharon Harley and Rosalyn Terborg-Penn, *The Afro-American Woman: Struggles and Images* (Baltimore: Black Classic Press, 1997), 53.

37. Isabel Wilkerson, *The Warmth of Other Suns: The Epic Story of America's Great Migration* (New York: Random House, 2010).

38. James Grossman, *Land of Hope: Chicago, Black Southerners, and the Great Migration* (Chicago: University of Chicago Press, 1991), 8.

39. Alain Locke, ed., *The New Negro* (New York: Albert and Charles Boni, 1925).

40. Grossman, *Land of Hope.*

41. Grossman, *Land of Hope*, 8.

42. Grossman, *Land of Hope.*

43. Grossman, *Land of Hope.*

44. Grossman, *Land of Hope.*

45. Reed, *Black Chicago's First Century*, 121.

46. Reed, *Black Chicago's First Century*, 40.

47. Richard Wright, *Black Boy (American Hunger)* (New York: Harper Perennial, 1944), 495–96.

48. O. S. Muelder, *The Underground Railroad in Western Illinois* (Jefferson, NC: McFarland, 2008).

49. Daniel J. Sharfstein, *The Invisible Line* (New York: Penguin, 2011).

50. Anna Julia Cooper, "Women's Cause Is One and Universal," 1893, BlackPast.org, www.blackpast.org/?q=1893-anna-julia-cooper-womens-cause-one-and-universal, retrieved April 4, 2012.

51. Booker T. Washington, quoted in Grossman, *Land of Hope*, 59.

52. W. E. B. Du Bois, quoted in Grossman, *Land of Hope*, 60.

53. W. Allison Sweeney, quoted in Grossman, *Land of Hope*, 63.

54. Reed, *Black Chicago's First Century*, 64.

55. Reed, *Black Chicago's First Century*, 64.

56. Reed, *Black Chicago's First Century*, 64.

57. W. H. Watkins, "Black Curriculum Orientations: A Preliminary," *Harvard Educational Review* 63, no. 4 (1993): 321–38.

58. Pattillo, *Black on the Block*, 52.

59. "Today's GI Bill," http://www.todaysgibill.org/todays-gi-bill/history-of-the-gi-bill, retrieved March 12, 2012.

60. Hilary Herbold, "Never a Level Playing Field: Blacks and the G.I. Bill," *Journal of Blacks in Higher Education* (1994–1995): 104–5, 107, 108.

61. G. Collison, *Shadrach Minkins: From Fugitive Slave to Citizen* (Cambridge, MA: Harvard University Press, 1997), 9.

62. bell hooks, *Where We Stand: Class Matters* (New York: Routledge, 2000), 2.

63. Wright, *12 Million Black Voices*, 145.

64. Davarian L. Baldwin, *Chicago's New Negroes: Modernity, the Great Migration, and Black Urban Life* (University of North Carolina Press, 2007).

65. *Chicago Defender*, "Story of Old Settlers Reads Like Fiction," May 3, 1930, 13.

66. *Chicago Defender*, "Story of Old Settlers," 13.

67. *Chicago Defender*, "Story of Old Settlers," 13.

68. "Jack Johnson," Wikipedia, http://en.wikipedia.org/wiki/Jack_Johnson_(boxer), retrieved December 23, 2011.

69. S. Barrett, "What the People Say," *Chicago Defender (National Edition)*, September 30, 1939, 14.

70. Barrett, "What the People Say."

71. Reed, *Black Chicago's First Century*, 64.

72. Baldwin, *Chicago's New Negroes*.

73. Reed, *Black Chicago's First Century*, 29.

74. Reed, *Black Chicago's First Century*, 29.

75. Wright, "Introduction."

76. Hunt, "Barack Obama Should Swap."

77. "Haymarket Affair," http://en.wikipedia.org/wiki/Haymarket_affair, retrieved July 24, 2012.

78. Richard Wright, "Blueprint for Negro Writing," *New Challenge* 1 (1937): 58.

79. Pattillo, *Black on the Block*, 44.

80. Beverly Guy-Sheftall, "The Women of Bronzeville," in *On Gwendolyn Brooks*, ed. Stephen C. Wright (Ann Arbor: University of Michigan Press, 1996).

81. From *Saturday Black Bridge: Vision of Black Women in Literature*, ed. Roseann P. Bell, Betty J. Parker, and Beverly Guy-Sheftall (New York: Doubleday, 1979), quoted in Guy-Sheftall, "The Women of Bronzeville," 233.

82. Quoted in Guy-Sheftal, "The Women of Bronzeville," 240.

83. Quoted in Guy-Sheftal, "The Women of Bronzeville," 241.

84. Quoted in Guy-Sheftal, "The Women of Bronzeville," 243.

85. Gwendolyn Brooks, *Bronzeville Boys and Girls*, ill. Faith Ringgold (1956; New York: Harper and Row, 1984). Reprinted by consent of Brooks Permissions.

86. C. C. De Santis, ed., *Langston Hughes and the Chicago Defender: Essays on Race, Politics, and Culture, 1942–62* (Urbana: University of Illinois Press, 1995), 26–27. Reprinted courtesy of the *Chicago Defender*.

87. *Hansberry v. Lee*, 311 U.S. 32 (1940).

88. *Burke v. Kleiman*, 277 Ill. App. 519 (1934).

89. Wright, *12 Million Black Voices*.
90. Wanda A. Hendricks, *Gender, Race, and Politics in the Midwest: Black Club Women in Illinois* (Bloomington: Indiana University Press, 1998). The "race man" was a concept put forth by Ida B. Wells-Barnett and others, arguing that African Americans needed to support the goal of electing black men who are race-conscious.
91. Suffrage Record, 18 March 1914 (1915), in Hendricks, *Race, Gender, and Politics in the Midwest*, 107.
92. Suffrage Record, 18 March 1914 (1915).
93. Pinderhughes, *Race and Ethnicity*, 95–96.
94. Reprinted courtesy of the *Chicago Defender*.
95. "Oscar DePriest," *Encyclopedia of Chicago*, www.encyclopedia.chicagohistory.org/pages/2402.html, retrieved May 5, 2012.
96. Elwood Watson, "DePriest, Oscar (1871–1951)," An Online Reference Guide to African American History, http://blackpast.org/?q=aah/depriest-oscar-1871-1951, retrieved June 8, 2012.
97. Neil Kraus, "The Significance of Race in Urban Politics: The Limitations of Regime Theory," *Race & Society* 7 (2004): 95–111, http://www.thecyberhood.net/documents/papers/kraus.pdf, retrieved June 3, 2011; Melissa Harris-Lacewell, "The Heart of the Politics of Race," *Journal of Black Studies* 34 (November 2003): 2.
98. Reprinted courtesy of the *Chicago Defender*.

# 3. THE BLACK CHURCH AND THE AFRICAN AMERICAN CHURCH IN CHICAGO

1. James Baldwin, *Notes of a Native Son* (New York: Beacon Press, 1995).
2. Jan Benzel, "New York Send Off," *New York Times*, August 30, 2010, http://cityroom.blogs.nytimes.com/2010/08/30/new-york-send-off-rise-up-singing.
3. Benzel, "New York Send Off."
4. Fiqah, quoted in Tami W. Harris, "Whitney's 'Homegoing' and the Spiritual Divide," February 27, 2012, http://www.racialicious.com/2012/02/27/whitneys-home-going-and-the-spiritual-divide.
5. Harris, "Whitney's 'Homegoing.'"
6. Harris, "Whitney's 'Homegoing.'"
7. Rob Kerby, "Tourists Pack the Pews of Harlem's Churches," Beliefnet, http://www.beliefnet.com/Entertainment/Home-Page-News-and-Views/European-tourists-pack-the-pews-of-Harlem-churches.aspx?p=1.
8. James Baldwin, "Stranger in the Village" (1955), in *Notes of a Native Son*.
9. "Whitney Houston's Funeral," uk.omg.yahoo.com/gossip/110--pop/whitney-houston-funeral-194001404, retrieved March 29, 12; Vanessa Greco, "Loved Ones Say Goodbye to Whitney Houston," CTV News, CA, February 12, 2012.
10. "Whitney Houston's Funeral."
11. Lia Eustachewich and Paul Milo, "Whitney Houston Celebrated in Rousing Funeral Service," February 18, 2012, http://hasbrouckheights.patch.com/articles/fans-media-prepare-for-whitney-houston-s-funeral#photo-9144455, retrieved March 15, 2012.
12. Gordon Allport, *The Nature of Prejudice* (Boston: Beacon Press, 1954).
13. C. Eric Lincoln, foreword to Wilmore, *Black Religion*, vii, in C. Eric Lincoln and Lawrence H. Maniya, *The Black Church in the African American Experience* (Durham, NC: Duke University Press, 1990).
14. Henry H. Mitchell, *Black Church Beginnings: The Long-Hidden Realities of the First Years* (Grand Rapid, MI: William B. Eerdmans, 2004), ix.
15. Pat McCaughan, "Black Clergy Charged to Live the Vision of God," *Episcopal News Archive*, October 31, 2005, http://archive.episcopalchurch.org/3577_69048_ENG_HTM.htm, retrieved June 26, 2012.

16. Quoted in M. C. Sernett, ed., *African American Religious History: A Documentary Witness* (Durham, NC: Duke University Press, 1999), 3.

17. Quoted in Sernett, *African American Religious History*, 4.

18. Laurie F. Maffly-Kipp, "The Church in the Southern Black Community," online introduction to the digital collection *Documenting the American South* (Chapel Hill: University Library at the University of North Carolina, 2001), http://docsouth.unc.edu/church/intro.html, retrieved May 19, 2011.

19. See W. E. B. Du Bois, "Of the Faith of the Fathers," in *The Souls of Black Folks* (Amherst: University of Massachusetts Press, 1973).

20. Maffly-Kipp, "The Church in the Southern Black Community."

21. Maffly-Kipp, "The Church in the Southern Black Community."

22. Maffly-Kipp, "The Church in the Southern Black Community."

23. Delma J. Francis, "The Church Was Everything," *Star Tribune*, February 8, 2003, Lexis-Nexis, retrieved May 8, 2011.

24. Francis, "The Church Was Everything."

25. Maffly-Kipp, "The Church in the Southern Black Community."

26. Mitchell, *Black Church Beginnings*.

27. Mitchell, *Black Church Beginnings*.

28. Sernett, *African American Religious History*, 67.

29. Peter Randolph, "Plantation Churches: Visible and Invisible," in *African American Religious History*, 2nd ed., ed. Milton C. Sernett (Durham, NC: Duke University Press, 1999), 263–68.

30. E. Franklin Frazier and C. Eric Lincoln, *The Negro Church in America/The Black Church Since Frazier* (New York: Schocken Books, 1974), 11.

31. Mitchell, *Black Church Beginnings*, 34.

32. Mitchell, *Black Church Beginnings*, 73.

33. Mitchell, *Black Church Beginnings*, 73.

34. Mitchell, *Black Church Beginnings*, 73.

35. Paul Oliver, *Savannah Syncopators: African Retentions in the Blues* (Worthing, UK: Littlehampton Book Services, 1970), 23.

36. Mitchell, *Black Church Beginnings*, 77.

37. Mitchell, *Black Church Beginnings*, 77.

38. Mitchell, *Black Church Beginnings*, 77.

39. Mitchell, *Black Church Beginnings*, 16.

40. Isaac Lane, "From Slave to Preacher among the Freedmen [1916]," in *African American Religious History*, 2nd ed., ed. Milton C. Sernett (Durham, NC: Duke University Press, 1999), 245–50.

41. St. Clair Drake and Horace R. Cayton, *Black Metropolis* (New York: Harcourt, Brace, 1945).

42. In Sernett, *African American Religious History*, 224.

43. In Sernett, *African American Religious History*, 224.

44. Jeremiah Asher, "Protesting the Negro Pew [1850]," in *African American Religious History*, 2nd ed., ed. Milton C. Sernett (Durham, NC: Duke University Press, 1999).

45. Frazier and Lincoln, *The Negro Church in America/The Black Church since Frazier*, 33–34.

46. Frazier and Lincoln, *The Negro Church in America/The Black Church since Frazier*, 107.

47. Richard Wright, *12 Million Black Voices* (New York: Thunder's Mouth Press, 1941), 68.

48. Drake and Cayton, *Black Metropolis*.

49. Woodson, *The History of the Negro Church*, quoted in Mitchell, *Black Chuch Beginnings*.

50. Anne Meis Knupfer, *The Chicago Black Renaissance and Women's Activism* (Chicago: University of Illinois Press, 2006), 27.

51. Knupfer, *Chicago Black Renaissance*, 27.

52. Delores S. Williams, *Sisters in the Wilderness: The Challenge of Womanist God-Talk* (Maryknoll, NY: Orbis, 1993), xiv, 243.

53. Paul Kroll, "The African American Church in America," http://www.gci.org/history/african, retrieved August 10, 2011.

54. See the discussion in Frazier and Lincoln, *The Negro Church in America/The Black Church since Frazier*, 17–19.

55. Sadena Thevarajah, "Religious Influences in the Anti-Slavery Movement," http://cghs.dadeschools.net/slavery/anti-slavery_movement/religious_origins.htm, retrieved February 24, 2012.

56. Thevarajah, "Religious Influences."

57. See the discussion in Frazier and Lincoln, *The Negro Church in America/The Black Church since Frazier*, 26–34, regarding how—in this example—the Anglican Church was not interested in changing the status of Negro slaves.

58. See Lane, "From Slave to Preacher," 245–50.

59. See Lane, "From Slave to Preacher," 245–50.

60. Reverdy C. Ransom, "The Race Problem in a Christian State [1906]," in *African American Religious History*, 2nd ed., ed. Milton C. Sernett (Durham, NC: Duke University Press, 1999), 339.

61. Martin Luther King Jr., Methodist Student Leadership Conference Address, 1964, www.americanrhetoric.com/speeches/mlkmethodistyouthconference.htm, retrieved March 21, 2012.

62. David Van Biema, "Can Megachurches Bridge the Racial Divide?" *Time*, January 11, 2010, www.time.com/time/magazine/article/0,9171,1950943,00.html#ixzz1MQvemJRA.

63. Van Biema, "Can Megachurches Bridge?"

64. Van Biema, "Can Megachurches Bridge?"

65. Van Biema, "Can Megachurches Bridge?"

66. Lynne Marie Kohm, "A Christian Perspective on Gender Equality," *Duke Journal of Gender and Law* 15 (2008), http://scholarship.law.duke.edu/cgi/viewcontent.cgi?article=1144&contex, retrieved May 3, 2012; Wiley Clarkson, "Where the Spirit Leads," 2011, http://www.clarksons.org/spiritleads/spiritleads.htm, retrieved May 14, 2012.

67. Micheal O. Emerson and Christian Smith, *Divided by Faith: Evangelical Religion and the Problem of Race in America* (New York: Oxford University Press, 2000).

68. Emerson and Smith, *Divided by Faith.*

69. Emerson and Smith, *Divided by Faith.*

70. Mitchell, *Black Church Beginnings*, 48.

71. Maffly-Kipp, "The Church in the Southern Black Community."

72. Emmett J. Scott, "Letters of Negro Migrants of 1916–1918," *Journal of Negro History* 4, no. 3 (July 1919): 290–340, article stable URL: http://www.jstor.org/stable/2713780; cited in *The Black Church in the African American Experience*, ed. C. Eric Lincoln and Lawrence H. Maniya (Durham, NC: Duke University Press, 1990), 118, 420.

73. Frazier and Lincoln, *The Negro Church in America/The Black Church since Frazier*, 52.

74. Drake and Cayton, *Black Metropolis*, 58.

75. Nikki Giovanni, *Quilting the Black-Eyed Pea: Poems and Not Quite Poems* (New York: HarperCollins, 2002), 8.

76. Drake and Cayton, *Black Metropolis.*

77. Drake and Cayton, *Black Metropolis.*

78. Alan H. Spear, *Black Chicago: The Making of a Negro Ghetto, 1890–1920* (Chicago: University of Chicago Press, 1967).

79. Charles M. Collins and David Cohen, *The African American* (New York: Viking Studio Books, 1993); Spear, *Black Chicago.*

80. Spear, *Black Chicago*, 91.

81. Christopher R. Reed, *Black Chicago's First Century, Vol. 1: 1833–1900* (Columbia: University of Missouri Press, 2005).

82. Reed, *Black Chicago's First Century.*

83. Christopher C. De Santis, *Langston Hughes and the Chicago Defender* (Urbana: University of Illinois Press, 1995), 199–200. Reprinted courtesy of the *Chicago Defender.*

84. Drake and Cayton, *Black Metropolis.*

85. "The Black Church as Civil Rights Headquarters and Community Center," *Black History Heroes* (blog), 2011, http://blackblackhistoryheroes.blogspot.com/2010/02/blackblack-church.html, retrieved May 15, 2011.

86. Reed, *Black Chicago's First Century*, 42.

87. Reed, *Black Chicago's First Century*, 42.

88. Francis, "The Church Was Everything."

89. Drake and Cayton, *Black Metropolis*, rev. ed. (New York: Oxford University Press, 1993).

90. *Encyclopedia of Chicago*, http://www.encyclopedia.chicagohistory.org/pages/27.html, retrieved May 2, 2011.

91. Latasha Chaffin, "Philanthropy and the Black Church," http://learningtogive.org/papers/paper47.html, retrieved June 27, 2012.

92. Francis, "The Church Was Everything."

93. Harry A. Ploski and James Williams, *African American* (Detroit: Gale Research, 1989).

94. "A Tale of Two Black Churches," CBS2: Chicago, February 18, 2011, http://chicago.cbslocal.com/2011/02/18/a-tale-of-two-black-churches/.

95. "A Tale of Two Black Churches."

96. "A Tale of Two Black Churches."

97. Dahleen Glanton, "More Black Churches Take on AIDS Battle," *Chicago Tribune*, June 6, 2010, http://articles.chicagotribune.com/2010-06-06/news/ct-met-blackaids-church-20100606_1_hiv-testing-black-churches-parishioners, retrieved May 15, 2011.

98. Glanton, "More Black Churches."

99. Jacqueline Trussell, "The Changing Face of Religion: The Suburbanization of the Black Church," www.blackblackandchristian.com/articles/academy/trussell-11-01.shtml, retrieved May 15, 2011.

100. Trussell, "Changing Face."

101. Trussell, "Changing Face."

102. Erica L. Ball, "African American Philanthropy," Philanthropy.Org, 2003, http://www.philanthropy.org/publications/online_publications/african_american_paper.pdf, retrieved April 30, 2003.

103. Pew Charitable Trust, "U.S. Religious Landscape Survey," http://www.pewtrusts.org/our_work_detail.aspx?id=568, retrieved March 21, 2012.

104. See Allport, *The Nature of Prejudice.*

105. Zinn, *People's History of the United States: 1492–Present* (New York: HarperPerennial, 2003), 658.

# 4. TRINITY UNITED CHURCH OF CHRIST

1. United Church of Christ, "Who We Are, What We Believe." The rest of statement reads as follows: "That we may all be one (John 17:21). This motto of the United Church of Christ reflects the spirits of unity on which the church is based and points toward future efforts to heal the divisions in the body of Christ. We are a uniting Church as well as a united church." http://www.ucc.org/about-us/what-is-the-united-church-of.html.

2. Julia Speller, *Walkin' the Talk: Keeping the Faith in Africentric Congregations* (Cleveland: Pilgrim Press, 2005), 78.

3. Speller, *Walkin' the Talk*, 79.

4. Speller, *Walkin' the Talk*, 80.

5. M. E. Martin, "Prophet and Pastor," *Chronicle of Higher Education*, April 11, 2008, http://chronicle.com/article/ProphetPastor/22067, retrieved June 12, 2012.

6. Trinity United Church of Christ, Manford Byrd Recognition Committee, "The Black Value System," http://www.bing.com/search?q=blackblack+value+system&form=MSNH14&qs=AS&sk=&pq=blackblack+value&sp=1&sc=6-11, retrieved June 27, 2001.

7. Barbara Hagerty, "A Closer Look at Black Liberation Theology," March 18, 2008, www.npr.org/templates/story/story.php?storyId=88512189, retrieved May 25, 2011.

8. Hagerty, "A Closer Look."

9. Hagerty, "A Closer Look."

10. Hagerty, "A Closer Look."

11. Hagerty, "A Closer Look."

12. Hagerty, "A Closer Look."

13. "Jeremiah Wright," Wikipedia, http://en.wikipedia.org/wiki/Jeremiah_Wright, retrieved August 28, 2011.

14. "Jeremiah Wright," Wikipedia.

15. "Jeremiah Wright," Wikipedia.

16. See, for example, a full-page *New York Times* ad titled "Black Power" in November 1967 by the National Committee of Negro Churchmen, and the publication of James H. Cone's *Black Theology and Black Power* in 1969.

17. Speller, *Walkin' the Talk*, 81.

18. W. E. B. Du Bois, *The Souls of Black Folks* (Millwood, NY: Kraus-Thomson, 1973).

19. Du Bois, *The Souls of Black Folks*.

20. Du Bois, *The Souls of Black Folks*.

21. Du Bois, *The Souls of Black Folks*, quoted in Jeremiah Wright Jr., *Sankofa Moment* (St. Paul, MN: St. Paul Press, 2010).

22. Speller, *Walkin' the Talk*, 82–83.

23. Speller, *Walkin' the Talk*, 82–83. See also Jeremiah Wright, "Doing Black Theology in the Black Church," in *Living Stones in the Household of God*, ed. Linda E. Thomas (Minneapolis, MN: Fortress Press, 2004), 16–17.

24. Wright, "Doing Black Theology," 16–17.

25. Speller, *Walkin' the Talk*, 86.

26. Wright, "Sankofa Moment," 48.

27. Speller, *Walkin' the Talk*.

28. Speller, *Walkin' the Talk*.

29. Speller, *Walkin' the Talk*.

30. Geoff Alexander, "Black Preaching Styles," 1986, http://www.afana.org/preaching.htm, retrieved March 27, 2012.

31. Alexander, "Black Preaching Styles."

32. Alexander, "Black Preaching Styles."

33. Alexander, "Black Preaching Styles."

34. Effie Rolfe, "The Rev. Otis Moss III to Be Installed at Trinity Church," *Chicago Defender*, May 27, 2009, http://www.chicagodefender.com/article-4703-the-rev-otis-moss-iii-to-be-installed-at-trinity-church.html, retrieved August 30, 2011.

35. Rhonda Gillespie, "Moss Officially at Helm of Trinity Church," *Chicago Defender*, June 3, 2009, http://www.chicagodefender.com/article-4818-moss-officially-at-helm-of-trinity-church.htm, retrieved August 30, 2011.

# 5. THE UNHEARD VOICES OF TRINITY CHURCH

1. E. A. Sovik, "Notes on a Sacred Space," *Christian Century*, 1982, 63, http://www.religion-online.org/showarticle.asp?title=1298, retrieved June 225, 2012.

2. Robin Kelley, "'We Are Not What We Seem': Rethinking Black Working-Class Opposition in the Jim Crow South," *Journal of American History* (June 1993).

3. David Abramtsov, "Behavior in the Church," http://www.stlukeorthodox.com/html/parishinfo/behavior.cfm, retrieved April 6, 2012.

4. David Hopkins, on *The Melissa-Harris Perry Show*, MSNBC, May 19, 2012.

5. Eli Saslow, "Congregation Defends Obama's Ex-Pastor," *Washington Post*, March 18, 2008, http://www.washingtonpost.com/wp-dyn/content/article/2008/03/17, retrieved July 10, 2011.

6. Larry Rohter and Michael Luo, "Groups Respond to Obama's Call for National Discussion about Race," *New York Times*, March 20, 2008, http://www.nytimes.com/2008/03/20/us/politics/20race.html, retrieved July 20, 2011; Howard Kurtz, "A Complex Speech, Boiled Down to Simple Politics," *Washington Post*, March 20, 2008, http://www.washingtonpost.com/wp-dyn/content/article/2008/03/19, retrieved July 20, 2011.

7. Barack Obama, "A More Perfect Union," speech, March 18, 2008, http://constitution-center.org/amoreperfectunion, retrieved June 26, 2012.

8. Mark Jurkowitz, "The Pastor's Press Tour Is the Week's Big Newsmaker," May 4, 2008, PEJ Campaign Coverage Index, http://www.journalism.org/print/10928, retrieved August 16, 2011.

9. *Bill Moyers Journal*, April 25, 2008, transcript, http://www.pbs.org/moyers/journal/04252008/transcript1.html, retrieved August 18, 2011.

10. Jeremiah Wright, speech to the NAACP, CNN.com, retrieved August 17, 2011.

11. Dan Balaz, "For Obama, Wright the Latest in a Long Line of Tests," *The Trail*, www.washingtonpost.com, retrieved April 11, 2008; Alessandra Stanley, "Not Speaking for Obama, Pastor Speaks for Himself, at Length," April 29, 2008, http://www.nytimes.com/2008/04/29/us/politics/29watc.html; Amy Sullivan-Washington, "Jeremiah Wright Goes to War," http://www.time/politics/article/0,8599,1735662,00.html.

12. Dana Milbank, "Could Rev. Spell Doom for Obama?" Rough Sketch, *Washington Post*, April 28, 2008, http://voices.washingtonpost.com/roughsketch/2008/04/obamas_pastor_reignites_race_c.html, retrieved April 28, 2012.

13. Nielsen Wire, "Nearly 37.8 Million Watch President Obama's Oath and Speech On TV," January 21, 2008, http://blog.nielsen.com/nielsenwire/media_entertainment/nearly-378-million-watch-president-obamas-oath-and-speech, retrieved April 28, 2012.

14. J. Gonzalez and J. Torres, *News for All the People: The Epic Story of Race and the American Media* (London: Verso, 2011), 1.

# Index

African American church. *See* black
church in America

Black Belt in Chicago, 35, 42; art and
literature of, 57–61; black race
consciousness, 56; diversity within, 52;
housing covenants, 44, 61; and Mayor
Richard Daley, 44–45; politics in, 57,
64–66; and the University of Chicago,
34. *See also* Brooks, Gwendolyn;
Dawson, William; De Priest, Oscar;
Great Migration to Chicago; Hughes,
Langston; media, *Chicago Defender*;
Wright, Richard
black church in America: activism, 86;
diversity in, 89; education, 74; HIV/
AIDS, 90; invisible institutions, 73, 74,
75–78; philanthropy, 90–91;
segregation in the North and, 79–80;
slavery and, 73–74, 75–79, 81–82, 84,
86, 87, 88; suburbanization, impact of,
90; tourism, 70–71; women in, 77,
80–81
"Black is Beautiful", 50, 56, 97. *See also*
Black Power
black liberation theology: Barack Obama
and, 4, 14; origins and meaning of,
103–104, 130–131; Reverend Wright
and, 1, 150; transcript of resistance,
xvii; Trinity UCC and, 99–100, 122
Black Power, 24, 97–98, 103, 106

Bronzeville. *See* Black Belt in Chicago
Brooks, Gwendolyn: life, 36, 41, 59;
poems, 41–42, 59–60
Byrd, Manford, 100. *See also* Trinity
United Church of Christ (Trinity UCC),
Black Value System

Clinton, Hillary: Father Michael Pfleger
and, 30–31, 146–147; Geraldine
Ferraro and, 7, 9; in the media, 6, 20,
23, 138–139

Dawson, William, 64
De Priest, Oscar, 61–64
DeSaible, Jean Baptist Pointe, 57
Du Bois, W. E. B., xv–xvi, 45, 74, 75, 107,
111

education: assimilation in, 97; segregation
in, 35–38

Farrakhan, Louis, 9, 121, 134, 140, 145

Great Migration to Chicago: black women
in, 46–47; *Chicago Defender* and,
85–86; John Anderson story, 49–50;
kitchenettes, 41–42; motivations for,
85; "old settlers" and "new arrivals",
40–41. *See also* Black Belt in Chicago

Hansberry, Lorraine, 61

Houston, Whitney, 71–72
Hughes, Langston, 60, 66–67, 87–88

media: biases, 10–11; black press, 55–56;
    *Chicago Defender*, xxi, 3, 36, 39, 47,
    48, 51, 54, 60, 63, 64, 65, 66, 85–86,
    113–114; democracy and, 3–4, 157;
    ethics, xv, xviii–xix, 2–3, 4–5; Fourth
    Estate, xv, 2; race, discussing, 19–20;
    social media, 10, 155; Trinity UCC,
    actions at, 124–130, 131–134
Minkins, Shadrach, 53–54
Moss, Reverend Otis, III: media, on the,
    123, 125, 132; Obama resignation,
    response to, 32; preaching style,
    114–115; transition to pastorship, 15,
    113–115, 122

Obama, Barack: "A More Perfect Union"
    speech, 15–16, 19, 134–138; attendance
    at Trinity UCC, 150–151; inauguration,
    149–150; Huffington Post essay,
    11–12; patriotism, 7–8; race as
    campaign issue, 7, 8–9; resignation
    from Trinity UCC, 30–31, 146–148
Olivet Baptist Church in Chicago, 87, 89,
    93

Pfleger, Father Michael, 30–31, 146–147
plight and protest literature. *See* Black Belt
    in Chicago, art and literature of
post-racial thesis, 34, 83, 134, 135, 136,
    137–138

Quinn Chapel AME, 87, 88

race-neutral and race-evading language, 65
racial divide in the church, 81–84

Sheares, Reverend Reuben A., 98, 99
"single story": of the black church, 71;
    Chimamanda Adichie on, xviii; of

Trinity UCC, xvii–xviii, 70, 116, 125,
    132, 145, 153–155, 157
Smith, Reverend Kenneth, 94–95, 97

Trinity United Church of Christ (Trinity
    UCC): Black Value System, 100–103;
    first building, 96; healing, 149–150;
    ministries, 110, 116; motto, 24–25,
    99–100, 107, 120, 122, 150; music,
    107; picketers, 120, 122–123; pro-
    black, 69, 152–153, 154; racism,
    accusations of, 69–70; reasons people
    joined, 110–112; resistance to media,
    124–130; sick and shut-in, 129–130.
    *See also* Smith, Reverend Kenneth;
    Sheares, Reverend Reuben A.; Wright,
    Reverend Jeremiah, Jr.; Moss,
    Reverend Otis, III

United Church of Christ (UCC): history of,
    93–94. *See also* Trinity United Church
    of Christ (Trinity UCC)

Wright, Reverend Jeremiah, Jr.: biography,
    2, 105; "God Damn America"
    statement, 2, 6, 130–131, 135, 139, 140,
    150; interview with Moyers, 24–26,
    139, 140–141, 142; at NAACP dinner,
    26–27, 28, 29, 139, 141; at National
    Press Club, 27–30, 139–145;
    pastorship, 104, 105–113; philosophy,
    110; social justice, 144. *See also* black
    liberation theology
Wright, Richard, xxii, 42, 49, 54, 57,
    58–59, 61, 65, 93

Xingjian, Gao, 1; Nobel Prize Lecture,
    16–17, 21

Zinn, Howard, xvii–xviii, 91